A Passion for Teaching

This book is a celebration and an acknowledgement of the contribution to high standards of teaching, learning and achievement of various forms of intellectual, physical, emotional, and passionate endeavour in which teachers at their best engage. Christopher Day demonstrates that teachers with a passion for teaching are those who are committed, enthusiastic and intellectually and emotionally energetic in their work with children, young people and adults alike. Passionate teachers are aware of the challenge of the broader social contexts in which they teach, have a clear sense of identity and believe they can make a difference to the learning and achievement of all their pupils.

A Passion for Teaching is a contribution to understanding and improving the teaching profession and brings new insights to the work and lives of teachers. It is for all teachers, teacher educators and intending teachers who have a passion for their teaching, who love learners, learning and the teaching life.

Christopher Day is Professor of Education and Co-director of the Centre for Research on Teacher and School Development at the School of Education, University of Nottingham.

A Passion for Teaching

Christopher Day

 RoutledgeFalmer
Taylor & Francis Group

LONDON AND NEW YORK

First published 2004
by RoutledgeFalmer
2 Park Square, Milton Park, Abingdon, Oxon, OX14 4RN

Simultaneously published in the USA and Canada
by Routledge
270 Madison Avenue, New York NY 10016

Reprinted 2005

RoutledgeFalmer is an imprint of the Taylor & Francis Group

© 2004 Christopher Day

Typeset in Baskerville by
Steven Gardiner Ltd, Cambridge
Printed and bound in Great Britain by
Biddles Ltd, King's Lynn, Norfolk

British Library Cataloguing in Publication Data
A catalogue record for this book is available from the British
Library

Library of Congress Cataloguing in Publication Data
Day, Christopher, ACP.
    A passion for teaching / Christopher Day.
        p.   cm.
    Includes bibliographical references and index.
    ISBN 0-415-25179-6 (Hardback: alk. paper)–
    ISBN 0-415-25180-X (Paperback: alk. paper)
    1. Affective education. 2 Effective teaching.
    3. Learning, Psychology of. I. Title.
    LB1072.D39 2004
    371.1 – dc22   2003020185

ISBN 0 415 25179 6 (hbk)
ISBN 0 415 25180 X (pbk)

To Simon and Tim

Contents

Figures and tables

Foreword

As a writer about 'passion' in teaching and learning, I have often felt myself something of an exile, a wanderer on the periphery of the Academy, a scholar too ragged of dress and wild of eye to be invited into the cosy companionship of the academic conversation.

For almost a decade now, I have been tempted to feel a bit self-conscious about having labelled my own book, *The Passionate Teacher*. My publisher, in 1995, insisted on adding a sub-title, *A Practical Guide*, which didn't make a lot of sense to me, but seemed to give it a harder, more pragmatic edge. When my book first appeared I feared that legitimate educators would give it a wide berth. And for years, it seemed that the latter part of the nightmare had come true. 'Passion' in the title seemed enough to keep the book from being reviewed or cited by serious university folk. Lots of teachers did buy the book, but didn't talk much publicly about it, or quietly presented a copy to family members or close friends entering or remaining in their profession.

But now that Christopher Day has brought together a rich and varied weaving of ideas and concepts and called it *A Passion For Teaching*, I feel redeemed. Passion is now definitely 'mainstream'. It seems it's OK for stolid academics to speak of 'passion' as an essential ingredient in successful educational scholarship, as well as in practice. 'Passion' has been invited to the ball, where only words like 'efficiency', 'rigour', and 'erudition' or corporate-sounding terms like 'outcome-based', 'achievement-oriented', and 'success-for-all' used to prance. Like it or not, we are entered into the Era of Passion.

All is not well, however. The legitimacy of passion as a participant in the academic conversation is not vouchsafed, not in the era of high-stakes testing, of the commercialization of the public learning arena, of one-size-fits-all, state-imposed curricular frameworks, of severe – if not draconian – manifestations of 'accountability'. Teachers are being exhorted to 'teach to the test', now that 'the test' has been politically mandated and bureaucratically sanctified. Odd as it may seem, even the champions of testing declare themselves as 'passionate' – about higher standards, about tougher measures, about leaving no child behind. We risk losing 'passion' to our adversaries at the very moment it has become acceptable to our learned colleagues.

Into this mixed world of competing motives and contending ideologies, Christopher Day has invited us to take part in an elegant buffet. He has laid out a magnificent table, eight courses/chapters in all, each with many dishes/sections, from scholars and teachers around the world – and all with 'passion' as the centrepiece. The breadth of his reading in the literature of teaching and learning is most impressive; he quotes from scholars on four continents and is most generous in searching out quotes from others wherever he feels they illuminate key aspects of his own contentions and beliefs about passion in teaching. One is tempted to linger on a number of these quotes, in contemplation of their depth and complexity, in the midst of this feast.

I am also much impressed with Chris Day's extension of the conversation about 'passion' into the full range of the life and work of teachers. Where I and other writers have often restricted ourselves mostly to classroom practice, and to the intellectual and emotional preparation for it, he has looked into the evolving life of teachers, from their early encounters with students, through mid-career challenges and dilemmas, on to their maturing years in the profession, and to the quality of their associations within schools. His concern with 'passionate learning communities', and with the 'development' of educators within their professions is welcome. And he reaches out to bring the work of others – of Howard Gardner's multiple intelligences and Daniel Goleman's emotional intelligence – into the framework of 'passion' without giving the reader the feeling that they are being expropriated to serve the author's passionate agenda.

Acting as the learned host, Chris Day may be at times a bit too modest about his own creative contributions. One begins to look for his voice in this chorus of worldly wisdom. When it is heard, it is a welcome addition to the banquet, as when he asserts his views on the preoccupation of schools with 'effectiveness':

> To be passionate about teaching is not only to express enthusiasm but also to enact it in a principled, values-led, intelligent way. . . . Passion is associated with enthusiasm, caring, commitment, and

hope, which are themselves key characteristics of effectiveness in teaching.

(p. 12)

And when he further cautions:

In recent years, there has been a proliferation of texts about school and teacher effectiveness. Yet each one has failed to acknowledge that effective teaching and learning relies, at its heart, on the exercise by teachers of sustained passion (as well as compassion) in the classroom; and that a key influence upon teachers' capacity to do this is the part played by the school context.

(p. 134)

Or when, in the closing pages of the book, he writes:

Passionate teaching does not claim to affect the historical constraints imposed by social, economic and political or indeed emotional orders. Its emancipatory function, however, is to tap into the capacity of pupils to become excited by learning, to help them raise their eyes beyond the immediate and to learn more about themselves, to build an identity grounded in new self-images.

(p. 176)

Christopher Day has done two especially important things in this book: He has made 'passion' the *chef d'oeuvre* of the entire movement to reform and improve teaching and learning, rather than treat passion as a garnish. And he has extended his inquiry into passion across a much wider spectrum of activity than anyone previously – his table of contents is itself a rich and varied menu of offerings on topics that speak to the centrality of passion.

This is not a book to race through. Read it leisurely, or risk a bout of indigestion. This is a book to savour. It is not a 'quick read,' no 'page turner.' If you're headed for the beach on holiday, find something else to bring along to collect sand between its pages. Save *A Passion for Teaching* for the quieter moments of contemplation. This book is a delight for the unself-consciously reflective, for the educator who already accepts the centrality of passion as a creative, interactive, moral force, and is curious as to just how widely the circle reaches, how many essential aspects of the craft, design, conceptualization, and interactive potential of teaching and learning can be illuminated by reference to passion.

One should not read this book as I did – all at once, under pressure of a deadline. In fact, this book should be banned from those pre-service courses, in-service workshops, or graduate seminars where readers are required to 'master' great quantities of material quickly. But this book is, in fact, an excellent introduction for novice educators into the world of humane scholarship in education as well as for experienced teachers who are seeking to revisit values and purposes. I can see many of his readers using this book, as did I, to discover new authors worth reading. Day tellingly ends each chapter with 'A Time to Reflect', and that is the watchword for this fascinating, intricate, idea-filled and thought-provoking volume.

Robert L. Fried
Northeastern University, Boston

Acknowledgements

I owe a debt of gratitude to many colleagues with whom I work, each of whom, in different but equally important ways, contributed to my thinking and writing. They include Judyth Sachs, a very special critical friend from Australia; Lesley Saunders and Ruth Leitch, who share my passion for teaching and the work of teachers; my close colleagues in the Centre for Research in Teacher and School Development here – Pat Thomson, Linda Ellison, Andy Townsend, and Mark Hadfield; my colleagues in the VITAE Project; and the many teachers, headteachers and teacher educators I meet who provide constant reminders of what passion, commitment, hard work, and hope look like in the practice of teaching. I am also indebted to Ikeke Wangboje and Claire Sullivan for their technical support on the long journey as the writing moved from first to final draft. Finally, I wish to acknowledge the patience and trust of Anna Clarkson, Publisher for RoutledgeFalmer, as deadlines for completion were extended to facilitate unanticipated challenges of other kinds.

Many thanks to the following for permission to use their material:

Table 2.1 From *Models of Learning – Tools for Teaching*, 2nd edition by Bruce Joyce, Emily Calhoun and David Hopkins, Open University Press, 2002. Reprinted as Table 5.2 with permission of the publisher.

Table 5.3 Reprinted by permission of the publisher from Silver, H. F., Strong, R. W. and Perini, M. J. (2000) *So Each May Learn: Integrating Learning Styles and Multiple Intelligences*, Alexandra, VA: Association for Supervision and Curriculum Development.

Table 5.4 Reprinted with permission of the publisher from Clark, C., *Thoughtful Teaching*, New York: Teachers College Press, © 1995 by Clark, C., all rights reserved, p. 27.

Figure 6.2 From Ralph Fessler, Judith Christensen, *The Teacher Career Cycle: Understanding and Guiding the Professional Development of Teachers*. Published by Allyn and Bacon, Boston, MA. Copyright © 1992 by Pearson Education. Reprinted with permission of the publisher.

Figure 6.3 Reprinted with permission of the publisher from Lieberman, A. and Miller, L., *Teachers – Transforming their World and their Work*, New York: Teachers College Press, © 1999 by Lieberman, A. and Miller, L., all rights reserved, p. 73.

Table 7.2 and Table 7.3 From McLaughlin, M. W. and Talbert, J., *Professional Communities and the Work of High School Teaching*, The University of Chicago Press, 2001. Reprinted with permission of the publisher.

Figure 7.4 From Imants, J., Tillema, H. H. and De Brabander, C. J., 'A Dynamic View of Teacher Learning and School Improvement', in F. K. Kieviev and R. Vandenberghe (eds), *School Culture, School Improvement and Teacher Development*, Leiden University, D.S.W.O. Press. Reprinted with permission of Jeroen Imants and Harm Tillema.

Table 8.4 From *Good Teaching and Learning* by Colin Morgan and Glyn Morris, Open University Press, 1999. Reprinted as Table 5.1 with permission of the publisher.

Christopher Day
University of Nottingham
July 2003

We should take care not to make intellect our god; it has, of course, powerful muscles, but no personality. It cannot lead; it can only serve.

Albert Einstein, 1950

Introduction
The need for passion

> Schooling is organized so that educational policies, curriculum, and instruction are interpreted and enacted by teachers. Teachers are the human point of contact with students. All other influences on the quality of education are mediated by who the teacher is and what the teacher does. Teachers have the potential for enhancing the quality of education by bringing life to curriculum and inspiring students to curiosity and self-directed learning. And teachers can also degrade the quality of education through error, laziness, cruelty or incompetence. For better or worse, teachers determine the quality of education.
>
> (Clark, 1995, p. 3)

This book is for those teachers, teacher educators and intending teachers who have a passion for their teaching; who love learners, learning and the teaching life; who acknowledge that teaching is not only about intellectual and emotional engagement with others – whether pupils, colleagues or parents – but also intellectual and emotional engagement with self through regular review and renewal of purposes and practices. It is intended as a contribution to understanding and improving the teaching profession and to bring new insights to the work and lives of teachers. It is also a celebration and an acknowledgement of the various forms of intellectual, physical, emotional and in particular, passionate endeavour in which teachers at their best engage and which form the core content of the book. It is for all those who recognize the limitations of reform that is only externally driven and who passionately assert the broader values and moral responsibilities that are internally driven and embedded in and expressed through good teaching.

The story this book tells is from the heart and the head. In its preparation, I found many who had written compellingly about one aspect or other of the passion of teaching. Some focused upon the teachers' self, others on their work, still others on the importance of commitment, job satisfaction, identity, and the influence of policy on these. Others wrote of emotional understandings, and teachers' moral purposes; and the importance of the collective passion in schools as learning communities. In most of the research and writing, these are discrete strands. Yet in practice, all these interact and, together, make up the whole. What I have tried to do here is to bring all these together in new ways, new relationships, and so to contribute to new understandings of what it means to become and remain a teacher with a passion for teaching.

The strongest memories of my schooling are of teachers who were more concerned with control than creativity and more interested in their subject than their pupils. Yet among them were some teachers who were passionately interested in enthusing their pupils with a love for learning, who noticed when something was amiss with individuals and acted upon it, who were intent on ensuring to the best of their ability that they communicated in ways that connected with pupils' interests and needs. It was these teachers who taught me the value of reflection, who showed me new worlds, who motivated me to explore them despite my over-whelming sense of alienation from the school experience. These teachers were not charismatic. One had a permanent stutter, another would appear impossibly vague in today's world of target setting, and another was a pedagogic despot in the classroom. Yet each showed by their actions a deep and sustained care for their charges, and, as I later came to realize, a passion for and understanding that their work went far beyond the transmission of curriculum and the assessment of measurable achievement.

Teachers with a passion for teaching are those who are committed, enthusiastic, and intellectually and emotionally energetic in their work with children, young people and adults alike. Yet these overt signs of passion are underpinned by clear moral purposes that go beyond the efficient implementation of set curricula. Passionate teachers are aware of the challenge of the broader social contexts in which they teach, have a clear sense of identity and believe that they can make a difference to the learning and achievement of all their pupils. They care deeply about them. They like them. They care also about how and what they teach and are curious to learn more about both in order to become and remain more than merely competent. They are aware of the role played by emotion in classroom learning and teaching. They are committed to working co-operatively and, at times, collaboratively with colleagues in their own and other schools and seek and take opportunities to engage in reflection of different kinds in, on and about their practices. For these teachers, teaching is a creative and adventurous profession and passion is not an option. It is essential to high-quality teaching.

> Passionately committed teachers are those who absolutely love what they do. They are constantly searching for more effective ways to reach their children, to master the content and methods of their craft. They feel a personal mission . . . to learning as much as they can about the world, about others, about themselves – and helping others to do the same.
>
> (Zehm and Kottler, 1993, p. 118)

Knowledge-creating schools

In his pamphlet on creative professionalism and the role of teachers in the knowledge society for DEMOS, an independent 'think tank', David Hargreaves sets out the need for knowledge-creating schools to be open to the outside world beyond the classroom; to develop a culture of commitment and enthusiasm for continual improvement; to encourage informal task-relevant, rather than hierarchical, relationships, and diversity rather than uniformity among staff; and demonstrate a readiness to encourage all to experiment with new ideas, in a culture within which mistakes are treated as 'paths to learning' (Hargreaves, 1998, p. 26). In such schools, new ideas will be supported, shared and exchanged – and, in the process, validated at individual teacher and school levels.

Yet without understanding the need for the active participation and emotional commitment of all teachers and associated staff, none of this will happen. Changes in structures will not be sufficient to ensure changes in cultures, both individual and collective, which for generations have encouraged isolation rather than collaboration and in which mistakes continue to be punished directly (by external inspection and league tables) and indirectly (through media criticism and selective funding based upon performance). When Hargreaves and many others before him lay out their vision for the future of schooling, they fail to grasp the need to bring the teachers with them in ways which do not simply ask for 'more' or 'different' but which acknowledge their primary need for self-fulfilment, job satisfaction, being valued; and which provide time and space to allow the creation, recreation and sustaining of the passion for teaching that enables them to teach at their best. Bullough and

Baughman (1997) express the issues of change well when they write that, 'for a change to stick it must find a place in teachers' thinking, in their belief systems, and in their habitual ways of acting and interacting within the classroom or grow out of their . . . [own] . . . thinking' (p. xv).

In my work with teachers across a range of primary and secondary schools over more than twenty years, I have witnessed what has been widely documented in surveys and smaller fine-grained research studies – a deterioration in morale and increases in workload for teachers of all ages and an accompanying crisis in recruitment and retention. There are many reasons for this, but perhaps the two most significant are the changes in society and what has come to be known as the 'standards' agenda. It is to these I now turn briefly, for it is impossible to write of a passion for teaching without taking them into account.

Changes in society

In writing of human nature and social order in the community, Fukuyama (1999) suggests that the consequences of the shift into an information society in which 'inexpensive information technology makes it increasingly easy to move information across national borders, and rapid communication by television, radio, fax, and e-mail erodes the boundaries of long-established cultural communities' (p. 3) are not entirely positive. He points to 'seriously deteriorating social conditions in most of the industrialized world . . . the decline of kinship as a social institute . . .' (p. 4) and, in parallel, the statistical increase in crime, fatherless children, HIV/AIDS, drug dependency and addiction. He adds to these reduced educational outcomes and opportunities, decline in trust and confidence in institutions and politicians, and the breakdown of generalizable rules of conduct as individuals maximize personal freedom.

When Fukuyama writes about the 'ligatures binding [individuals] in webs of social obligation [being] . . . greatly loosened' (p. 47, op. cit.), this has implications for the social functions of schools and, therefore, for teachers, in school environments that are socially disadvantaged and with pupils 'whose parents have failed to provide . . . [them] . . . with adequate social capital and are not managing to keep up' (ibid., p. 259). This is compounded in places where there are diminished opportunities for high quality education caused by problems of staff recruitment, lack of appropriately qualified specialist teachers in key areas, retention, and issues of quality, which, it seems, are becoming permanent features in the landscape of some schools in many countries.

The standards agenda

Concerns with the need to raise standards of achievement and improve their positions in the world economic league tables have prompted governments to intervene more actively in all aspects of school life to improve school systems over the last twenty years; and financial self-reliance and ideological compliance have become the twin realities for many of today's schools and their teachers (Hargreaves, 1994). One characteristic of this movement to reform schools is an international trend towards the development of measurable teaching competencies as a means of assessing teaching standards. This has powerful consequences for teacher professionalism. Elliott (1991, p. 124), for example, argues that at stake in competency-based assessment are the ways in which quite separate views of teaching – teaching as a technology and teaching as a moral practice – are applied to judge teachers' effectiveness and worth. Being competent in both is part of a professional's practice but if the view of teachers as skilled technicians in the classroom whose only purpose is to implement the set curriculum prevails, then the complex art and science of teaching may be downgraded to possession of a cluster of baseline technical skills. Over time, the temptation for managers to judge teachers exclusively against sets of competences, rather than using them as benchmarks, may become as overwhelming as it is for teachers to judge pupil progress only against their results in tests that focus upon a relatively narrow range of achievements. It is important, then, that the limitations of output achievement competences as they are currently conceived as a means of both judging teachers' work and of planning their development, are recognized, and that teachers have a critical view of their worth that is set within a broader educational vision.

I would make six observations on the government standards agenda and its effects on schools, teachers and students:

1   As they are constituted, measurable standards account for a relatively limited amount of teaching, learning and achievement.
2   In those areas that are central to the standards agenda for students in England, i.e. literacy, numeracy, science, there was initial evidence of increased attainment by pupils. This has now plateaued and observers note a 'ceiling' effect.
3   Try as teachers may, there are certain year cohorts and individual pupils for whom accidents of birth, family and peer influences and motivation persistently prevent all efforts to educate to nationally prescribed standards.

4   The use of behavioural competences to measure the abilities of
      teachers does not account for their broader, moral purposes.
5   It is by no means certain that the reduction of teacher autonomy
      has resulted in better teaching or more committed teachers.
6   There is a continuing crisis in recruitment and retention. Yet
      without committed teachers of the highest quality, standards are
      unlikely to be raised and the challenges presented by changes in
      society will not be met.

The chapters in this book do not offer a set of prescriptions for
so-called 'effective' teaching. There are many books and a plethora of
other documents, reports, papers, and articles that do – so many, in
fact, that it is difficult to believe that schools are not by now filled with
effective teachers! Of course, they are not, simply because schools and
classrooms are complex organizations and the quality of teaching and
learning depends more on the teacher and the learner than on policies
and prescriptions.

Rather, the chapters focus upon the qualities, values, purposes,
characteristics, and practices of teachers, in different contexts and phases
of their lives, who are, have been or wish to be again passionate in their
teaching. It is a broad and rich agenda, and I make no apology for
my inclusion of a range of sources and references to the many wise,
knowledgeable, skilful, and passionate authors who have informed and
stimulated my thinking. Wisdom does not reside in a single person! I
hope, therefore, that it will be used both as a reference book to be 'dipped
into' from time to time and as an aid for reflection. It is for this reason that
each chapter ends with a short 'Time to reflect' section. It is my hope,
also, that its style of presentation will lend itself to visits from the busy
educator. Above all, I hope that it will refresh and stimulate all those who
give of their heads and their hearts to the call of teaching.

The chapters move from a focus on the individuals' inner selves, their
moral purposes, emotions, commitments, to their own learning and
practices in the communities that influence the way these are constructed,
and finally to the challenges of sustaining their passion for teaching. In
Chapter 1, Why Passion is Essential, I focus upon the characteristics of
passionate teaching, the broad economic, social and policy contexts in
which it occurs, and the association between passionate teaching and
effectiveness, the 'good' teacher, passion, hope, and ideals. The chapter
concludes with an holistic agenda for the education of the passionate
teacher. In Chapter 2, Moral Purposes: Care, Courage and Pupils' Voices,
I discuss first the core values, virtues and responsibilities associated with

the passionate teacher, and the connections between these and the care and compassion that permeates classrooms in which motivation and learning are recognized as essentially endeavours closely connected with human relationships. I conclude with a range of pupils 'speaking' of their experiences and adults sharing memories of their teachers. In Chapter 3, Emotions and Identities, I draw together and discuss literature from a wide range of perspectives that recognizes the essential role played by emotion in teaching and its connection also with the 'standards' agenda in schools. I discuss the place of emotions in decision-making and teaching that is both emotional labour and emotional work. The self is a crucial element in the way teachers construe and construct the nature of their work. It matters enormously to pupils and parents also what kind of person the teacher is, and so the second part of the chapter focuses on the importance of personal and professional identities to teachers in enabling them to understand and manage themselves, their pupils and external influences. In Chapter 4, The Passion of Commitment: Job Satisfaction, Motivation and Self-Efficacy, I suggest that commitment is the quality that separates those who care, who have moral purposes and are passionate about their pupils, their subjects, and their own learning and achievement as well as those of their pupils, from those for whom teaching is just a job. The chapter provides examples of the way teachers feel about their commitment and points to the challenges of sustaining it across different phases of their teaching lives in different contexts. In relation to this, I discuss 'self-efficacy' (the belief that you can make a difference in pupils' learning), and the importance to good teaching of motivation, morale and job satisfaction.

In Chapter 5, Building Knowledge about Practice, I bring together selected research intended to add to, reinforce and stimulate passionate thinking about teaching and learning: research on multiple intelligences, models of teaching, emotional intelligence, spiritual intelligence, and pupil learning styles and their implications for practice. I suggest ways of looking 'beneath the surface' in order to identify and meet pupils' class-room learning needs in creative ways. The focus for Chapter 6, A Passion for Learning and Development, is on teachers' own learning. The maintenance of good teaching demands that all teachers revisit and review regularly the ways they are applying principles of differentiation, coherence, progression, and continuity and balance, not only in the 'what' and 'how' of their teaching but also the 'why' in terms of their moral purposes. To be a professional means having a lifelong commitment to inquiring practice. We know that teachers' self-knowledge, commitment, enthusiasm, and emotional intelligence contributes to student learning. Yet research suggests that routines, school cultures, policy environments, and personal histories can often work against the fulfilment of this aspiration. In the chapter, I propose that investment in different forms of professional development is essential if teachers are to sustain the quality of their work through all phases of their teaching lives. In the second part of the chapter, I focus upon the purposes and challenges of different modes of reflective practice that engage the mind and the emotions, and I present models for organizing professional development activities appropriate to these.

Because teachers work in social settings and because these can affect their commitment and their teaching both positively and negatively, Chapter 7, Passionate Learning Communities, focuses upon the school as an influence on teachers' capacities to build and sustain their passion for teaching. As an intellectual and emotional arena, the school may bond or divide its members. I discuss the characteristics and cultural norms of schools as learning communities for teachers as well as pupils. Passionate teachers do not, I suggest, work in isolation either from colleagues or pupils. So it may be expected that their classrooms will be places in which pupils will be active participants in decisions about their own learning; that teachers' practices will be shared through school leadership that encourages peer observations and other forms of collegiality; and that there will be a collective sense of efficacy and trust. Of particular interest is networked learning between schools, which encourages and supports teachers in learning together and from each other through sustained practical inquiry. The final chapter focuses upon Sustaining the Passion because there is never a time in teaching when one can say that there is nothing more to do. For some, passion begins to fade as the teacher becomes debilitated by the daily demands of pupils, the environment and personal life factors. Yet this is not inevitable. With good leadership in the school, and an awareness of the need for life–work balance, support from colleagues and others, regular review of purposes, values and practices, and renewal of commitment, it is possible to sustain passion. The chapter contains examples of teachers who have 'thrown in the towel' and those who continue to 'stay connected' and express a passion for teaching throughout the length of their careers in challenging contexts.

Essentially, I remain hopeful for the teaching profession and for its continuing contributions to the complex art of educating children and young people who do not choose to be educated. Teaching, I believe, is a courageous occupation and the best teachers are those who are committed and passionate, and able to sustain these over their careers.

Professionalism describes the quality of practice. It describes the manner of conduct within an occupation, how members integrate their obligations with their knowledge and skill in a context of collegiality, and of contractual and ethical relations with clients. . . . Teaching in an educational context is strongly connected to the betterment of individuals. It is therefore impossible to talk extensively about teachers and teaching without a language of morality.

(Sockett, 1993, p. 91)

Teachers, now, are potentially the single most important asset in the achievement of the vision of a democratically just learning society. They must, more than ever before, be more than transmitters of knowledge. In this century they need to play more complex roles if students' creativity, intellectual curiosity, emotional health, and sense of active citizenship are to be realized. More then ever before, also, it is teachers who hold the key to students' growing or diminishing self-esteem, achievement, and visions of present and future possibilities for learning through their commitment, knowledge and skills. It is the kinds and quality of the education, training and development opportunities throughout their careers and the cultures in which they work that will influence their ability to help students to learn how to learn to succeed.

We know that the odds against success are often high. For some teachers, the hope, optimism and self-belief that are the vital 'wellsprings' of successful learning and positive educational change (Hargreaves and Fullan, 1998, p. 1) are being eroded by the combined pressures of increased accountability, student testing, school inspection, performance management, and accompanying bureaucratization by governments who pay lip service to the importance of teachers and the complexity of teaching whilst continuing to increase workload in the name of raising standards.

The best teachers at all levels are those who have strong intellectual and emotional identities and commitments both to their subject(s) and to their students. Accounts by students of all ages across the world about their most successful teachers point to their passionate involvement as a key factor, for:

The example we set as passionate adults allows us to connect to [pupils'] minds and spirits in a way that we can have a lasting, positive impact on their lives . . . by . . . working with the [pupils] at the frontier of their own individual and collective experiences, feelings and opinions.

(Fried, 1995, pp. 27–8)

It is this passion that is rarely acknowledged as being at the heart of the intellectual endeavours and commitment to service of teachers as they work towards the moral purposes of society through students and young people. It is the drive to understand and articulate this passion and the ways it is socially constructed and mediated through the various experiences of teachers, their personal histories and biographies, their values and beliefs and the contexts in which they work, that is at the heart of every chapter. This book is for and about teachers for whom teaching is more than just a job, more than an intellectual challenge, more than a management task, for whom vocation and commitment are essential features of their professionalism. It is for teachers who are concerned, through their work, with education in its broader sense, who acknowledge that emotional engagement and care are essential to good teaching, who are committed to service, and who are, have been or wish to be again, passionate.

Why passion is essential

In our rush to reform education, we have forgotten a simple truth: reform will never be achieved by renewing appropriations, restricting schools, rewriting curricula, and revising texts if we continue to demean and dishearten the human resource called the teacher on whom so much depends . . . if we fail to cherish – and challenge – the human heart that is the source of good teaching.

(Palmer, 1998, p. 3)

Passion is defined in the *Oxford Dictionary* (1989) as 'any kind of feeling by which the mind is powerfully affected or moved'. It is a driver, a motivational force emanating from strength of emotion. People are passionate about things, issues, causes, people. Being passionate generates energy, determination, conviction, commitment, and even obsession in people. Passion can lead to enhanced vision (the determination to attain a deeply desired goal) but it can also restrict wider vision and lead to the narrow pursuit of a passionately held conviction at the expense of other things. Passion is not a luxury, a frill, or a quality possessed by just a few teachers. It is essential to all good teaching. It is

not just a personality trait that some people have and others lack, but rather something discoverable, teachable or reproducible, even when the regularities of school life gang up against it. Passion and practicality are not opposing notions; good planning and design are as important as caring and spontaneity in bringing out the best in students. Although not the whole story, passion, uncomfortable as the word may sound, is at the heart of what teaching is or should be.

(Fried, 1995, p. 6)

Passion, therefore, may lead to positive, committed behavioural outcomes on the one hand, or negative, destructive ones on the other, depending on the internal rational–emotional balance. The positive–negative balance does rest on neat division, for example the presumption that anger is a negative emotion and love a positive one. Indeed, current theoretical models arising from neurophysiology (van der Kolk, 1994), cognitive psychology (Metzger *et al.*, 1990; Goleman, 1995) and various therapies (Jackins, 1965, 1973, 1989) observe that intensity of emotion has a high tendency to interfere with rational thinking. Thus, passionate feelings are just as likely to cloud judgement and lead to extremes of behaviour that may not be rational. Often what drives passionate feelings is unconscious. As Nias observes:

> Behind the ordered control and professional calm of all the teachers . . . bubble deep, potentially explosive passions, emotions bringing despair, elation, anger and joy of a kind not normally associated in the public mind with work.
>
> (Nias, 1996, p. 226)

Yet good teachers invest large amounts of their substantive emotional selves in pursuing their work with students. Not only are they accountable for their work to parents and their employers; they are also responsible to the students they teach.

To be passionate about teaching is not only to express enthusiasm but also to enact it in a principled, values-led, intelligent way. All effective teachers have a passion for their subject, a passion for their pupils and a passionate belief that who they are and how they teach can make a difference in their pupils' lives, both in the moment of teaching and in the days, weeks, months and even years afterwards. Passion is associated with enthusiasm, caring, commitment, and hope, which are themselves key characteristics of effectiveness in teaching. For teachers who care, the student as a person is as important as the student as a learner. That respect for person-hood is likely to result in greater motivation to learn. Caring teachers who know their students create relationships that enhance the learning process (Stronge, 2002). Passion is also associated with fairness and understanding, qualities constantly named by students in their assessments of good teachers, and with the qualities that effective teachers display in everyday social interactions – listening to what students say, being close rather than distant, having a good sense of playfulness, humour, encouraging students to learn in different ways, relating learning to experience, encouraging students to take responsibility for their own learning, maintaining an organized classroom environment, being knowledgeable about their subject, creating learning environments that engage students and stimulate in them an excitement to learn.

It is only when teachers are able and enabled to nurture and express their passions for their field of knowledge, and about learning, to bring these to their work, to break through 'the fog of passive compliance or active disinterest' (Fried, 1995, p. 1) that sometimes seems to envelop so many students, that they will meet with success.

> It is the teachers' passions that help them and their students escape the slow death of 'busyness at work', the rituals of going through the motions, which in schools usually means checking that the homework was done, covering the curriculum, testing, grading, and quickly putting it all behind us.
>
> (Fried, 1995, p. 19)

Passionate teaching and effectiveness

Teachers in all classrooms are expected to be knowledgeable and skilled practitioners, accountable for raising standards of achievement of all students in ways that will stimulate pupils' interests in learning. They are expected, also, to promote school–parent relationships, address issues of culture and language, environmental concerns and social, citizenship and moral issues, issues of equity, social justice, participative democracy, and lifelong learning. In other words, teachers' work is complex, and located in contexts that are both demanding (of knowledge, classroom management and teaching skills) and emotionally and intellectually challenging. They are confronted in their work, it is said, by a number of external imperatives that lead to contradictory demands: on the one hand, there is a growing recognition of the importance to the economy, to life-long education, and to the society, of teamwork and co-operation, tolerance and mutual understanding. On the other, there is an increase in alienation of students from formal schooling, increasing emphasis on competition and material values, and growing inequalities, deepening social differences and a breakdown in social cohesion (UNESCO, 1996; Bentley, 1998). It is important to remember that it is teachers who must bear major responsibility for managing these demands. They are 'one of our last hopes for rebuilding a sense of community' (Hargreaves and Fullan, 1998, p. 42).

Government reforms have also transformed the way teachers teach in schools in England and made them more publicly accountable for pupils' results. The so-called 'performativity' agenda (Lyotard, 1979; Ball, 2001) that has been established is not all bad – teachers and schools now plan for and monitor pupil progress much more systematically. However, its broader bureaucratic, managerialist implementation has exhausted many teachers so they have lost that passion to educate with which they first entered the profession. The space formerly available for spontaneity, creativity and attending to unanticipated learning needs of children and young people has contracted as teachers struggle to attain government targets for achievement and fulfil associated bureaucratic demands.

Bringing a passionate self to teaching every day of every week of every school term and year is a daunting prospect. Having a good idea about what to do in the classroom is only the beginning of the work of teaching. It is the translation of passion into action that embodies and integrates the personal and the professional, the mind and the emotion, that will make a difference in pupils' learning lives.

> Teachers have hearts and bodies, as well as heads and hands, though the deep and unruly nature of their hearts is governed by their heads, by the sense of moral responsibility for students and the integrity of their subject matter which is at the core of their professional identity. They cannot teach well if any part of them is disengaged for long. Increasingly, social and political pressures give precedence to head and hand, but if the balance between feeling, thinking and doing is disturbed too much or for too long, teaching becomes distorted, teachers' responses are restricted, they may even cease to be able to teach. Teachers are emotionally committed to many different aspects of their jobs. This is not an indulgence; it is a professional necessity. Without feeling, without the freedom to 'face themselves', to be whole persons in the classroom, they implode, explode – or walk away.
>
> (Nias, 1996, p. 305)

At their best, however, teachers display, through who they are and how they act, a deep and passionate commitment to their work. Under such circumstances and faced with such challenges, it is vital that they sustain their passion for teaching. In a comparative study of policies that aimed to increase teacher quality, the common factor among excellent teachers identified in studies in New Zealand (Ramsay, 1993), Italy (Macconi, 1993), America (White and Roesch, 1993), Sweden (Lander, 1993) and

France (Altet, 1993) was that they had a passionate desire for the success of all their students. This was communicated through the classroom ethos – their sense of humour, interpersonal warmth, patience, empathy and support of their pupils' self-esteem; through classroom practices – they employed a broad range of teaching approaches that promoted semi-autonomous and collaborative learning; through collaboration with other teachers; and through a capacity for continued reflection of different kinds (Hopkins and Stern, 1996).

Fried (1995) argues that there is a clear connection between passionate teaching and the quality of students' learning:

1   When students can appreciate their teacher as someone who is passionately committed to a field of study and to upholding high standards within it, it is much easier for them to take their work seriously. Getting them to learn then becomes a matter of inspiration by example rather than by enforcement and obedience.

2   Without a trusting and respectful relationship among students and teachers, everyone's ability to work collaboratively and to take the kind of risks that learning requires is minimized.

3   Unless students are able to see the connection between what they are learning and how they might put such learning to work in a real life context, their motivation to excel will remain uneven at best.

(Fried, 1995, p. 47)

Teaching and learning at its best is not, then, an entirely rational set of processes. High-quality input does not always result in high-quality output. Good teaching can never be reduced to technique or competence.

There are many factors that help or hinder effective teaching and learning. Not least among these are the family histories and circumstances of the parents and the students; the leadership and learning culture of the school; the effects of government policies; the perceived relevance and value of the curriculum; behaviour in the classroom and staff room; relationships with parents and the wider community; and teachers' knowledge, skills and competencies. Yet the primary factors in good teaching that is effective are much more than these. They are the inner qualities of the teacher; a continuing striving for excellence (in herself and others); a caring for and fascination with growth; and a deep commitment to providing the best possible opportunities for each pupil. Good teaching is to do with teachers' values, identities, moral purposes, attitudes to learning (their own as well as those of their students), their caring and commitment to be the best they can at all times and in every circumstance for the good of their students. It is about their enthusiasm and their passion.

The call of teaching

Haavio, a Finnish educator, identified three key characteristics of the good teacher:

(i) *Pedagogical discretion* – the ability to use the most appropriate teaching for each individual

(ii) *Pedagogical love* – the caring instinct, i.e. the desire to help, protect and support

(iii) *Vocational awareness* – it seizes the teachers' personality in such a way that he is ready to do his utmost for it and finds in it internal gratification and the purpose of his life.

(Haavio, 1969)

Such ethical and moral dimensions of teachers' lives distinguish committed teachers who 'educate', whose work is connected to their whole lives, from those who 'teach', for whom teaching is a job rather than a vocation. For the former, emotional engagement, love of children/ young people, caring and critical thinking are essential complementary components of teaching. In observing passionate teachers at work in classrooms, there is no disconnection between the head and the heart, the cognitive and the emotional. None is privileged over the others.

David Hansen (1995, 1999, 2001) conceives teachers' work as a calling, a moral and personal commitment that has to do with 'cultivating students' minds and spirits:

Teaching is a continuous activity of encouraging or fuelling attitudes, orientations, and understandings which allow students to progress rather than to regress as human beings, to grow rather than to become narrow in their outlook and range of capabilities. . . . Other things being equal, a person with a sense of calling comes to inhabit the role of teacher more fully than does an individual who treats it as only a job . . . will be more likely to exert a broader and more dynamic intellectual and moral influence on students. . . . As a calling teaching is a public service that also yields personal fulfilment to the person who provides that service. . . .

(Hansen, 1999, pp. 94–6)

It is clear from this and a variety of other research that while the *origins* of passion lie in the 'call' to serve, in the belief that we can make a difference in the quality of students' lives, its *renewal* relates to student behaviour, self-esteem, support through the school culture and colleagues, and a sense of being valued by the community. In studying the art of teaching in primary schools, Peter Woods and Bob Jeffrey were clear that emotions figured prominently in teachers' work:

> they were passionate about their own beliefs . . . they cared for their children; and their teaching had a high emotional content.
>
> (Woods and Jeffrey, 1996, p. 54)

One of the teachers interviewed in Woods and Jeffrey's study, for example, talked of her enthusiasm:

> Enthusiasms rub off on kids. I don't very often go into a class and do things I'm not interested in because I know that I don't do it well. But if I am interested in a particular subject or area and I go in and do it, I find that the children actually pick that up in a way. They actually get enthusiastic as well. . . .
>
> (Nicola, quoted in Woods and Jeffrey, 1996, p. 67)

Thus, when they see themselves failing, a sense of frustration, sadness or anger develops:

> So many kids go from day to day and they don't realise how important education is. . . .
>
> (Ibid., p. 15)

> I tend to feel sadness when we learn something about a student and their family situation, things we can't control or have any impact on. . . .
>
> (Ibid., p. 17)

All those who work with children and young people, all those who have observed and listened to many teachers who, quite clearly 'love' their job and the children and young people they teach, will recognize that the call of teaching is, perhaps above all, about love:

> . . . love of learning, of students, of the process of being fully human. Teaching is about love because it involves trust and respect, and

> because at its best teaching depends upon close and special relationships between students and teachers. It is, in a word, a vocation based on love.
>
> (Nieto *et al.*, 2002, p. 350)

Time to exercise such love is at a premium in the busyness of teachers' work and lives. Yet because clarity of purpose and passion, and hope that they and their teaching will make a difference to the learning lives of their students, are at the core of good teaching, it is essential that teachers are encouraged to and supported in finding time to revisit and review these. Since good teaching is fundamental to raising standards, it is clearly both the responsibility of the teacher and the school to ensure that teachers are able to continue to sustain passion, to exercise the love, care and respect necessary to good teaching, to strive to 'go deeper', to hold on to hope for a better future.

> Going deeper means hard thinking and soul searching about the fundamental value and purpose of what we do as educators. It means reaching into our hearts to care more deeply for those we teach and forge stronger emotional bonds with other people, such as parents, who share in the educational responsibility. Going deeper means staying optimistic and hanging on to hope, even in the most difficult circumstances, not as futile indulgence, but as active commitment that helps make real differences in young people's lives. Going deeper, in other words, involves purpose, passion, and hope.
>
> (Hargreaves and Fullan, 1998, p. 29)

Passion, hope and ideals

Teaching is a values-led profession concerned, at its heart, with change, directly for the betterment of pupils but ultimately for the betterment of society as a whole. Halpin contrasts Godfrey's definition of 'ultimate hope' as 'entailing social objectives, . . . a core of trust' (Halpin, 2003, p. 2) with Milan Simecka's assertion that a world without such hope 'would be a world of resignation to the status quo' (Simecka, 1984, p. 175, cited in Halpin, p. 2). In the context of this book, it is easy to relate Godfrey's definition of ultimate hope to those who are passionate about their work and their students. Vision, in particular, is an expression of hope, an 'affirmation that despite the heartbreak and trials that we face daily . . . we can see that our actions can be purposeful and significant . . .' (Sockett, 1993, p. 85). There is a need for vision, as a part of hope, to be re-visited regularly. For both:

> . . . are not a simple, unified view of what this school [or classroom] . . . can be, but a complex blend of evolving themes of the change programme. Visioning is a dynamic process, no more a one-time event that has a beginning and an end than is planning. Visions are developed and reinforced from action, although they may have a seed that is based simply on hope.
>
> (Louis and Miles, 1992, p. 237)

A passionate teacher can never, by definition, be resigned to the status quo. Yet hope, the bedrock of passionate teaching, can be hard to sustain:

> The alarm goes off at six and I haul myself out of bed at the start of another week. I try to do half an hour's work before setting off to school. I am still managing to get a decent night's sleep most nights, but the cumulative effect of the workload is taking its toll. I constantly feel the dull weight of deep fatigue . . . what strikes me is how little slack there is in the system. Every teacher seems to be working flat out all of the time; so much so that when for one reason or another a teacher is absent for any prolonged period, the strain is felt immediately . . . I've seen it happen in one department in this school recently and, were it not for the selfless and voluntary effort by all members of the department and the large amount of time and extra organization by the faculty head there would have been numerous times in which pupils were little more than baby-sat. And this is a very popular comprehensive [school] with a stable and experienced teaching staff in a comfortable teaching area with largely well-motivated pupils and parents. I shudder to think how things are in less fortunate schools . . . where a third of the staff are leaving at the end of the school year, and where it is not unusual for the police to be called to sort out any incidents. . . .
>
> (McCormack, 2001, pp. 6–7)

Given that this was written by a mature, new entrant to the teaching profession, it is easy to imagine how experienced teachers can have their initial hope in their ability to make a difference in students' lives eroded, their initial passion drained. The headline on the front page of the *Guardian* newspaper, 7 January 2003, which reported the findings of the General Teaching Council for England (GTCE) commissioned poll of 70,000 teachers – the largest ever undertaken – that 'A third of teachers plan to quit', was shocking but not surprising. Yet to be passionate is to retain hopefulness, to possess a disposition

> which results in them being positive about experience or aspects of that experience . . . the belief that something good, which does not presently apply to one's own life, or the life of others, could still materialize, and so is yearned for as a result.
>
> (Halpin, 2003, p. 15)

Teaching is, by definition, a journey of hope based upon a set of ideals, for example that I, as a teacher, can and will make a difference to the learning and the lives of the students I teach and the colleagues with whom I work – despite an acute awareness of obstacles to motivation and commitment (my own and others), the socio-economic circumstances of students, resource constraints, and policy factors over which I have no control. Teachers who are passionate about what, how and who they teach remain hopeful. Arguably it is our ideals that sustain us through difficult times and challenging environments; and it is our ideals that commit us to changing and improving our practice as the needs of students and the demands of society change. From the perspective of emotional intelligence,

> having hope means that one will not give in to overwhelming anxiety. . . . Indeed, people who are hopeful evidence less depression than others as they manoeuvre through life in pursuit of their goals, are less anxious in general, and have fewer emotional distresses.
>
> (Goleman, 1995, p. 87)

Those who hope, who have ideals and are passionate about teaching are, contrary to the popular image, highly practical in the way they prepare for and go about ensuring the betterment of their students.

> Holding ideals is not exhibiting warm and fuzzy feelings but needs to be valued as part of intensive educational debate about fundamental purposes . . . the absence of which undermines the heart of professionalism. . . .
>
> (Sockett, 1993, pp. 138–9)

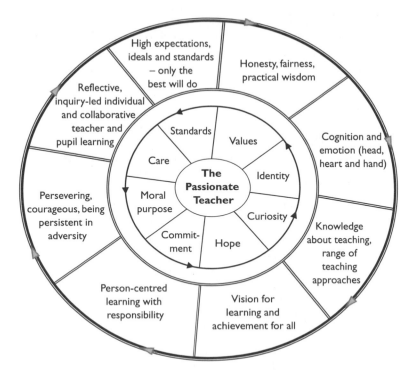

Figure 1.1 The Passionate Teacher.

Idealists also exhibit the courage to stand up for their beliefs and be prepared to argue for their views, not dogmatically, but as part of regular staff conversation about the aims of teaching in 'our' school and the ways practices do or do not reflect these.

In Figure 1.1, I bring together the hopes, values, identities, commitments, care, motivations, emotions, curiosities, moral purposes, and standards associated with the passionate teacher. It represents an agenda for inquiry and development that provides an alternative version of teaching qualities and characteristics to those that focus only upon teachers' technical competencies. It relates the personal and professional, the ideological and the practical, the mind and the heart, to form an holistic agenda for the initial and continuing development of all teachers – which the following chapters in this book will elaborate.

Time to reflect

These questions are drawn from the work of Geert Kelchtermans, a Belgian educator who from analysis of intensive interviews with beginning and experienced teachers identified five components in the teacher's self:

1   *Self-image*

   - Who am I as a teacher?
   - What are the connections with who I am as a person?

2   *Self-esteem*

   - How well am I doing my job as a teacher?
   - How do I feel about my work as a teacher?
   - Am I satisfied with myself as a teacher?
   - What are the sources of joy and contentment?
   - What makes me doubt my own personal and professional qualities?

3   *Job motivation*

   - What motivated me to become a teacher?
   - What motivates me to remain a teacher?
   - What could contribute to increasing (or sustaining) my motivation as a teacher?
   - What can I do to make this happen?
   - How can others help?

4   *Task perception*

   - What must I do to be a good teacher and how?
   - Do I feel that the emotional or relational problems of my students are my concern and to what degree?
   - Is it sufficient that all my students achieve the minimum goals for my classes?
   - What is my personal professional development programme?
   - What is it that I currently do that is a part of my job as a teacher?
   - What is it that is not?
   - What actions can I take to improve my situation?

5   *Future perspective*
    • What are my expectations for the future and how do I feel about them?
    • How do I look forward to the rest of my years in teaching?
    • What actions can I take to ensure that the future is bright?
                                             (Kelchtermans, 1999, p. 10)

Chapter 2

Moral purposes

Care, courage and pupils' voices

> What makes teaching a moral endeavour is that it is, quite centrally, human action undertaken in regard to other human beings. Thus, matters of what is fair, right, and virtuous are always present. Whenever a teacher asks a student to share something with another student, decides between combatants in a schoolyard dispute, sets procedures for who will go first, second, third and so on, or discusses the welfare of a student with another teacher, moral considerations are present. The teacher's conduct, at all times and in all ways, is a moral matter. For that reason alone, teaching is a profoundly moral activity.
>
> (Fenstermacher, 1990, p. 133)

Moral purposes

Moral purposes are at the heart of every teacher's work. They underpin their sense of commitment to their pupils, which includes but goes beyond the instrumental policy agendas of governments. In this chapter, I will discuss the kinds of care and courage which good teachers demonstrate in their everyday work, and what pupils have to say about their experiences of passionate teaching and its effects upon their learning.

Teaching is moral in the sense that it is designed to benefit humankind, but teachers may often be blind to their influence on students. Perhaps they are too busy, preoccupied with classroom management and subject-content coverage. This will be more so in secondary than in primary schools, where teachers spend almost every day with the same students. Countless stories by students or ex-students point to the importance, for good and bad, of the teacher's personal and interpersonal attributes. Classic films about the influence of teachers – *Goodbye, Mr Chips*, *The Blackboard Jungle*, *The Dead Poets' Society* as well as numerous texts – are testimonies to the 'moralness', moral complexity and powerful effects of teachers' beliefs, style, manner, and values upon students. While it is important not to 'sentimentalize' (Jackson, 1999, p. 88), it is necessary to acknowledge that moral purposes are an essential part of all teachers' roles. Those with a passion for teaching are not content with teaching the curriculum to students. For passionate teachers, professional account-ability is about far more than satisfying externally imposed bureaucratic demands or annually agreed targets for action linked to government and school improvement agendas. While these may be important, they do not touch upon the ethical or moral character of the teacher's work. Rather, such teachers understand that the nature of teaching, the terms of their work, oblige teachers to 'place the intellectual and moral well-being of students first and foremost' through their actions and interactions (Hansen, 1998, p. 651). They know they have a broader influencing role on students' ways of thinking, feeling and behaving,

Sockett argues that techniques of teaching are always subservient to a moral end and, therefore, that the moral character of the teacher is of prime importance. He identifies five major virtues: honesty, courage, care, fairness, and practical wisdom.

> *Honesty*   Central to teachers' professional expertise are an ability to differentiate between fact and fiction, a concern for the search for truth, an ethic of belief, creation of trust, and a *passion* for truth.
>
> *Courage*   'A continuing determination to stick to one's principles in the face of all kinds of adversity' . . . [courage is] . . . not related solely to fear or physical action; demands the use of practical reason and judgement, *either* in a situation of immediate danger *or* in the pursuit of long-term commitments that are morally desirable; [it] will be found in different sorts of social and institutional practices' (pp. 72–3).
>
> *Care*   Teachers must want children to care for what they learn and for each other. . . . 'They are not afraid of showing that they care, nor are they ashamed of wanting students to appreciate them, to like them, to reciprocate care. . . . They get to stretch the capacities and responsibilities of their role, understanding that it has to be a professionally personalized role' (p. 79).
>
> *Fairness*   'Teachers represent adult life. Their determination to instil a sense of justice alongside a sense of caring is an initial model of the outside world . . . in practice, teachers assume at least three roles that involve questions of fairness: distributing time and attention,

imposing discipline and sanctions, and monitoring fairness as a member of the school' (p. 82).

Practical wisdom   'Requires qualities of reflectiveness and judgment to be interwoven with the four other virtues enabling the teacher to know what to do when and why, in terms of pedagogical skill and content knowledge, with enthusiasm and authenticity so that the teaching role is congruent with personal values' (p. 85).

Like Sockett, Bottery argues that 'altruism' is essential to all versions of professionalism. He points to five essential ethics:

- *Truth disclosure*, which must override personal advantage
- *Subjectivity*, in which individuals must recognise the limits of their perceptions and the individuality of personal values
- *Reflective integrity*, in which individuals acknowledge the limits of personal perception and thus the need to incorporate different understandings of a situation into their work
- *Humility*, in which personal fallibility is recognised not as failure but as a condition of being human
- *Humanistic education*, in which the individual's duty is to help the clients help themselves.

(Bottery, 1996 p. 193)

While these are at the heart of the work of the passionate teacher, they cannot be taken for granted. The ethic of truth, reflective integrity and humanistic education – even fairness – may become eroded over the years as the people for whom we care change and teaching becomes routinized. Courage to teach in ways that are relevant to each child's motivational and learning needs may also become difficult to sustain with the inhibiting pressures of prescribed curricula, standardized tests and achievement agendas.

Care

Teachers who wish to exert personal agency and creativity in cultivating the intellectual and moral learning of their students will, by definition, be passionate about what they do and how and who they teach. They will display high levels of skill in a variety of contexts and exercise great care. In research with secondary school teachers, Gill Helsby and her colleagues noted that they developed

. . . appropriate and caring relationships with students which gave priority to their interests and well being, as well as dealing 'professionally' with colleagues, parents and other agencies where appropriate. Finally, because of the complexities of the task of teaching and the obligation to meet varying individual needs, high levels of skill were necessary to respond intelligently to multiple demands in a complex and changing environment. . . .

(Helsby *et al.*, 1997, pp. 9–10)

It is difficult to envisage a passionate teacher without such professional skill and integrity and whose first priority is not 'connectedness' with pupils, colleagues and self. Without this, motivation, trust and enthusiasm cannot be nurtured. In teaching, especially, it is impossible and undesirable to sustain divisions between the personal and professional. In teaching, care and compassion are essential features of becoming and remaining connected to students and colleagues. Teachers and students alike work better when they are cared 'about': an expression of teachers' personal beliefs and emotional commitment that goes beyond the contractual obligation of caring 'for' (Fletcher-Campbell, 1995). Children especially are 'emotionally attuned to be on the look out for caring, or lack thereof, and they seek out and thrive in places where it is present' (Elias *et al.*, 1997, p. 6). Yet to care for someone, teachers (and headteachers), need to know who they are, their strengths and limitations, how they can grow in order to respond to their needs. They need to be reflective in three ways: deliberative, relational, and critical.

In the *deliberative approach* they will reflect on their own roles (since teaching entails engaging in particular interpersonal relationships); on not just how they teach but whether what they teach is worthwhile and 'for the good' of students; and on the influences of the contexts in which they teach. Valli (1990) contrasts this with the *relational approach*, which is rooted in 'receptivity, relatedness and responsiveness' rather than in moral reasoning or deliberation. Here, 'relationships are more important than rationality, empathetic understanding more important than abstract principles' (p. 43). The *critical approach* entails a responsibility to interrogate broader social and structural inequalities that affect schooling and act to rectify these by changing institutional norms and practices, where appropriate. There can be no doubt that without such reflection and action, teachers are unlikely to connect with their students and teaching is unlikely to improve.

Talk to almost any pupil about good teachers and you will hear the word 'care'. It is a key construct by which good teachers are identified.

Indeed, the nature of good teaching presupposes a care for the one taught as well as respect for the integrity of what is taught (Sergiovanni and Starratt, 1993). In this one statement, the case for the education of the spirit (care), and the teacher as a critical rather than compliant educator is made. While teachers should not be expected to be therapists, there is a need to acknowledge that at times during the teaching process they will be engaged, as part of their continuing efforts to 'connect' with their students in order to 'teach them', in therapeutic acts. They know, also, that who they are as well as what they teach must connect emotionally with each student. This suggests a deep level of intimacy and what Daniel Goleman calls 'synchrony':

> The synchrony between teachers and students indicates how much rapport they feel; studies in classrooms show that the closer the movement co-ordination between teacher and student, the more they feel friendly, happy, enthused, interested, and easygoing while interacting. In general the high level of synchrony in an interaction means the people involved like each other . . . synchrony reflects the depths of engagement between the parties; if you're highly engaged, your moods begin to mesh, whether positive or negative.
>
> (Goleman, 1995, pp. 116–17)

Teachers with a passion for teaching *like* children and young people, feel comfortable in teaching them, are interested in learning about their backgrounds and present realities, treat them as individuals, and listen actively to what they say and how they act. In short, a core part of passion is care. Such care is complex and requires considerable empathy. Nel Noddings describes this as one-caring, in which

> Apprehending the other's reality, feeling what he feels as nearly as possible, is the essential part of caring from the view of the one caring. For if I take on the other's reality as possibility and begin to feel its reality, I feel, also, that I must act accordingly; that is, I am impelled to act as though on my own behalf, but on behalf of the other.
>
> (Noddings, 1984, p. 228)

Caring, as part of a passion for teaching, is far from being a sentimental ideal. It is essential. It is a key construct in the accounts given by pupils of all ages of good teachers. They are 'helpful', 'fair', 'encouraging', 'interested and enthusiastic', as against bad teachers who are 'indifferent' to the individual (Nash, 1976; Hargreaves, D., 1972; Woods, 1979).

Caring relationships between teachers and students, then, are fundamental to successful teaching and learning. They are the glue that
binds the two together and are the abiding expression of the teacher's
commitment to the student as person.

Because caring demands personal as well as professional investment in
the classroom, teachers run the risk of being personally and professionally vulnerable:

> . . . to reach out to children and develop genuine, warm relationships
> with them may compromise one's ability to control them. Much of
> what is wrong with our schools can be traced back to the fact that
> when these two objectives clash, connection frequently gives way to
> control.
>
> (Kohn, 1996, p. 112)

They need courage!

Courage

> I am a teacher at heart, and there are moments in the classroom when
> I can hardly hold the joy. When my students and I discover uncharted
> territory to explore, when the pathway out of the thicket opens up before
> us, when our experience is illuminated by the lightening-life of the mind
> – then teaching is the finest work I know. But at other moments, the
> classroom is so lifeless or painful or confused – and I am powerless to do
> anything about it – that my claim to be a teacher seems a transparent
> sham. Then the enemy is everywhere: in those students from some afar
> planet, in that subject I thought I knew, and in the personal pathology that
> keeps me earning my living this way. What a fool I was to imagine that
> I had mastered this occult art – harder to divine than tea leaves and
> impossible for mortals to do even passably well!
>
> (Palmer, 1998, p. 1)

Parker J. Palmer's words, taken from his book, *The Courage to Teach*,
portray the excitement of teaching at its best – when the minds and
spirits of teacher and students are mutually engaged in learning – and at
its most frustrating, when connections between teaching and learning,
the teacher and the learner seem to be impossible to make. There will be
few in the human services professions who read this book who have not
experienced these highs and lows; and few who have not been tempted,

at one time or another, to rein in the passion with which they entered their work.

Palmer explores the intellectual, emotional and spiritual landscape of teaching. At the heart of his book is the question, 'Who is the self that teaches?' In recognizing the importance of well-developed individual identities and a 'connectedness' to others, MacIntyre, like Palmer, links care, identity and concern with courage:

> If someone says that he cares for some individual, community, or cause but is unwilling to risk harm or danger on his, her or its own behalf, he puts into question the genuineness of his care and concern. Courage, the capacity to risk, harm or damage oneself, has its role in human life because of this connection with care and concern.
>
> (MacIntyre, 1981, p. 192)

Courage, like fairness, honesty, care, and practical wisdom, is a necessary virtue in teaching (Sockett, 1993). Sockett defines courage as: 'a virtue that describes how a person, often selflessly, behaves in difficult and adverse circumstances that demand the use of practical reason and judgement in pursuit of long-term commitments that are morally desirable' (ibid., p. 74). For much of the time, teachers work in situations that may reasonably be described as difficult, personally, emotionally and cognitively challenging, sometimes turbulent and occasionally violently disruptive. It requires courage to maintain a commitment over time, courage to persist in caring for every student in the class, those who are able, those who are not, those who are interested and those who are alienated. It takes courage to continue to believe in and be actively engaged in one's moral purposes and not to default under pressures of effort and energy.

> Entropy, or evil, is the default state, the condition to which systems return unless work is done to prevent it. What prevents it is called 'good' – actions that preserve order while preventing rigidity, that are informed by the needs of the most evolved systems. Acts that take into account the future, the common good, the emotional well-being of others. Good is the creative overcoming of inertia, the energy that leads us to the evolution of human consciousness. To act in terms of new principles of organization is always more difficult, and requires more effort and energy. The ability to do so is what has been known as virtue.
>
> (Csikszentmihalyi, 1997, p. 143)

It takes courage not to be discouraged when teaching practices must be changed, new curricula absorbed, new rules of conduct met that seem to emphasize bureaucracy at the expense of teaching. Teaching well, over time, is a struggle and it takes courage to continue to encourage self and others to learn in changing personal, professional, social, and organizational contexts.

Three cautionary notes

There are three cautionary notes for the passionately caring teacher, however, in the exercise and management of care. The first concerns the relationship between care and achievement, the second the consequences of care, and the third, the negative results of compassion that is unmanaged by the teacher:

1 Care and achieving the task

The challenges of maintaining teaching in which there is both care and concern for the processes of learning and the rewards of achievement are considerable. Nias reports that she has visited primary schools in which 'preservation of a warm and social climate seemed to have become an end in itself' (Nias, 1999a, p. 68). Yet she also observes that without continuing to express and articulate affection for pupils, both they and their teachers' lives would be morally as well as emotionally and educationally impoverished.

2 The limits of care

One of the greatest single complaints by pupils in schools is that some teachers do not care. Yet there is a limit to the care that teachers are able to provide. It cannot be unconditional. Unconditional care is a part of a loving relationship, while care as part of a loving pedagogical relationship is part of the teacher's responsibility to educate. Many children

> . . . feel alienated from their school work, separated from the adults who try to teach them, and adrift in a world perceived as baffling and hostile. At the same time, most teachers work very hard and express deep concern for their students. In an important sense, teachers do care, but they are unable to make the connections that would complete caring relationships with their students.
>
> (Noddings, 1992, p. 2)

Perhaps the fear of these kinds of feelings, along with a recognition that it is impossible to teach and fully care for each and every student all the time, is what causes some teachers to maintain personal and professional distance from their students (Laskey, 2000).

3 Compassion fatigue

> Caring and compassion are not soft, mushy goals. They are part of the hard core of subjects we are responsible for teaching. Informed and skilful care is learned. Caring is as much cognitive as affective. The capacity to see the world as others might is central to unsentimental compassion and at the root of both intellectual skepticism and empathy.
>
> (Meier, 1995, p. 63)

Passionate teaching is guided by principles of compassion that overcome the vagaries of time pressures at work, cultures that promote division rather than collaboration and do not support the building of learning communities that, by definition, are compassionate organizations.

At the heart of any successful teacher–learner relationship is compassion, defined as 'other-oriented feelings that are most often congruent with the perceived welfare of the other person' (Batson, 1994, p. 606), and often seen when the teacher recognizes a student's emotional difficulty in coping with being at school, in being expected to learn while, for example, suffering a crisis at home. Teaching is hugely challenging and complex at a personal level not least because many young people today face problems, difficulties and challenges ranging from family conflict to relationships, academic pressures, racism, substance abuse, poverty, life-stage transitions, etc. However, these are circumstances in which the need to care and sustain care for students in order to encourage them to learn is so great that teachers' emotional selves may be overwhelmed, their own well-being compromised. Working alongside, encouraging, teaching such young people takes its toll over time. Figley (1995) coined the term 'compassion fatigue' to describe the condition resulting from exposure to and empathy with people's traumatic issues. Engaging with others empathetically (passionately) – listening to stories, pupils' stories of fear, abuse, worry, and suffering (so much part of the pastoral role of teaching for those who really engage) – carries risks. 'Trauma is contagious' (Herman, 1992, p. 140).

Individuals can respond to high or chronic stress by displaying changed behaviour, such as increased alcohol intake, or suffer psychological symptoms, including sleep problems, irritability or burn-out; and develop health problems like backache, peptic ulcers or a depressed immune system. Within the organization there could be many indicators, including increased levels of absenteeism, high staff turnover, poor time-keeping, bullying, and disciplinary problems.

Compassion fatigue is a form of stress that develops when care-givers have become so involved with providing care to others that they become emotionally and spiritually exhausted themselves. Symptoms are similar to those suffered as a result of overwork, and may include:

- *Physical*: sleep difficulties, headaches
- *Emotional*: irritability, anger, anxiety, depression and guilt, withdrawal
- *Behavioural*: impatience, aggression, pessimism, defensiveness and cynicism
- *Work-related*: lowered concentration, poor work performance, apathy, absenteeism, perfectionism, workaholism
- *Interpersonal*: perfunctory communication with others, inability to concentrate on relationships, withdrawal, distancing from friends
- *Intrapersonal*: loss of confidence, self-esteem, and patience with self

Ways of countering or avoiding this form of fatigue include: management of too-close personal (as distinct from professional) emotional involvement with pupils; engaging the support of others; and regular review of the career trajectory in order to assess the experiences that may contribute to compassion fatigue. Energy and enthusiasm for teaching, learning and living must be sustained if passion is to survive.

Zehm and Kottler suggest guidelines to follow along the path to becoming a passionate, committed teacher:

1   *Take care of yourself*   Teachers with higher levels of self-esteem are more flexible in their thinking, more willing to learn and more effective in applying what they learn to improve the learning of their students.
2   *Be interested and interesting*   Take risks, let your passion for lifelong learning fuel your pursuit of new knowledge, experiences, opportunities to learn . . . infect your students with natural curiosity to ask questions. Make education interesting.

3　*Find a mentor/critical friend*　Teachers who work in isolation from others are more susceptible to burnout and lower levels of self-esteem.

4　*Make learning meaningful*　Spend time helping students to understand why they are studying a particular subject and how it will benefit them . . . infuse them with a passion to learn.

5　*Balance care and control*　Care and controlling are mutually supportive . . . establish classroom boundaries to support self-discipline, mutual respect and care.

6　*Cultivate your cultural sensitivity*　It is part of the passionately committed teacher's moral responsibility to cultivate knowledge and appreciation of cultural diversity, and to teach others to do the same.

7　*Become active in professional organizations*　Enrich your personal–professional life.

(Zehm and Kottler, 1993, pp. 120–4)

Passionate voices

The final part of this chapter focuses upon what pupils and ex-pupils say about their teachers. What pupils say about teachers, teaching, learning and schooling provides an important means of thinking about improving schools and classrooms (Rudduck *et al.*, 1996), and it is clear from a number of studies that they are eminently competent to perceive teachers' attitudes, intentions and behaviour accurately. We should, therefore, take time to listen to them.

> Passionate people are the ones who make a difference in our lives. By the intensity of their beliefs and actions, they connect us with a sense of value that is within – and beyond – ourselves. Sometimes that passion burns with a quiet, refined intensity; sometimes it bellows forth with thunder and eloquence. But in whatever form or style a teacher's passion emerges, students know they are in the presence of someone whose devotion to learning is exceptional. Even when that devotion has an intensity that may make students feel uncomfortable, they still know it's something important. It's what makes a teacher unforgettable.
>
> (Fried, 1995, p. 17)

There have been a number of research studies on pupils' perspectives on good schools and teachers (Blishen, 1969; Nash, 1973; Meighan,

1977; Woods, 1979; Beynon, 1985) in addition to those of Rudduck and her colleagues (1996). Yet while the wise teacher will always seek feedback and note pupil response to him/her and his/her teaching as an informal means of gauging effect, there is still little evidence of pupils' views being taken into account in systematic, regular ways. Morgan and Morris (1999), in interviewing more than 200 pupils and 133 teachers in comprehensive schools, recognized the importance attached by governments to raising standards in schools in response to the need for competitive economic advantage. However, they suggest that:

> . . . of equal, if not greater, importance is education's role in equipping each of its citizens with the character of autonomous thought and action, with the moral sense and civic confidence that they collectively are the ultimate government. Quality in education is then about character and skills, about the architecture of the soul and the standard of living.
>
> (Morgan and Morris, 1999, p. 16)

In response to the question, 'What makes *the difference* between lessons where you learn a lot and those where you don't learn very much?', most pupils (60 per cent), in their study, not surprisingly, cited the teacher. While more than half of these cited teaching methods, almost 20 per cent cited the teachers' interpersonal relationships and 25 per cent the teachers' control and order as being influential. In a chapter that focuses on why some teachers are better than others, Morgan and Morris (ibid.) report that whilst 59 per cent of pupils' responses related to their class-room practices (task), 37 per cent related to teacher relationships (op. cit., p. 36). The overwhelming majority of these statements related to aspects of enthusiasm expressed by teachers. Below is a selection from those quoted:

> How they present the work to you so it is not tedious and boring . . . making the work interesting . . . more exciting . . . make it fun . . . make things exciting, rather than someone who talks and we just write . . . explain things . . . not bothered if you ask them questions. . . . Keeping order; making lessons fun and not 'that's your work get on with it'. . . . Helpful and encourage you when you have a problem. . . . Care . . . have time . . . are humorous . . . will talk personally and confidentially with pupils . . . make you believe in yourself. . . .
>
> (op. cit., pp. 38–50)

These responses reflect those of countless international research studies of pupils' perspectives on good teaching. They provide a set of standards that teachers who are passionate about their work relish; for without the passion for subject and pupil it will be difficult to sustain the levels of planning, intelligent interaction and emotional engagement necessary to merit the title 'good' teacher.

In a recently reported research project into potential models for the successful teaching of 'Personal Development', Key Stage 3 students expressed enthusiasm for the work of their teachers, who taught a range of subjects. They found the lessons to be:

> Fun, interesting opportunities to get to know people better . . . to learn about how other people think . . . to learn what happens in your own life and therefore begin to understand it. . . .

The research found that teachers who were perceived by students to be most successful were *passionate* and *enthusiastic*:

> You know as soon as they come through the door that they really want to make these classes work for everyone.

> She's not afraid to share her personal life with us because she knows she can trust you and we can trust her.
>
> (in Leitch *et al.*, 2003)

This kind of teaching demands that teachers use a range of personal and pedagogical approaches. The teacher who demonstrates initial enthusiasm is likely to create a positive ethos, but sustaining the enthusiasm will need skilful practice. Here are some more words from the pupils interviewed by Morgan and Morris (1999, p. 56):

> History teacher explains really thoroughly, uses colourful words and is dramatic, and it's a bit more fun, we might do posters or write letters. . . .

> Science teacher took us down to the canal, we had nets and had to catch the insects and tested the water sample. . . .

> In English . . . *Treasure Island*, we had a film we discussed then wrote our own scripts in groups.

In German the teacher explains things deeply. We go around the room and say words. . . .

When all is said and done, teachers cannot teach effectively without the full co-operation of their pupils. Yet to achieve the co-operation of every student all the time is almost impossible. Metz (1993) points to the limitations of authority, the benefits of academic and social competences, and the exchange of goods through which the teacher holds out the reward of achievement (or the fear of non-achievement) in exchange for co-operation.

> Because teachers' work consists of creating rather complex changes in children's cognitive understandings and skills on the one hand and in their developing characters on the other, it is nearly impossible for teachers to be effective without at least passive acquiescence from students. To be fully effective, teachers need each student's hearty co-operation.
>
> (Metz, 1993, p. 104)

However, even this will not be sufficient to win the hearts and minds of students who see school education as a waste of time, who do not want to co-operate with school or classroom agendas or who lack the skills or motivation to do so, especially in schools where demands for raising achievement may appear so stringent and time-consuming that their value as a person seems to come second to the achievement of a targeted set of results.

There is no doubt that pupils are, like teachers, under increasing stress to perform. Bendelow and Mayall argue that 'because of the authority and control adults exercise over all aspects of children's lives, adult models importantly affect children's experience, knowledge and identity' (op. cit., p. 243). Relationships between children and adults, or 'generational proximity' may be

> a continuum ranging from conflict to harmony in child–adult relations. At one extreme, the generations may be experienced as separate, firm, congealed, and standing face to face in opposition to each other, to the extent that the child feels controlled, excluded or defined as an object. At the other extreme, children and adults may be engaged in a joint enter-prise, in harmony, with similar goals, and with a mutual emotional reinforcement of their satisfaction with the enterprise

and the social relationships embedded in it and strengthened through it.

(Mayall, 1998, p. 138,
cited in Bendelow and Mayall, 2000, p. 244)

In a study carried out in a range of primary schools, Bendelow and Mayall found that, for most children, friendships and companionships were critical to their enjoyment, together with work in which they could participate actively (e.g. problem solving).

Yet just as teachers may make a positive difference, so they may achieve the reverse. Twenty years ago, John Goodlad wrote of a thousand classrooms he and his colleagues had visited that they were:

> almost completely devoid of outward evidences of effect. Shared laughter, overt enthusiasm, or angry outbursts were rarely observed. Less than three per cent of classroom time was devoted to praise, abrasive comments, expressions of joy or humor, or somewhat unbridled outbursts such as 'wow' or 'great'.
>
> (Goodlad, 1984, pp. 229–30)

Today there are still stories of humiliation, hate and fear in classrooms:

> I remember in my elementary school there was one teacher famous for his slapping. I hated him. All the kids feared and avoided him.
>
> (Andrea, quoted in Mitchell and Weber, 1999, p. 38)

> One day in music class, the teacher caught me giggling as we sat cross-legged on the floor around the piano. As a punishment she made me sit scrunched up under her piano bench for the rest of the music lesson. I felt like an animal.
>
> (Jan, quoted op. cit., p. 38)

> One student . . . said she could not describe her good teachers because they differed so greatly. . . . But she could describe her bad teachers because they were all the same: 'Their words float somewhere in front of their faces, like the balloon speech in the cartoons'.
>
> (Palmer, 1998, p. 11)

A survey by Campaign for Learning in England found that a high proportion of 14–16-year-old students claimed that 'poor teaching' –

associated with teachers who were distant, patronizing and not interested in them as people – was a cause for their underachievement:

> The teachers never explain anything, they're always on people's backs like 'that's wrong', 'that's pathetic', 'you're thick'.

> Teachers favour the more intelligent students in our class and don't help us less intelligent students enough.

> Basically, we are patronized and treated as though we are little kids.

> The teachers don't even try to understand us.
>
> (Reported in Bentley, 1998, p. 80)

What qualities, then, do teachers who are able to connect with, inspire and interest students have?

Memories

> Often the stories that we remember and tell about our own schooling are not so much about what we learned, but how we learned and with whom. There are stories about teachers we loved, teachers we hated and those we feared. . . . There were good days and others full of tears and broken hearts, and many, many days of boredom, monotony and endless repetition.
>
> (Ronsmaniere *et al.*, 1997, p. 4, cited in Boler, 1999, p. 18)

In the most extensive empirical research into pupil perspectives on teachers in England, Rudduck, Chaplain and Wallace (1996) provide a synthesis of how pupils would like teachers to be. They should provide:

1   Respect for pupils as individuals and as a body occupying a significant position in the institution of the school.
2   Fairness to all pupils irrespective of their class, gender, ethnicity or academic status.
3   Autonomy – not as an absolute state but as both a right and a responsibility in relation to physical and emotional maturity.
4   Intellectual challenge that helps pupils to experience learning as a dynamic, engaging and empowering activity.

5   Social support in relation to both academic and emotional concerns.
6   Security in relation to both the physical setting of the school and in interpersonal encounters (including anxiety about threats to pupils' self-esteem).

(Rudduck, Chaplain and Wallace, 1996, p. 174)

Yet missing from this summary is the way teachers' passion for their work can affect the students. Here are just a few memories from teachers and pupils of their best teachers and best lessons:

Makes me feel important

She [the teacher] had an ability to make us all feel important. I thought she was my friend, everyone in the class did too. I hated history but liked her, and so I paid particular attention.

(Debbion, quoted in Cotton, 1998, p. 35)

The good teachers are the ones who know how to listen as well as talk, who don't make you feel that your opinion isn't worth anything. It's not age that's important; it's their attitude to young people. There are some who don't seem to enjoy what they're doing, and there are others who seem so enthusiastic about their subjects. It's brilliant being with those sort of teachers.

(Gillian, in White, 2000, p. 18)

My teacher . . . was the catalyst for my interest in the teaching profession as well as the match that lit my fiery passion for European history. . . . He was so full of knowledge . . . that . . . he would just tell us stories off the top of his head. . . . He was the first teacher to ever make me feel as though I was as intelligent as the other students in the class . . . he seemed to really value what I had to say . . . he was a very kind and intelligent man as well as an excellent teacher.

(Sandra, quoted op. cit., pp. 159–60)

Inspirational

Mrs Jones . . . demystified Shakespeare for me, translating it with inspiration. I remember it taking a long time to understand and come to like the plays we studied, but when I finally did it was thrilling and I scribbled for hours at home. She showed me how to read a story and make it come alive. . . .

> (Vicky, quoted in Cotton, 1998, p. 38)

There's no substitute for the infectious human element of a teacher deeply in love with his subject. He alone will set fire to my soul. I need guidance to mould my chalky dreams into a rich and satisfying adulthood. My need is now, today. Tomorrow is somewhere else. . . .

> (Susan, in Blishen, 1969, p. 20)

A small, rather comical looking man enters my classroom, . . . and what follows is almost literally a dance of ideas. His energy captures me even after ten years – wow! Almost twenty years later. At that moment I was seduced into following the path of truth. . . . I will never forget this teacher. . . . You felt his joy, you believed in his commitment to the subject because it was manifest in the very air of the classroom. . . . After this class, I was frequently exhausted and exhilarated by the energy of both the ideas and the expression of those ideas. Emulating this total joy coupled with such total physical and mental concentration and commitment has since been [my] ideal.

> (Harrell Carson, 1996, p. 13, cited in McWilliam, 1999, p. 111)

Belief

– was my best teacher because he believed in me. . . . By believing in me he taught me to believe in myself.

> (Dorothy, quoted in Cotton, 1998, p. 40)

Being a human being

When you go back to a list of qualities that made your best teachers so effective, you probably noticed that so much of what made them significant in your life was not what they did, but who they were as human beings. . . .

> (Zehm and Kottler, 1993, p. 2)

The best teachers are those who have worked hard not only to develop themselves as experts in their fields, but also to practice what they know and understand in their own personal lives.

> (op. cit., p. 16)

Enthusiasm

They've got to be enthusiastic about what you do as well as what they're teaching. . . . As you grow up the teacher has to change with you. . . .

(Joshua, in White, 2000, p. 52)

Going the extra mile

Mrs D. knew that something was bothering me. One day, after class, she asked me to stay behind so she could speak to me. . . . I broke down and told her about my father (who was an alcoholic) . . . for two years (after leaving school) we wrote to each other. I really think she was a terrific teacher and I will always remember what she did for me!

(Janine, quoted op. cit., p. 37)

Passionate

What matters is that they have a passion for their subject and a way of motivating you. Some teachers have the ability to motivate people, to know just how far they can push it, how provoking they can be to make you this close to giving up, but then you decide: 'I'm going to show this teacher'.

(Julia, in White, 2000, p. 159)

Teachers who just burn for their subject are the best. There are some who are boring and kind of, 'I am here today, I get my pay, and you are sitting there trying to learn . . . I do not care'. Those are the worst.

(Ola, in White, 2000, p. 159)

These words provide powerful evidence of the lasting effects and influence of teachers on the emotions of students, which relates as much to the person of the teacher as the professional.

Time to Reflect

Fried identifies ten characteristics of 'The Passionate Teacher'. Passionate teachers:

- Love to work with young people, but also care deeply about knowledge and ideas
- Try never to let their compassion for a student serve as a reason for excusing that student's ignorance or lack of skill
- Can be hard taskmasters precisely because they care for kids so deeply
- Are alive to events both in the classroom and in the world outside school, and they bring those perspectives together in their work with students
- Have the capacity for spontaneity and humour and for great seriousness, often at almost the same time
- Join with kids in appreciating the abundant absurdity of human nature but are also sensitive to issues that deserve to be taken seriously, particularly fairness and decency in how people treat one another
- Build a culture of mutual respect amid societal pressures to stigmatize and condemn unpopular persons and ideas and to dismiss young people and their concerns
- Are always taking risks, and they make at least as many mistakes as anybody else. . . . What's different is how they react . . . they choose to acknowledge and learn from them, rather than ignore or deny them
- Help to make the classroom a safer place for students to make their own mistakes and learn from them
- Take their mission seriously and communicate their beliefs.

(Fried, 1995, pp. 26–7)

1   Which of these characteristics do you identify with and which do you not?
2   Which of these characteristics do you display in your teaching now?
3   Are there any you used to have but you no longer use or use less often?
4   Which of these characteristics would you like to introduce or emphasize more in your teaching?

Chapter 3

Emotions and identities

In Western thought affect and emotion have been distrusted, denigrated or at least set aside in favour of reason. The tendency to distrust – even deplore – emotion has been aggravated by the rise of professions with their insistence on detachment, distance, cool appraisal, and systematic procedures.

(Noddings, 1996, p. 435)

Emotions

Antonio Damasio (1994, 2000), one of the world's leading neurologists, suggested that emotion is part and parcel of cognition. In doing so, he challenged the received wisdom that emotion (as distinct from extreme emotions) interferes with wise decisions. In *The Feeling of What Happens: Body and Emotion in the Making of Consciousness*, Damasio (2000) suggests that we need to overcome the 'obstacle of self' (ibid., p. 8) by under-standing three closely related phenomena:

- An emotion
- The feeling of that emotion
- Knowing that we have a feeling of that emotion.

Primary emotions are viewed as intrinsic states, natural responses triggered by circumstances or events (e.g. happiness, sadness, fear, anger, surprise). Secondary emotions, on the other hand, are a more complex amalgam of primary emotions. They are socially acquired, inextricably linked to our social and self-development in particular contexts (e.g. embarrassment, jealousy, guilt, pride). Because survival in complex environments (e.g. classrooms) depends upon teachers not only doing things right but doing the right things, and because emotions are integral to processes of reasoning and decision-making, we must understand them and identify their origin, in order to educate them as an integral part of the education of our minds:

> When consciousness is available, feelings have their maximum impact, and individuals are also able to reflect and to plan. They have a means to control the pervasive tyranny of emotion: it is called reason. Ironically, of course, the energies of reason still require emotion, which means that the controlling power of reason is often modest.
>
> (Ibid., p. 58)

Teaching itself has long been acknowledged as work in which emotions are central (Fineman, 1993; Nias, 1996; Day, 1998). Teachers invest their personal and professional selves in their workplace. Thus, because their work is a principal location for teachers' sense of self-esteem and personal as well as professional satisfaction, it is inevitable that they will have deeply felt emotions. Maintaining an awareness of the tensions in managing our emotions is part of the safeguard and joy of teaching. In focusing upon the role of emotions in teaching, the assumptions are that:

1   Emotional intelligence is at the heart of good professional practice (Goleman, 1995).
2   Emotions are indispensable to rational decision-making (Damasio, 1994; Sylwester, 1995; Damasio, 2000).
3   Emotional health is crucial to effective teaching over a career.
4   Emotional and cognitive health are affected by personal biography, career, social context (of work and home) and external (policy) factors.

Yet talking about emotion generates strong feelings and its relevance to teacher education continues to be perceived by many to be controversial. Indeed, in many instances, emotions are managed and regulated to ensure the efficient and effective running of the organization. They

> . . . are usually talked about only insofar as they help administrators and reformers 'manage' and offset teachers' resistance to change or help them set the climate or mood in which the really important business of cognitive learning or strategic planning can take place.
>
> (Hargreaves, 1998, p. 837)

The same is true for the consequences of the intensification and attempted 'technicization' of teachers' work in many countries. For example, while the New Right managerialist agendas now recognize the existence of widespread teacher stress and acknowledge its effects upon the quality of teaching and learning, there are no signs that they seek to look beyond this 'crisis' to attend the underlying emotional repertoire required by teachers if they are to sustain high-quality, enthusiastic teaching on a daily basis over a career. External policies, school and/or departmental cultures, too, may exercise both positive and negative effects on the emotional state of their teachers and, thus, on the ways in which they act in the classroom. Andy Hargreaves' studies have shown that when teachers' work is speeded up or intensified, many teachers become overwhelmed by the demands of externally imposed change, and that 'those who invest themselves most heavily in the emotional labour of the work are likely to become racked by guilt, feeling that they are hurting those for whom they care' (Hargreaves, 1997, p. 19). Where curricula are closely scripted and where school cultures inhibit the expression of certain kinds of emotion, there may be less room, for example, for spontaneity, risk-taking or improvization in teaching. To be warm and encouraging to a student who is persistently rude or uninterested requires emotional work, and there are few classrooms that are not inhabited by at least some students of these kinds. Yet, with the popularizing of such concepts as 'emotional intelligence' (Goleman, 1995) and 'multiple intelligences' (Gardner, 1983), increasing support is being added to the arguments of those who believe 'a view of human nature that ignores the power of emotions is sadly short-sighted' (Goleman, op. cit., p. 4):

> . . . we know emotion is very important to the educative process because it drives attention, which drives learning and memory. . . . By separating emotion from logic and reason in the classroom, we've simplified school management and evaluation, but we've also then separated two sides of one coin – and lost something important in the process. It's impossible to separate emotion from the other important activities of life. Don't try. . . .
>
> (Sylwester, 1995, pp. 72, 75)

Emotions and cognition

A significant and ongoing part of being a teacher is the experiencing of strong emotions. We know, for example, that the emotional climate of the school and classroom will affect attitudes to and practices of teaching and learning. Teachers (and their students) experience an array of sometimes contrasting emotions in the classroom. In a review of empirical research, Sutton (2000) found that love (as a social relationship) and care, job satisfaction and joy, pride, excitement, and pleasure in students' progress and achievements are among the most commonly cited positive emotions. Because of their emotional investments, teachers also inevitably experience a range of negative emotions when control of long-held principles and practices is challenged or when trust and respect from parents, the public and their students is eroded. In a study of Belgian teachers, Kelchtermans (1996) reported on teachers' feelings of *vulnerability*, engendered when professional identity and moral integrity are questioned either by policy changes, parents, inspectors, or colleagues in the light of unrealistic expectations or their failure to help students achieve higher standards. In England, Jeffrey and Woods (1996) found *professional uncertainty*, confusion, inadequacy, anxiety, mortification, and doubt among teachers when they investigated primary school teachers' responses to an OFSTED inspection, associating these with 'dehumanization' and 'deprofessionalism'. Other negative emotions are: frustration; anger exacerbated by tiredness, stress and students' misbehaviour; anxiety because of the complexity of the job; guilt, sadness, blame and shame at not being able to achieve ideals or targets imposed by others. As Boler reports:

> Each of us can recount at least one if not many horror stories about our schooling experience which exemplify humiliation, shame, cruelty, fear and anger – and sometimes joy, pleasure and desire.
>
> (Boler, 1999, p. xvii)

Less well documented are the negative emotions that can result from gender-related bias. Megan Boler writes of her exclusion by male colleagues:

> I discovered that the exclusion was part of an ancient historical tradition. The boundary – the division between 'truth' and reason on one side, and 'subjective bias' and emotion on the other – was not a neutral division. The two sides of this binary pair were not equal. Emotion had been positioned on the 'negative' side of the binary division. And emotion was not alone on the 'bad' side of the fence – women were there too.
>
> (Boler, 1999, p. xv)

The same may be true for some male colleagues in female-dominated primary schools or secondary-school departments. Where negative emotions outnumber positive ones, self-efficacy may be low and this can leave teachers with a sense of helplessness and hopelessness in carrying through work that relies upon hope and help for its success.

Sutton interviewed thirty teachers with a range of 1–28 years' experience from a range of schools. Of these, 63 per cent were female. She found that 'joy', 'anger', 'surprise' and 'excitement', 'love', 'sadness', and 'fear' were the most-cited core emotions. Two-thirds of the teachers said that they experienced surprise, excitement and enthusiasm (Nias, 1989; Tickle, 1991):

> The way I thought about enthusiasm in the emotions in teaching is my enthusiasm that I bring to the classroom. . . . I think it's my continued excitement when I walk in, the students know that I have a bubbly personality, I smile, greet the students every day . . . they know that's my love for teaching.
>
> (Sutton 2000, p. 13)

Because teaching is an intense job that demands huge amounts of physical, intellectual and emotional energy (PriceWaterhouseCoopers, 2001; Jackson, 1968), it is vital that the positive emotions always outweigh the negative if passion is to be sustained. Lazarus, Kanner and Folkman (1980) suggested that positive emotions have three functions:

- They can provide a '*breather*', through humour
- They can '*sustain*', helping individuals feel effective and valued
- They can be '*restorative*', helping individuals feel connected and cared for.

Emotional labour, emotional work

> The more the heart is managed the more we value the unmanaged heart.
>
> (Hochschild, 1983, p. 192)

Hochschild's classic research on emotional work and emotional labour carried out with university students, flight attendants and bill collectors seems at first sight not to relate well to teachers. Yet there are some similarities. For example, education is a long journey, not all students want to buy into the experience, and 'the emotional style of offering the service is part of the service itself' (op. cit., p. 5). Hochschild defines the work done by flight attendants as 'emotional labour', where 'seeming to love the job' becomes part of the job (ibid., p. 6). Such labour requires the worker to induce or suppress feeling in order to sustain the outward appearance that produces the proper state of mind in others. In other words, emotional labour is sold for a wage. She distinguishes this from emotional work or emotion management to describe acts that have 'use' rather than 'exchange' value.

Teaching calls for and, at its best, involves daily, intensive and extensive use of both emotional labour (e.g. smiling on the outside while feeling anything but happy on the inside) and emotional work that enables teachers to manage the challenges of teaching classes containing students with a range of diverse motivations, personal histories and learning capacities. However, too much of the former leads to a disengagement from the complexities of teaching and learning, and a loss of trust by students; and too much investment of one's emotional self may lead to personal vulnerability, feelings of inadequacy at being unable to engage everyone in learning all the time and, in extreme cases, overwork and breakdown. It may lead teaching to become predominantly 'emotional labour', where the smile of communication is about business not the person, where 'How are you today?' does not require a response, and where even acts of care are understood as devices to progress rather than emanating from genuine respect and care.

> When we sell our personality in the course of selling goods or services we engage in a seriously self-estranging process. . . .
>
> (Hochschild, 1983, p. ix)

Generations of teachers and teacher educators have debated the question of how much of one's emotional self to give to the role and how much of this should be protected. Students, however, suggest that regardless of how each individual manages emotion, it must never be regarded as a commodity. Their descriptions of 'good' teachers refer to the virtues of caring, fairness, justice, and personal concern (see Chapter 2). One's own personality must be managed, but not to the extent that emotions become commodities to be used in the interests of the employer or in the efficient implementation of policy. Hochschild illustrates her point using Stanislaviski's (1965) differentiation between 'surface' acting, where actors only act *as if* they have the particular feelings, and 'deep' acting:

This type of act (of the Coquelin school) is less profound than beautiful. It is more immediately effective than truly powerful; [its] form is more interesting than its content. It acts more on your sense of sound and sight than on your soul. Consequently it is more likely to delight than to move you. You can receive great impressions through this act. But they will neither warm your soul nor penetrate deeply into it. Their effect is sharp but not lasting. Your astonishment rather than your faith is aroused. Only what can be accomplished through surprising theatrical beauty or picturesque pathos lies within the bounds of this act. But delicate and deep human feelings are not subject to such technique. They call for natural emotions at the very moment in which they appear before you in the flesh. They call for the direct co-operation of nature itself.

(Stanislavski, 1965, p. 22)

Yet while it is the possession and willing application of natural emotions that arise from a real rather than forced or artificial passion for teaching and the taught by which good teachers may be recognized, it is also the case, as we have seen in the preceding discussion, that such natural emotions, which express themselves on a daily basis in the processes of teaching and learning, do need to be managed. Thus, both 'surface' and 'deep' emotions have their place in teaching. To identify so closely with the job that it becomes the centre of one's life is to risk burn-out; and although taking the opposite stance, regarding teaching as 'just a job', avoids that risk, the emotional estrangement from self and others that is a necessary corollary may result in cynicism and alienation. Passionate teachers do not accept the tenets of the rationalistic streams of management that suggest either implicitly or explicitly that 'ego detach-ment' (ibid., p. 264) is necessary in order to increase control over feelings in work that involves the emotions. Rather, they recognize that emotional engagement is, more often than not, an essential part of processes of effective teaching and learning, that it is important to have access to the part played by emotion in their decision-making and judgement, and that the emotional relationship between the teacher and the learner is as important to raising standards as is the intellectual content of the lesson. While the heart must be managed, it must also be allowed to beat freely.

Emotions and the standards agenda

There are two fundamentally different ways of knowing and under-standing that interact to construct our mental life. First, there is the application of the rational mind: we use the logical, deductive mode of comprehension, which is careful, analytic, reflective, and frequently deliberate. Alongside, there is another way of knowing by applying the emotional mind, which is powerful, impulsive, intuitive, holistic and fast – and often illogical. Usually there is a harmony between the two – head and heart operating together, one informing the other. However, when we are upset, distressed by strong emotions or indeed in touch with our passions, the emotional mind swamps the rational mind (Day and Leitch, 2001). It is clear from memory, neuroscientific and psychotherapeutic research (Jackins, 1973; Evison and Horobin, 1988; Epstein, 1986) that powerful, extreme emotions do disrupt thinking and, therefore, learning and teaching practices. Strong emotion – anxiety, love, anger, and the like – can create neural static in the pre-frontal cortex that can sabotage the capacity for attention in 'working memory'. According to Goleman (1995), 'That is why when we are emotionally upset we say "we can't think straight" – and why continual emotional distress' (p. 2) can cripple the capacity to learn.

From a neuroscientific perspective, Le Doux (1998) argues that the emotional brain may act as an intermediary between the thinking brain and the outside world. There is an interplay between thought and feeling, and between feeling and memory. When feelings are ignored, they can act unnoticed and thus have unacknowledged negative or positive influences.

> Our capacity to function intellectually is highly dependent on our emotional state. When we are preoccupied our minds are literally occupied with something and we have no space to pay attention, to take in and listen to anything else. When we are frightened we are more likely to make mistakes. When we feel inadequate we tend to give up rather than struggle to carry on with the task.
>
> (Salzberger-Wittenberg, 1996, p. 81)

When flooded by our emotional brain, our 'working brain' may have little capacity for attention to hold in mind the facts necessary for the completion of a task, the acquisition of a concept, the making of an intelligent decision, or the maintenance of relationships.

> When teachers' emotional scanning goes awry, however, what they actually experience is emotional misunderstanding – they think they know what their students are feeling, but are completely wrong . . .

students who seem studious are actually bored; ones who appear hostile are really embarrassed or ashamed that they cannot succeed! Because emotional misunderstanding leads teachers to misread their students' learning, it seriously threatens learning standards. In this sense, emotion as well as cognition, is foundational to the standards agenda.

(Hargreaves, A., 2000, p. 815)

Positive emotional relationships with students are also likely to reduce the incidence of behavioural problems and increase students' motivation to learn, for:

it is the affective component that guides a student's attention and is the primary determinant of achievement in school.

(Oatley and Nundy, 1996, p. 258)

Such relationships are characterized by genuine interest and regard, care, and the creation of a classroom ethos that is learner-orientated.

Research on the effects of emotions on memory has led to the conclusion that they can and do enhance memory retention (McGaugh, 1989). If this is so, then engaging the emotions, making learning personally intriguing and deeply felt is essential to good teaching. Feeling and emotion, then, have a vital role in the quality of teaching and learning since it is through our subjective emotional world that we develop our inner and outer realities, and make sense of our relationships and eventually of our place in the wider world (p. 42). To succeed in this, however, it is necessary for teachers to have a clear sense of identity. Knowing who you are, in what circumstances you teach and what are the influences on your teaching is essential to the practice of passionate professionalism.

Professional and personal identities

> When I do not know myself, I cannot know who my students are, I will see them through a glass darkly, in the shadow of my unexamined life – and when I cannot see them clearly, I cannot teach them well. When I do not know myself, I cannot know my subject – not at the deepest levels of embodied, personal meaning.
>
> (Palmer, 1998, p. 2)

Teachers' professional identities – who and what they are, their self-image, the meanings they attach to themselves and their work, and the meanings that are attributed to them by others – are, then, associated with both the subject they teach (this is particularly the case with secondary school teachers), their relationships with the pupils they teach, their roles, and the connections between these and their lives outside school.

The concepts of self and identity are often used interchangeably in the literature on teacher education. Identity as a concept is closely related to the concept of self. Both are complex constructs, not least because they draw on major research and theoretical areas of philosophy, psychology, sociology, and psychotherapy. Referring specifically to 'professional identity', Ball (1972) usefully separates *situated* from *substantive* identity. He views the situated identity of a person as a malleable presentation of self that differs according to specific definitions of situations (e.g. within schools), and contrasts this with the more stable, core presentation that is fundamental to how a person thinks about himself or herself.

Much research literature demonstrates that knowledge of the self is a crucial element in the way teachers construe and construct the nature of their work (Kelchtermans and Vandenberghe, 1994), and that events and experiences in the personal lives of teachers are intimately linked to the performance of their professional roles (Ball and Goodson, 1985; Goodson and Hargreaves, 1996). In her research on the 'realities of teachers' work', Acker (1999) describes the considerable pressures on teaching staff that arise from their personal lives. Complications in personal lives can become bound up with problems at work. Moreover, constructing, sustaining and renewing identity in changing circumstances involves, according to Palmer, re-membering:

> Re-membering involves putting ourselves back together, recovering identity and integrity, reclaiming the wholeness of our lives. When we forget who we are, we do not merely drop some data. We dis-member ourselves, with unhappy consequences for our politics, our work, our hearts.
>
> (Palmer, 1998, p. 20)

Several researchers (Nias, 1989, 1996; A. Hargreaves, 1994; Sumsion, 2002) have noted that teacher identities are not only constructed from the more technical aspects of teaching (i.e. classroom management, subject knowledge and pupil test results), but also

> . . . can be conceptualized as the result of an interaction between the personal experiences of teachers and the social, cultural, and institutional environment in which they function on a daily basis.
>
> (Sleegers and Kelchtermans, 1999, p. 579)

A sense of personal and professional, intellectual, social and emotional identity is at the core of being an effective teacher. It has been defined as 'the process by which a person seeks to integrate his (her) various statuses and roles, as well as his (her) diverse experiences, into a coherent image of self' (Epstein, 1978, p. 101).

The activist identity

Sachs (2003) identifies two contrasting forms of professional identity. The first is *entrepreneurial*, which she associates with efficient, responsible, accountable teachers who demonstrate compliance to externally imposed policy imperatives with consistently high-quality teaching as measured by externally set performance indicators. This identity may be characterized as individualistic, competitive, controlling and regulative, externally defined, standards-led. The second is *activist*, which she sees as driven by a belief in the importance of mobilizing teachers in the best interests of student learning and improving the conditions in which this can occur. In this identity, teachers will be primarily concerned with creating and putting into place standards and processes that give students democratic experiences (Sachs, 2003). The entrepreneurial identity, she suggests, is the desired product of the performativity, managerialist agendas, while the activist identity suggests inquiry-oriented, collaborative classrooms and schools in which teaching is related to broad societal ideals and values, and in which the purposes of teaching and learning transcend the narrow instrumentalism of current reform agendas.

Yet even to entertain the idea of an activist agenda suggests the need for courage, confidence, and a clear understanding of and passionate commitment to a set of moral purposes. To be a passionate activist teacher is to eschew the inward-looking isolated teaching profession described by Bottery and Wright, which:

> . . . not only serves controversial and political and economic ends. It is also limited in its ability to develop a generation that can adequately respond to complex and changing demands of a more

global environment, as well as to provide the sorts of skills and attitudes required for a more empowered and participative citizenry.

(Bottery and Wright, 2000, p. 100)

Judyth Sachs agrees and suggests that what is needed are professionals who resist the temptation to accept 'dull routine' and 'homogeneity of practice' (Sachs, 2003, p. 15). These professionals do not allow the physically and emotionally demanding contexts of teaching to dampen the passion and hope that are essential to good teaching.

There are unavoidable interrelationships between professional and personal identities, if only because the overwhelming evidence is that teaching demands significant personal investment:

> The ways in which teachers form their professional identities are influenced by both how they feel about themselves and how they feel about their students. This professional identity helps them to position or situate themselves in relation to their students and to make appropriate and effective adjustments in their practice and their beliefs about, and engagement with, students.
>
> (James-Wilson, 2001, p. 29)

Geert Kelchtermans (1993) suggests that the professional self, like the personal self, evolves over time and that it consists of five interrelated parts:

- *Self-image*: how teachers describe themselves though their career stories
- *Self-esteem*: the evolution of self as a teacher, how good or otherwise as defined by self or others
- *Job motivation*: what makes teachers choose, remain committed to or leave the job
- *Task perception*: how teachers define their jobs
- *Future perspective*: teachers' expectations for the future development of their jobs.

(Kelchtermans, 1993, pp. 449–50)

In his (1996) study of the career stories of ten experienced Belgian primary school teachers, Kelchtermans found two recurring themes:

- *Stability in the job*: a need to maintain the status quo, having achieved their ambitions, led to job satisfaction

- *Vulnerability* to the judgements of colleagues, the headteacher and those outside the school gates, such as parents, inspectors, media, which might be based exclusively on measurable student achievements. As vulnerability increased, so they tended towards passivity and conservatism in teaching.

A positive sense of identity with subject, relationships and roles is important to maintaining self-esteem or self-efficacy, commitment to and a passion for teaching. Yet, although research shows that identity is affected, positively and negatively, by age, experiences, organizational culture, and situation-specific events that may threaten existing norms and practices (Nias, 1989; Kelchtermans, 1993; Flores, 2002), few programmes of professional development acknowledge this explicitly. Research in The Netherlands, for example, found that the 'working climate', especially the ways teachers co-operated and expressed appreciation for each other, and active involvement in the development of school policy, impacted positively on teachers' sense of identity (Beijaard, 1995).

Changing identities

[T]he maintenance of a coherent story about the self is no longer a matter of occasional fixing if something goes wrong, but it is a continuing process in need of continual 'reskilling'. This is deemed necessary in order to weather transitions that are part and parcel of everyday life.

(Biggs, 1999, p. 53)

Identity is made up of mind, heart and body. For example, the novice teacher may find her identity by adapting to the expectations and directives of others in what Lacey (1977) called strategic compliance. Later, however, imitation and conformity may give way to invention and originality as she moves from taking on an identity to constructing her own. Identities are an amalgam of personal biography, culture, social influence, and institutional values, which may change according to role and circumstance. They depend upon:

the sustaining of coherent, yet continuously revised, biographical narratives, [which] takes place in the context of multiple choice. . . .

> Reflexively organized life planning . . . becomes a central feature of
> the structuring of self identity.
>
> (Giddens, 1991, p. 5)

Like Giddens (1991), Coldron and Smith (1997) consider that the
experience of teaching is one of continually constructing a sustainable
identity as a teacher.

Identities are not stable but discontinuous, fragmented and subject to
change (Day and Hadfield, 1996). Indeed, today's professional has been
described as, 'mobilizing a complex of occasional identities in response
to shifting contexts' (Stronach *et al.*, 2002, p. 117). Such mobilizations
occur in the space between the 'structure' (of the relations between power
and status) and 'agency' (the influence we and others can have), and it is
the interaction between these that influences how teachers see themselves, i.e. their personal and professional identities. Emotions play a
key role in the construction of identity (Zembylas, 2003). They are the
necessary link between the social structures in which teachers work and
the ways they act:

> . . . emotion is a necessary link between social structure and social
> actor. The connection is never mechanical because emotions are
> normally not compelling but inclining. But without the emotions
> category, accounts of situated actions would be fragmentary and
> incomplete. Emotion is provoked by circumstance and is experienced
> as transformation of dispositions to act. It is through the subject's
> active exchange with others that emotional experience is both
> stimulated in the actor and orienting of their conduct. Emotion is
> directly implicated in the actor's transformation of their circum-
> stances, as well as the circumstances' transformation of the actor's
> disposition to act.
>
> (Barbalet, 2002, p. 4)

Peshkin (1984) observes that 'we . . . have many subjective selves.
Which one comes to the fore depends on the situation in which we
find ourselves' (p. 234). Past and present personal, professional and
organizational contexts too are, therefore, important. Teachers will
define themselves not only through their past and current identities, as
defined by personal and social histories and current roles, but also
through their beliefs and values about the kind of teacher they hope to
be in the inevitably changing political, social, institutional, and personal
circumstances:

For a given individual, or for a collective actor, there may be a plurality of identities. Yet, such a plurality is a source of stress and contradiction in both self representation and social action. This is because identity must be distinguished from what, traditionally, sociologists have called roles, and role sets. Roles . . . are defined by norms structured by the institutions and organizations of society. Their relative weight in influencing people's behaviour depends upon negotiations and arrangements between individuals and those institutions and organizations. Identities are sources of meaning for the actors themselves, and by themselves, constructed through the process of individuation. The construction of identities uses building materials from history, from geography, from biology, from productive and reproductive institutions, from collective memory and from personal fantasies, from power apparatuses and religious revelations.

(Castells, 1997, pp. 6–7)

Because teaching well depends not only upon knowing what to teach but also knowing those who are taught, and because the teacher and those who are taught will themselves change over time as a result of life changes and changes in our society, teachers need to revisit their own identities in order to continue to connect. Reporting research with teachers in The Netherlands, Douwe Beijaard illustrated the different patterns of change in teacher identities:

Mary remembers her satisfaction about her own teaching in the beginning because she experienced it as a challenge. This challenge disappeared when she had to teach many subjects to overcrowded classes. The second lowest point in her story line was caused by her time-consuming study and private circumstances at home. Now she is reasonably satisfied, due to a pupil-centred method she has developed together with some of her colleagues. Peter is currently very satisfied about his own teaching; he qualifies his present teaching style as very adequate. In the beginning of his career, however, it was very problematic for him to maintain order. In this period he considered leaving the profession several times. The second lowest point in his story line refers to private circumstances and to problems in the relationship with colleagues.

(Beijaard, 1995, p. 288)

Here we see the ways personal and professional environments can affect teachers both positively and negatively. This interplay between the private and public, personal and professional lives of teachers is a key factor in their sense of identity and job satisfaction and, by inference, in their capacity to maintain their passion for teaching. In Mary's case, increases in class size and role diversification and intensification decreased the keen challenge she had felt on her entry into teaching; in the case of Peter, 'painful beginnings' (Huberman, 1993) had made it difficult even to survive. Common to both were the times when personal problems in their lives outside the classroom affected adversely their attitudes to teaching. Good teaching *is* a complex job that makes exacting demands upon the heart and soul as well as the mind, which few other jobs can claim to do.

Hope and courage, care and compassion are not, then, associated with role, but rather with teachers' identities. Activist identities focus upon the broader purposes of education in democratic communities:

1   The open flow of ideas, regardless of their popularity, that enables people to be as fully informed as possible.
2   Faith in the individual and collective capacity of people to create possibilities for resolving problems.
3   The use of critical reflection and analysis to evaluate ideas, problems, and policies.
4   Concern for the welfare of others and the 'common good'.
5   Concern for the dignity and rights of individuals and minorities.
6   An understanding that democracy is not so much an 'ideal' to be pursued as an 'idealized' set of values that we must live by and that must guide our life as a people.
     (Apple and Beane, 1995, pp. 6–7 cited in Sachs, 2003, p. 131)

Her theme is not passion, but Sachs recognizes that her notion of an activist teaching profession would be difficult to sustain in practice without it. She outlines nine principles:

1   Inclusiveness rather than exclusiveness – emphasizing the need for networks and partnerships.
2   Collective and collaborative action – interactions, sharing ideas and debating issues helps to sustain interest and works against disillusionment.
3   Effective communication of aims and expectations – people need to know what is expected of them, what the risks and personal costs might be.
4   Recognition of the expertise of all parties involved.

5   Creating an environment of trust and mutual respect – activism requires trust in people and process. Trust in times of passion and concerted efforts galvanize people.

6   Ethical practice – recognizes the needs, interests and sensitivities of various parties, acknowledges that no-one is culturally neutral.

7   Being responsive and responsible – expedience or opportunism for self promotion is best avoided.

8   *Acting with passion – activism requires commitment, courage and determination . . . involves high levels of emotional energy, demands that participants believe strongly in their convictions and have the best interests of the group clearly in mind.*

9   Experiencing pleasure and having fun – while the importance of the issues is to be taken seriously, the camaraderie of the group is essential.

(Sachs, 2003, pp. 147–9, italics added).

Although Sachs' notion of the activist professional was created out of a critical analysis of the current state of the teaching profession, it is essentially one of hope in the triumph of democratic discourse and faith in the individual and collective capacity of teachers and schools to be creative, communicative, critically appreciative, values-led, ethically centred, socially aware and inquiry-orientated.

Time to reflect

Hargreaves, Shaw and Fink (1997) have identified seven leadership 'frames', which focus upon purpose, culture, politics, organizational learning, structure and leadership as a means of examining change through multiple lenses. One of these is the 'Passion Frame', in which they, rightly, identify the importance of attending to feeling. The questions they pose form a useful means of reflection on the role of the teacher as passionate leader.

Passion Frame

The Passion Frame is about feelings – understanding other people's, creating environments that generate positive feelings of your own, and knowing how to avoid and deal with negative ones.

Teaching and learning are profoundly emotional activities.

- Are we paying proper attention to students' emotions in our work?
- Do we cultivate students' emotional intelligence? How? How could we?
- Does our school and its classrooms support, neglect or interfere with caring relationships with all students?
- How do change efforts affect teachers' emotional relationships with students, parents and colleagues?
- How can change efforts rekindle teaching as a passionate profession?
- Are our change processes (e.g. planning, implementation) positively emotional in their design?
- How do schools as workplaces and our attempts to change them promote 'positive' emotions like exhilaration and enjoyment, or negative ones like guilt, shame and frustration?
- How do we try and develop our colleagues' emotional intelligence (or do you assume they should already have it and just get angry if they don't)?
- Does our change effort, leadership style, etc. actively attend to the emotions of students, colleagues and parents? How?

(Hargreaves, Shaw and Fink, 1997)

Chapter 4

The passion of commitment

Job satisfaction, motivation and self-efficacy

Commitment is seen as the quality which separates the 'caring' or 'dedicated' from those 'who are not concerned about the children', who 'put their own comfort first'. It is also the characteristic which divides those 'who take the job seriously' from those who 'don't care how low their standards sink', and those who 'feel a loyalty to the whole school' from the teachers 'who only care about their own classes'. Further it distinguishes those who see themselves as 'real teachers' from those whose main occupational interests lie outside the school.

(Nias, 1989, pp. 30–1)

In Chapters 2 and 3, I discussed the importance of passion to teachers' work in terms of their moral purposes, care, and emotional understandings and identities. It is easy to see how these may be associated with commitment. In her reflexive account of research over a twenty-year period with 54 primary school teachers, Jennifer Nias (1989) wrote that the word 'commitment' appeared in almost every interview. It was a term used to distinguish those who were caring, dedicated and who took the job seriously from those who put their own interests first. Some teachers derived satisfaction from their commitment, while others found the demands too great a burden and reported that teaching was too absorbing and could take over their lives (Nias, 1989). Such teachers often placed limits on their commitment as a means of survival, or in some cases, chose to leave the profession altogether. Teacher commitment is closely associated with job satisfaction, morale, motivation, and identity, and a predictor of teachers' work performance, absenteeism, burn-out, and turnover, as well as having an important influence on students' achievement in and attitudes toward school (Firestone, 1996; Graham, 1996; Louis, 1998; Tsui and

Cheng, 1999). It may be enhanced or diminished by factors such as student behaviour, collegial and administrative support, parental demands, national education policies, and their own professional histories and career phase (Day, 2000; Louis, 1998; Riehl and Sipple, 1996).

It has also been associated with teacher professionalism. Helsby *et al.* (1997) established that behaving as a professional in secondary schools involved:

> Displaying . . . degrees of dedication and commitment, working long hours as a matter of course and accepting the open ended nature of the task involved . . . [making] . . . the maximum effort to do the best you possibly can and a constant quest for improved performance. . . .
>
> (Helsby *et al.*, 1997, pp. 9–10)

Nor should we forget the more obvious signs of commitment such as enthusiasm for the job and the people with whom one works. Witness, for example, comments by a school principal in a recent multiperspective study of successful head teachers:

> Every day's a challenge . . . I've no wishes to do anything other than what I'm doing. . . . Over the years, enthusiasm seems to grow rather than wane. . . .
>
> (Day *et al.*, 2000, p. 44)

Like this head teacher, many teachers have somehow found 'room to manoeuvre' as external reform initiatives (which have the effect of reducing teachers' range of discretionary judgements) are imposed and as the bureaucracy associated with increased contractual accountability begins to bite. Such teachers survive and once again flourish in the most challenging circumstances, principally because of the strength of the values they hold.

As Stephen Ball observed:

> Responses [to policy] must be 'creative'. . . . Given constraints, circumstances and practicalities, the translation of the crude, abstract simplicities of policy texts into interactive and sustainable practices of some sort involves productive thought, intervention and adaptation. Policies . . . create circumstances in which the range of options available in deciding what to do are narrowed or changed,

or particular goals or outcomes are set. . . . All of this involves creative social action, not robotic reactivity.

(Ball, 1994, p. 19)

It is precisely because of such changes that students need teachers who are able to be themselves in the classroom, who combine the person with the professional, who are passionate about what and who they teach, who have moral purposes, who are committed to teaching creatively, who will never describe themselves only in terms of their technical competences; and who will acknowledge that teaching and learning is work that involves the emotions and intellect of self and student.

Characterizing commitment

In research on enduring commitment (Day, 2001), one experienced educator reported that:

> I give my whole heart to my work. . . . I love challenge . . . and I feel satisfied with having put my all into it. . . . I've been in teaching 27 years and up to this point I've never considered any other work, because I'm committed to helping every individual child achieve their potential.
>
> (Day, 2001)

While not all participants echoed the *intensive dedication* of this, all talked of the most important commitment as being

> to the individual kids.

> It's based on my desire to enable all children to reach their potential . . . it comes from the heart . . . and I want to be able to be at my best both technically . . . (and) to bring a reflective approach. I don't believe in teaching that you can just be a technician.

A more complex view of commitment was expressed by an LEA adviser:

> At the moment there are various aspects of my work that I don't feel committed to at all, there are others that I do. I am committed to supporting schools in a way that helps them to improve. But I don't feel committed to some of the tasks I'm asked to do, involving

monitoring and paper-chasing to fulfil bureaucratic exercises that don't make any difference . . . so there's a real tension.

One of the participants defined commitment as *values based*:

a value, a virtue. It is the combination of having a sense of responsibility, loyalty and hard work. . . . I try to give my best performance, though I'm aware that I have good and bad days.

Another elaborated:

I think there's almost a 'sliding scale' of commitment. There are people who are prepared to invest heart and soul when you know you might not get much of a personal return. Children can be really rewarding but also frustrating if you invest a lot of yourself. . . . I've got a commitment above and beyond delivering a curriculum, to developing children as people . . . but also a commitment to developing myself as a professional, to widening my knowledge so that I can be really effective in what I do.

Another perspective on commitment is the '*ideological*':

an ideological approach to my teaching which is to do with belief in the dignity of the individual and the integrity of the comprehensive (school) ideal. . . .

Commitment, then, means different things to different people, though generic features are enthusiasm, care, belief in an ideal (vision), hard work, a sense of social justice, and an awareness of the need to attend to their own continuing development as well as that of their pupils.

The uncommitted

There are also those who are not committed. They may be:

just not very good at what they're doing . . . a lack of 'spark', that extra quality that's intangible . . . sloppy preparation, sloppiness in their interactions with students, poor timekeeping . . . someone who has lost that lust for life . . . children pick up on it and staff do. . . .

> People who are not committed tend to go in (the classroom) just
> before the bell in the morning, do their job, don't interact socially or
> emotionally with the children. . . . Teaching can't be just a job . . .
> you've got to have a passion for it as well. . . .

> There's a light on but nobody at home.

There is a recognition here of the loss of the 'emotional engagement'
so essential to good teaching.

These echo Evans' (1998) findings that:

> Teachers do not all share the same levels of commitment to their
> job. For some, it is a major part of their lives; . . . and they afford it
> extensive consideration and high priority. Others may perceive it
> differently. To them, teaching is just a job. . . . They may carry out
> their duties conscientiously and they may enjoy the work, but it is not
> their 'centre of gravity'. . . .
>
> (Evans, 1998, p. 103)

Change over time: the maturing of commitment[1]

A key issue for all teachers is how to maintain commitment over time:

> Most teachers come into teaching because they have a commitment.
> But we all have a certain level and some of us plateau earlier or later
> than others . . . people who are committed don't ever stop wanting
> to learn . . . so I'd characterize someone who is not committed as
> being stuck . . . not moving on. . . .

The passing of time and the changing environment may result in a
diminished commitment and job satisfaction. It was clear that although
these experienced educators had *maintained their commitment*, their understanding of the job, changes over which they had no control and changes
in their own life had caused them to *modify their approach* to their work, to
'channel' their commitment in different ways. One head suffered from ill
health but was determined to 'keep fighting' for the things she believed
in:

1 I develop this theme further in Chapter 8.

> In the last couple of years (of headship of a primary school) . . .
> there has been a little bit of ill health. . . . My attitude to the work
> has changed because of a growing understanding of things I hold
> dear, believe in and value . . . and because of that there are areas
> now that I don't like. . . . I now seem to spend a good deal of
> time fighting for the things I believe in and shall continue to do
> that. . . .

Although this seems to confirm Huberman's (1993) findings that in the
'final phase' of teaching, many teachers find satisfaction principally in
the classroom, it can be complicated by the effects of changes outside the
classroom:

> I find that increasingly difficult . . . you can start a lesson and within
> ten minutes you can have at least six interruptions. People come
> in and out and it's not fair on the kids . . . and I feel that my quality
> of teaching has deteriorated . . . and that's not because I don't
> prepare my lessons, it's because of all the forces that come in from
> outside. . . .

Almost all the teachers spoke of a tension between their commitment
to long-held core values and changes in the environment in which they
worked. However, they appeared to have been able to hold on to their
commitment – 'I've always maintained my belief at the same level
because its my passion'. While personal circumstances had affected the
balance of work and personal life (e.g. having a family) their beliefs had
not. Some talked about the origins of commitment as being vocational
('I always wanted to be a teacher'), while others talked of the 'supportive
environments' in which they had worked:

> [I] had a really good headteacher, worked with some exceptionally
> good teachers who have remained lifelong friends. . . .

All spoke of the ways their 'growing understanding of things I hold
dear, believe in and value' had caused them to 'take a more longitudinal
approach' to their teaching and the wider implications of what they did
in terms of management structures and external forces:

> I think about school-wide issues a lot more. . . . I like to get involved
> in meetings . . . the overall running of the school and where our
> department fits into that. . . .

Experience seemed to have played a key role in their continuing growth and ability to keep wanting to effect change and be an effective teacher:

> . . . the more experience you have and the people you come into contact with, things that you hear about, read about, have meant that I have more of a bank of knowledge and understanding to be committed and effect improvement than I did have . . . but I've always wanted to do this job and do it well. . . .

Personal investment in the professional task

There was also a positive association between their *personal* commitment and maintaining *professional* standards of practice, sometimes 'against the odds':

> My practice comes out of my commitment, not the other way around. Because I'm committed, I take my role very seriously. . . .

> I know that I have a bad day when I'm exhausted and not giving my best. I know that I need to take a bit of space so I can pull back that level of commitment.

> I have very high standards of myself and that can inevitably lead to frustration when the pressure on your time makes you do things in a less reasoned and thought-out way than you would have liked because sometimes the practicalities of the busy workplace environment make you do things . . . and sometimes you're not given the reflective space in which to think about issues more deeply . . . but you've got to move on, you can't be racked with guilt and self-loathing because my level of commitment would suggest that I always work with care and sensitivity and integrity and honesty . . . and that's the best I can do. . . .

> . . . You can't go at it like a 'bull in a china shop' because you'd wear yourself out. I try to be professional in my dealings with kids and staff at all times, though there are times when I feel like being less than professional.

These teachers seemed to possess a deep knowledge of their core values and acceptances of themselves, their strengths and weaknesses.

They were also prepared to move on in ways others were perhaps not:

> There are teachers who I would consider to be committed to their jobs . . . but not prepared to alter the way they do things, and accept changing situations and environments and take the ideas on board . . . and I think of how much I've been prepared to change and develop my own practice. . . .

Committed to learning

> Passionately committed teachers are those who absolutely love what they do. They are constantly searching for more effective ways to reach their children, to master the content and methods of their craft. They feel a personal mission . . . to learning as much as they can about the world, about others, about themselves – and helping others to do the same.
>
> (Zehm and Kottler, 1993, p. 118)

Part of the reason that many teachers are able to continue to adapt, to move on in changing circumstances, is their awareness of and adherence to particular core values that focus upon 'making a positive difference' in the learning lives of those with whom they work; and they associate this with the *enduring capacity to reflect*:

> I like to think that I am both committed and reflective . . . that they have a concomitant relationship. . . .

> You can't have one without the other . . . the school needs to recognize this. . . .

> Good teachers are all the time looking at what they do, reflecting on what they do . . . looking at weaknesses and recognizing strengths. . . . I have colleagues who . . . don't reflect, just carry on being mechanistic in what they do. Reflective people have a commitment to what they do. . . .

> . . . one of the commitments is giving time and space to mull over ideas and think about what's happening and what isn't happening.

. . . If you're committed to your students and want to see them develop, you're committed to think about what's working and how you can move them on . . . So reflective practice has got to be an integral part of that relationship.

. . . I think when you're more experienced you can work on intuition, you can work on bringing past experience to bear. But there is a danger in all of that, that you repeat patterns. It's hard work, but you do have to question why you're doing what you're doing . . . the day you get to the point where you think that you know it all, is the day you should retire. . . .

Continuing to learn is one way of maintaining a sense of self, self-esteem and a continuing commitment to do the job as well as possible in all circumstances:

I don't think commitment is just doing the job. I see it as a much more personal, emotional entanglement. To me, reflectivity is commitment and commitment is reflectivity. . . .

Differences in support

Much has been written about the relationship between effective teaching and school culture. It is now the 'received wisdom', for example, that collaborative cultures enhance teacher participation, and that this is likely to lead to and sustain teacher commitment.

I work in a good management team. They acknowledge my level of commitment . . . they understand that I work hard . . . they support me by giving me time and space to attend courses. . . . I don't think many management teams have thought carefully about how committed professionals can sustain their work rate over a great length of time.

Yet collaboration itself is not a rational process. The necessary emotional as well as intellectual commitment to working closely with others will be weakened without appreciation:

My commitment is not recognized, acknowledged in many ways . . . I'm not bitter . . . it's just basic people-management skills that are lacking.

I don't know how far they value my commitment. I don't feel under valued in that respect . . . [but] . . . we need to get more involved in the wider educational debate.

. . . nobody really questions it. They know that what is expected is being done, achieved. . . .

I suspect they have a different definition of commitment than I do . . . that they would define my role as somebody who has got to help the school to achieve its academic targets. . . .

This last comment was echoed by another teacher:

Judgements are placed upon you as to how well the children perform in their SATs (national tests). It feels like there's a whole staircase of people looking down on you . . . that are going to make these judge-ments on what you do, and the initiatives they've invested money in . . . there's a real climate of academic-driven syllabus in primary schools.

While these comments suggest that support is welcomed, it is clear that, as in some classrooms, there is a *felt lack of appreciation from others* of the work that these teachers do, day in, day out in their schools.

It seems, then, that 'commitment' is made up of a combination of factors and that the most important of these are:

1   A clear, enduring set of values and ideologies that inform practice regardless of social context.
2   The active rejection of a minimalist approach to teaching (to just doing the job).
3   A continuing willingness to reflect upon experience and the context in which practice occurs and to be adaptable.
4   A sustained sense of identity and purpose, and an ability to manage tensions caused by external change pressures.
5   Intellectual and emotional engagement.

How experienced professionals manage to maintain their commitment over the years remains a mystery further research may need to resolve. Although there are many examples of narratives of individuals that provide clues, there has as yet been little systematic research over time with teachers of different age and experience working in different circumstances. What is clear is that many teachers experience 'highs' and 'lows', are affected by life-cycle and contextual circumstances but remain, nevertheless, called to continue to do the best they can in making a difference.

Efficacy²

Although commitment is essential to the passion of teaching, there is a good argument for preventing it from taking over so much of your life that you eat, breathe and sleep teaching. Paradoxically, teachers' lives outside the school and classroom must be safeguarded so they can give their whole self to their students during school time (rather than what is left after a long night of planning or assessing, coupled with fatigue and a headache!). This is not to support those who preach the distancing of 'self' from work. On the contrary, the 'I – Thou' (intimate) as distinct from the 'I – It' (distant) relationship (Buber, 1965) is essential to good teaching. Yet what Nias (1996) terms the 'total fusing of personal and occupational self-image' (p. 42) can be unhealthy. It might be expected that teachers who are new to teaching, to the school or to a new role in the school will work longer hours during their first period as they seek to address early concerns and to 'measure up' to the job. However, to be working excessively as a matter of routine, to become permanently tired or exhausted after working a sixty-plus hour week, is likely to damage rather than enhance occupational effectiveness and consequently enjoyment, satisfaction, self-esteem, and, ultimately, commitment.

Among the mechanisms of personal agency, none is more central and pervasive than people's beliefs about their ability to exercise control over events that affect their lives. Thus self-efficacy (Ashton and Webb, 1986; Rosenholtz, 1989), the self-belief of teachers that they can exert a positive effect on their students' success, is a key mediating factor in sustaining a passion for teaching. High and low teacher self-efficacy have strong emotional components. Teachers who, for example, emphasize that the environment overwhelms their ability to have an impact on student's learning, 'exhibit a belief that reinforcement of their teaching

2 I am indebted to my colleagues on the VITAE project for their contributions to this section.

efforts lies outside their control, or is external to them' (Tschannen-Moran *et al.*, 1998, p. 204). Alternatively, teachers who 'express confidence in their ability to teach difficult or unmotivated students evidence a belief that reinforcement of teaching activities lies within the teacher's control, or is internal' (ibid.).

Teachers' sense of efficacy and willingness to confront new challenges, then, will depend on the meanings they give to their own teaching failure or success:

> Those who are confident about their instructional practices and students' capabilities are likely to attribute successful or unsuccessful performance to something they have done rather than to luck, chance or an easy undertaking. They confront new challenges, therefore, with great optimism and effort. Low-efficacy teachers more readily attribute teaching success and failure to outside causes, such as having a 'good' class in the former case and a lack of administrative or parental support in the latter. Believing that outside factors make teaching success beyond their professional grasp, inefficacious teachers shy away from new job challenges that seem likely to produce the same low performance-based self-esteem.
>
> (Rosenholtz, 1989, p. 425)

Rosenholtz's (1989) research was also concerned with the workplace conditions of teachers. Her prime focus was on the workplace conditions that produce high attrition rates in beginning teachers. In this work she acknowledges and endorses teacher-efficacy research by arguing that people will confront new challenges only if they believe they have a reasonable chance of success in producing the outcomes they seek. Based on their sense of efficacy, individuals exert (or do not exert) substantial effort in pursuit of goals, persist in the face of diversity, rebound from setbacks and exercise control over events that affect their lives (Bandura 1997).

There is a crucial relationship between teachers' sense of efficacy and the psychic rewards of teaching. If teachers begin to doubt that they can help students learn – because of the students themselves or because they feel unable to meet external demands they find unreasonable or in conflict with teachers' broader moral purposes – then their personal investment in their work will decline and dissatisfaction and defection will result. Improved teacher efficacy has been associated with reduced stress among teachers (Parkay *et al.*, 1998). Teachers leaving teaching have been 'found to have significantly lower teacher efficacy than teachers either in their first year or their fifth year of teaching' (Glickman and Tamashiro, 1982; Tschannen-Moran *et al.*, 1998, p. 205). Some research has focused on school-context effects. For instance, Raudenbush *et al.* (1992) found teachers' 'level of personal teaching efficacy depended on the subject matter being taught and the particular group of students they worked with each lesson. Teachers tended to be less efficacious for non-academic track classes than for academic and honours classes' (in Tschannen-Moran *et al.*, 1998, p. 220).

Personal and general teaching efficacies have been consistently related to student achievement. Moore and Esselman (1992) found that teachers who had a greater sense of general teaching efficacy outperformed their peers in mathematics teaching. High levels of student achievement are also associated with teachers having higher personal and general teaching efficacy (Ross, 1992). In addition to student achievement, teacher efficacy is reported to impact on students' attitudes towards school, the subject matter taught and the teacher (Woolfolk *et al.*, 1990).

Just as identities change, so a person's sense of efficacy varies from one situation to another according to context and task. Ashton and Webb (1986) found teachers' sense of efficacy and competence to be influenced by one or more of seven contextual factors that relate to classroom and organizational conditions and external influences:

1 Excessive role demands
2 Inadequate salaries and low status
3 Lack of recognition and professional isolation
4 Uncertainty
5 A sense of powerlessness
6 Alienation
7 The decline in teacher morale.

In order to teach effectively, teachers must not only feel psychologically and emotionally 'comfortable', they must also have some sense of belief that they can make a difference in the lives of children they are teaching and that those children are learning. They must feel their professional work is bringing about positive change in their pupils. Teachers need to feel wanted and important, and require affirmation of this by those with whom they live and work (Rudow, 1999).

Job satisfaction, morale and motivation

> Motivation is concerned with the degree of inclination towards an activity, but that degree of inclination is determined by the pursuit of goals which will satisfy needs. What motivates, therefore, in a work context, is the desire for job satisfaction. . . . Morale levels are determined by expectancy of continued job satisfaction, and high morale, resulting from high expectations, motivates individuals towards goal-focused activity which is expected to sustain, and increase, job satisfaction, which, in turn, raises morale.
>
> (Evans, 1998, p. 40)

There is mounting evidence in England that rapid changes in the external and internal conditions of schools and nature of teaching are producing conditions of extreme uncertainty and identity crises among what historically has been for many teachers a stable profession. There is a continuing premature loss of able, experienced teachers on grounds of ill-health (Troman and Woods, 2001). The years between 1989 and 1998 show a 43 per cent increase (DfEE, 1998). Attrition is high in the first ten years and after 25 years plus (DES, 1990; Arnold, 1993). Teacher morale is reported to be at a low ebb, and this is not restricted to older teachers. Stress and burn-out are high (Travers and Cooper, 1993, 1996). There is a growing number of teachers on temporary and short-term contracts (Lawn, 1995), and in many areas recruitment of new teachers is not increasing at the rate required to replace those who are leaving. A recent opinion poll (*Guardian*, 29 February 2000, p. 1) estimated that 50 per cent of teachers were planning to leave within ten years and that of those, more than 30 per cent of those under 35 years old were expecting to leave within ten years and 46 per cent within fifteen years. There is, therefore, a need to conserve and enhance human-resource investment and effectiveness. Research throughout Europe and Scandinavia has also shown increasing levels of teacher stress, fatigue and burnout as a result of the changes that have affected their work lives (Klette, 2000; Moller, 2000; Esteve, 1989; Jesus, 2000). The extent to which job satisfaction is achieved is, from the employers' perspective, likely to affect retention, and from the individual teacher's perspective, continuing commitment to their work (Hall, Pearso and Carroll, 1992). Significantly, a large-scale American study in the late 1990s found that:

The most satisfied teachers worked in a more supportive, safe, autonomous environment than the least satisfied teachers.

(NCES, 1997, p. 32)

Evans distinguishes two factors that contribute to job satisfaction among primary school teachers:

- *Job comfort*: the extent to which teachers are satisfied with the conditions and circumstances in which they work
- *Job fulfilment*: a state of mind encompassing all the feelings determined by the extent of the sense of personal achievement that teachers attribute to their performance of those aspects of their job which they value.

(Evans, 1998, p. 11)

She found that these not only related to classroom relationships but were also affected by the kinds and qualities of school leaders and relationships with colleagues.

The research literature suggests that some teachers' commitment and self-efficacy tend to decrease progressively over the course of the teaching career (Fraser, Draper and Taylor, 1998; Huberman, 1993) but that these can be sustained by a strong sense of values, purposes and identity, school cultures that are caring, supportive and challenging, and by continuing satisfaction gained from successful teaching and learning relationships with pupils. Teachers who, for example, regularly change roles, work in a supportive culture, and are reflective and able to participate in significant decision-making in school, maintain their motivation and satisfaction in the essential core of their work – classroom teaching (Huberman, 1993; Helsby and McCulloch, 1996). There is no doubt, however, that external factors exercise significant influence for better or worse, such as the nature of the children they teach, teachers' energy levels, health, and increasing concerns with family matters. It remains the case, then, that after an early stage of commitment to teaching associated with the choice of professional identity, followed by a stage of experimentation and search for new challenges, a significant minority of teachers often experience a phase of uncertainty and self-doubt, followed by phases of distance, conservatism and eventual disengagement (Huberman, 1993). Indeed, it is widely reported that some teachers aged 45-plus find continuing commitment to classroom teaching problematic, partly for reasons of time, energy and health, but also because they have become emotionally exhausted or 'disenchanted' (Raudenbush *et al.*, 1992; Vandenberghe and Huberman, 1999). Life-cycle and career factors are known also to play an increasingly important role in the lives of teachers of this age and beyond (Fessler, 1995; Huberman, 1993; Ball and Goodson, 1985). While research into teachers' lives and careers has identified the possibilities over the last ten to fifteen years for the plateauing of development, growing frustration because of lack of promotion, loss of self-confidence and disenchantment, this can also be the case among younger teachers as a result of an increasingly alienating environment.

It is not only the external conditions that affect job satisfaction. Leadership and management, and relationships with colleagues also make a difference. In small-scale qualitative research on primary school teachers with a range of experience in English schools, Cockburn (2000) found, unsurprisingly, that the majority enjoyed their work because of the satisfaction they gained from the challenges of contributing to the academic and social progress of their students, and because of relationships with colleagues:

> I love getting a new class in September, thinking by the time they leave me at the end of the year they would know so much more and it would be because of what I could tell them.
>
> (Nancy, quoted in Cockburn, ibid., p. 227)

> You just know you have made a difference in their lives.
>
> (William, ibid., p. 229)

In contrast, where feelings are trivialized, ignored or constantly criticized, self-esteem and their feelings of worth as people can be destroyed.

> [If] our feelings are trivialized, ignored, systematically criticized, or extremely constrained by the poverty of our expressive resources, this situation can lead to a very serious kind of dismissal – the dismissal of the significance to a person of his or her own life, in a way that reaches down deeply into what the significance of a life can be to the person whose life it is.
>
> (Campbell, 1997, p. 188)

Vandenberghe (1999) investigated the reasons given by Flemish primary school teachers for leaving teaching. He found that those who left were first, less hopeful that they could overcome routine; second, were pessimistic of achieving promotion; third, had poor relationships with their headteachers; and fourth, worked in non-cooperative environments. Their overwhelming feeling was that their professional growth was 'stuck'. This relates to earlier research in schools in America on the importance to teacher satisfaction of school cultures and school leadership that encourage reflection and collaboration (Rosenholtz, 1989).

It is likely that where teachers cannot satisfy their emotional and intellectual needs in their teaching, their efforts to teach well and their ability to contribute to the raising of standards will be hindered. For most teachers, it is their *classrooms* that represent the main source of self-esteem and job-fulfilment. Dinham and Scott's (1996) study of teacher satisfaction, motivation and health in 71 Australian schools found that the two major satisfiers were pupil achievement and professional self-growth. However, if they are not 'comfortable' in the departmental or school-wide conditions in which they work, this may also affect their classroom practice.

There is a relationship, then, between a sense of personal professional agency, identity, commitment, job satisfaction, and organizational cultures and structures. Professional fulfilment will be achieved in full only when the relationship between these is positive. For example, a number of studies have charted the consequences for the work lives of teachers of the growing emphasis upon results-driven curricula and performativity over the last fifteen years (Ball, 2000; Woods, 1999). They have found that these reforms have led many to take fewer risks in their teaching, that creative teaching and learning and time to respond to the spontaneously expressed needs of individual pupils have become squeezed, and that the curriculum has been 'delivered' through more use of more traditional teaching styles (Francis and Grindle, 1998).

In Nias' (1989) study of primary school teachers' accounts of work in England, she found some who were 'guilty', 'inferior', 'ashamed' because they felt they were not measuring up to their own standards (ibid., p. 36). Yet despite self-expenditure, exhaustion, disappointment and despair, 'survival against the odds was a matter of pride' (ibid., p. 37).

Hargreaves (1994) has also examined the emotional dynamics, meaning and consequences of guilt for teachers and teaching, and concludes that it is a central preoccupation for most teachers. Drawing on the work of Alan Davies, he identifies two kinds of guilt: '*persecutory*' and '*depressive*'. The former arises from 'doing something which is forbidden or failing to do something which is expected by one or more external authorities' (p. 143). The latter is at its most intense 'when we realise we may be harming or neglecting those for whom we care, by not meeting their needs or by not giving them sufficient attention' (p. 144). He writes of '*guilt traps*' and '*guilt trips*'. The former are the social and motivational patterns that delineate and determine teacher guilt. The latter are 'the different strategies that teachers adopt to deal with, deny or repair this guilt' and . . . 'burn-out, exit, cynicism and denial are among these major guilt trips of teaching' (p. 142).

'Depressive' guilt is often associated with the caring commitment through which many who are 'called to teach' express their core moral purposes as an essential quality alongside their knowledge and pedagogical organization and teaching skills.

In England, the recently established General Teaching Council (GTCE), as a result of extensive consultation with teachers, teachers' associations and a range of other stakeholders, has acknowledged the importance of teacher commitment and has begun to articulate a clear set of values. It has embedded these in two documents: a *Code of Professional Values and Practice*, and *The Teachers' Professional Learning Framework (TPLF)*. The *Code of Professional Values* refers to the competence and 'high levels of commitment, energy and enthusiasm' needed by teachers to achieve success for their pupils (p. 1); and the *TPLF*, recognizing that, 'teachers' commitment to developing their own learning directly affects levels of school and pupil performance' (p. 3), outlines a professional development entitlement for all teachers in which they have time to engage in sustained reflection and structured learning through a range of development activities.

> Time to plan, act, evaluate, reflect, and modify practice, and encourage risk taking and innovation and further learning are all features of schools which are focused on pupils and teacher learning.
>
> (GTCE, 2003, p. 14)

Such documents explicitly acknowledge that commitment needs to be nurtured, supported and challenged through continuing professional development, and that central to this endeavour is reflective practice.

Time to reflect

1

> All of us begin our work in education with a 20/20 personal vision
> about the way we would like a school to be. This is what we value and
> are prepared to work and even fight for. . . . Then . . . something
> devastating and apparently inevitable begins to happen. Our
> personal vision becomes blurred by the well-meaning expectations
> and lists of others. . . . The capacity to retain and adhere to a
> personal vision becomes blunted by exhaustion and compliance.
>
> (Barth, 1990, p. 148)

Questions

* What was my personal vision when I began teaching?
* Does it remain? Has it changed? What is it now?
* Do I want to renew/recommit to it?
* What do I need to do to achieve this?
* Who can help me?

2   Veninga and Spradley (1981) suggest a five-stage model by which it
is possible to identify physical and emotional signs of stress:

1   *Eustress*, characterized by a 'healthy sense of being stretched
and challenged and sufficiently well-supported to meet the
challenge'.

2   *Fuel shortage*, marked by job dissatisfaction, inefficiency at work,
fatigue, sleep disturbance, and escape activities such as excessive
eating or drinking, leisure taken in 'overdrive'.

3   *Development of symptoms* (e.g. headache, back pain, fatigue,
digestive disorders, anxiety, anger), that become more frequent
and intense.

4   *Crisis*, marked by acute symptoms, pessimism, self-doubt, a
sense of being trapped, and an obsessional concern with all of
these.

5   *'Hitting the wall'*, at which point external help is usually needed
to effect recovery'
(Veninga and Spradley, 1981, cited in Nias, 1999, pp. 229–30)

* Where would you rate yourself on this model?
* Have you ever visited other stages?

- What were the causes?
- How did you deal with it? Who helped?
- What kind of interpersonal relationships and cultures support you in sustaining your passion for teaching?
- What contributes most to your self esteem?

And finally:

- If you are at Stage 1, 2, 3, 4, or 5 of the model, what are you doing about it? Make an action plan, preferably with a friend, and ask that friend to help you follow it.

Chapter 5

Building knowledge about practice

> If we want all students to actually learn in the way that new standards suggest and today's complex society demands, we will need to develop teaching that goes far beyond dispensing information, giving a test, and giving a grade. We will need to understand how to teach in ways that respond to students' diverse approaches to learning, that are structured to take advantage of students' unique starting points, and that carefully scaffold work aimed at more proficient performances. We will also need to understand what schools must do to organize themselves to support such teaching and learning . . . 21st century schools must shift from a selective mode – characterized by minimal variation in the conditions for learning in which 'a narrow range of instructional options and a limited number of ways to succeed are available' – to an adaptive mode in which 'the educational environment can provide for a range of opportunities for success'.
>
> (Darling-Hammond, 1996a, p. 7)

The passionate teacher will not only recognize the need for, but will also want to employ a range of teaching approaches that take account of the most up-to-date knowledge of teaching and learning. Such approaches will most effectively stimulate and support students' learning, are fit for purpose and relate to teachers' moral imperatives. This chapter, therefore, examines different models of teaching, intuition, expertise and tact, and pupil learning; and knowledge of different kinds of multiple, emotional, spiritual and ethical intelligences that inform and influence these.

Models of teaching

In their report on extensive research on good teaching and learning with 133 teachers and 207 pupils, Morgan and Morris (1999) conclude that

Table 5.1 Teachers' classroom perspectives.

Teacher perspective towards classroom	Related view of pupil identity	Pupil response perspective
Reliance on survival and control (shouts at pupils)	Adversary	'Opposition' behaviour and reluctant learner
High reliance on transmission of knowledge (talks at pupils)	Receiver of truth and wisdom	Passive learner, sometimes bored
Reliance on transaction (talks with pupils)	Co-partner in learning achievement	Co-partner and active learner, takes ownership for own learning achievement

(Ibid., p. 133)

the main message is that pupils, 'set great store by teachers' ability to affect their learning'. They draw three broad implications:

1   Teachers need significantly more belief in themselves with regard to the amount of difference they can make.
2   There is more room (than teachers perceive) for a general shift to greater eclecticism in classroom teaching, with greater awareness and use of a wider range of activity methods, and more open discussion of pedagogical concepts and practice.
3   There is a need to raise awareness and to apply interpersonal relationship strategies to ensure a better balance between the affective and technical aspects of their teaching.

(Morgan and Morris, 1999, pp. 132–3)

Table 5.1 is their initial attempt to construct a simple model of teachers' classroom perspectives based upon their research.

The table provides an interesting perspective on the relationships between teachers' views of their role, the ways these might be received by their pupils, and the effects upon the quality of learning.

To mark the learner's mind we need to know its intricacies, its preferred learning styles, its different sorts of intelligence. . . . We

Table 5.2 A selection from the four families of models of teaching.

Model	Developer (redeveloper)	Purpose
Information processing models		
Inductive thinking (classification)	Hilda Taba (Bruce Joyce)	Development of classification skills, hypothesis building and testing, and understanding of how to build conceptual understanding of content areas
Concept attainment	Jerome Bruner Fred Lighthall (Bruce Joyce)	Learning concepts and studying strategies for attaining and applying them. Building and testing hypotheses
Advanced organizer	David Ausubel (and many others)	Designed to increase ability to absorb information and organize it, especially in learning from lectures and readings
Mnemonics	Michael Pressley Joel Levin (and associated scholars)	Increase ability to acquire information, concepts, conceptual systems, and meta-cognitive control of information processing capability
Social models		
Group investigation	John Dewey Herbert Thelen Shlomo Sharan Rachel Hertz-Lazarowicz	Development of skills for participation in democratic process. Simultaneously emphasizes social development, academic skills and personal understanding
Role playing	Fannie Shaftel	Study of values and their role in social interaction. Personal understanding of values and behaviour
Structured social enquiry	Robert Slavin and colleagues	Academic enquiry and social and personal development. Co-operative strategies for approaching academic study
Personal models		
Non-directive teaching	Carl Rogers	Building capacity for personal development, self-understanding, autonomy and esteem of self

Table 5.2 (cont.)

Model	Developer (redeveloper)	Purpose
Behavioural models		
Direct teaching	Thomas Good, Jere Brophy (and many others)	Mastery of academic content and skills in a wide range of areas of study

(Source: Joyce *et al.*, 1997, Chapter 2, cited in Hopkins, 2001, p. 87)

> need to know that the pupil's mind stands ready to do a deal with the other end – the teacher's extraordinary skill as an alchemist to the mind in transforming mental slavery to freedom. At this end lies the golden cusp of the teacher's skill: his or her ability to open the mind.
>
> (Brighouse, 1994, p. 29)

There are different models of teaching that move teachers beyond the more traditional teaching perspectives outlined in Table 5.1 in order to help students to become more effective learners. Some of these are based on new understandings derived from brain research (Sylwester, 1995; Wolfe, 2001). Hopkins (2001) summarizes these, while emphasizing that they should not be regarded as panaceas or followed uncritically (p. 89) in Table 5.2 above.

The families of models of teaching identified by Joyce, Calhoun and Hopkins (1997), i.e. information processing, social, personal, and behavioural and cybernetic, provide a useful reference point in building and sustaining a repertoire of teaching approaches that relate closely to students' learning needs. However, they cannot be used mechanically or prescriptively. To be effective, teachers need to place the various teaching approaches within an understanding of the context of learning. Teachers need first to be able to interpret the local situation in order to determine what possible actions can be taken (Doyle, 1997). Teachers need, in other words, to be close to learning and the learners.

Flow, creativity and being close to learning

> Flow describes the spontaneous, effortless experience you achieve when
> you have a close match between a high level of challenge and the skills you
> need to meet that challenge. Flow happens when a person is completely
> involved in the task, is concentrating very deeply, and knows moment by
> moment what the next steps should be. . . .
>
> (Csikszentmihalyi, in Scherer, 2002, p. 14)

All teachers will have experience of 'flow' – when, for example, half an
hour has passed and neither pupils nor teacher has noticed, so engrossed
are they in teaching and learning. It is what others describe as powerful
teaching, when the desire to learn is mobilized and sustained, when
the whole physical, emotional and intellectual selves of all those in the
classroom are animated, elated by the experience. It is the antithesis
of 'teaching-as-usual'. It occurs when teachers are being at their most
creative, when they are:

- Open to new ideas and situations, encouraging challenges to
  themselves and their view of the world
- Adaptable, able to transfer knowledge from one context to use
  in another
- Predisposed hopefully to new challenges and thus motivated to
  overcoming these
- Tenacious in their approaches to resolve problems
- Willing to engage the learner in the context of the learner's own
  intentions, interests and desires
- Being passionate about learning.

(Adapted from Seltzer and Bentley, 1999, pp. 26–9)

Thoughtful tact

Van Manen, a Canadian educator, distinguishes four abilities among
what he calls pedagogically tactful teachers:

(i) Sensitive ability to interpret inner thoughts, understanding,
feelings, and desires from indirect clues such as gestures,
demeanour, expression, and body language . . . the ability to
immediately see through motives or cause and effect relations;

(ii) The ability to interpret the psychological and social significance of the features of the inner life, e.g. the deeper significance of shyness, frustration, interest, difficulty, tenderness, humour, discipline;

(iii) [Having] . . . a fine sense of standards, limits and balance . . . knowing how far to press, how close to get to students;

(iv) Moral intuitiveness . . . instantly sensing what is the right or good thing to do on the basis of perceptive pedagogical understanding of children's nature and circumstances.

(van Manen, 1995, pp. 44–5)

All teachers would wish to claim 'tact' as central to their work. Yet it is not taught, cannot be easily achieved, and requires immense amounts of intellectual and emotional energy to be exercised in the crowds and immediacy of classrooms.

The exercise of thoughtful tact requires understanding, knowledge, and a capacity for and disposition to engage in practical reasoning. It is called *phronesis* by Aristotle, to distinguish it from *episteme*, which is regarded as true and certain knowledge. In contrast:

Practical reasoning is deliberative, it takes into account local circumstances, it weighs tradeoffs, it is riddled with uncertainties, it depends upon judgement, profits from wisdom, addresses particulars, it deals with contingencies, is iterative and shifts aims in process when necessary. Practical reasoning is the stuff of practical life. . . . Its aim is to arrive at good but imperfect decisions with respect to particular circumstances.

(Eisner, 2002, p. 375)

Intuition and expertise

Teaching is a hugely complex and skilled activity. It is simultaneously both a science and an art – it requires scholarship, rigorous critical enquiry, collective creation of educational knowledge according to collegial and communal norms, *and* it requires intuition, imagination, improvization: all those spur-of-the-moment, not-to-be-predicted, instinctive and idiosyncratic decisions that more than one commentator has likened to a performance art. . . .

(Saunders, 2002, p. 6)

As teachers' experiences of subject, pupil and the social contexts in which they work increase, alongside the necessary challenge and support through continuing professional development, it is likely that their pedagogical, intellectual and emotional growth will be accompanied by the development of expertise and intuition. While these will not be available to all teachers in equal measures in all circumstances and while they are not necessarily age related, they will be invaluable allies in the work of all successful teachers, especially those who wish to maintain their passion.

In a study of Nobel science laureates, Lorenz, who received the Nobel prize for medicine in 1973, spoke of the value of intuition:

> This apparatus which intuits has to have an enormous basis of human facts at its disposal with which to play. And it plays in a very mysterious manner, because . . . it sort of keeps all human facts afloat, waiting for them to fall into place, like a jigsaw puzzle. And if you press . . . if you try to permutate your knowledge, nothing comes of it. You must give a sort of mysterious pressure, and then rest, and suddenly BING!, the solution comes.
>
> (Cited in Fensham and Marton, 1992, p. 116)

This suggests that intuition, in the exercise of pedagogical tact for example, is based upon knowledge, and that it cannot be applied in any pre-planned way. Yet intuition is an essential facet of passionate teaching. Just as passion will be affected by learned history and current personal, social and cultural contexts, so it is also played out in an arena in which knowledge of self, pupils and subject are essential ingredients. Thus intuition is a product of social context, social interaction and individual histories. It is both a disposition and it can be developed. In discussing complex decision-making in the secondary school classroom, Brown and Coles (2000) identified intuitive practitioners as those who are able to:

- Stay with the complexity of the situation
- Adapt their lessons to the contributions of their students
- Provide the grit in the oyster and then work with the consequences
- Subordinate their teaching to their pupils' learning.

(Brown and Coles, 2000, p. 174)

Lorenz, and Brown and Coles all acknowledge intuition as an essential quality in creative work that involves problem seeking and problem solving. Whereas Lorenz accepts that patience is required for intuition to occur, Brown and Coles use it in a more active sense. Both regard it as being the process of holistic perception, the ability to make connections and relationships between previously unrelated events – and most certainly not an entirely rational planning activity! Although writing primarily about leadership of organizations, Wheatley's words could equally be applied to the ways passionate teachers approach their work:

> My growing sensibility of a quantum universe has affected my organizational life in several ways. First, I try hard to discipline myself to remain aware of the whole and to resist my well-trained desire to analyze the parts to death. I look now for patterns of move-ments over time and focus on qualities like rhythm, flow, direction, and shape. Second, I know I am wasting time when I draw straight arrows between two variables in a cause and effect diagram, or position things as polarities, or create elaborate plans and time lines. Third, I no longer argue with anyone about what is real. Fourth, the time I formerly spent on detailed planning and analysis I now use to look at structures that might facilitate relationships. I have come to expect that something useful occurs if I look at people, units, or tasks, even though I cannot determine precise outcomes. And last, I realize more and more that the universe will not co-operate with my desires for determinism.
>
> (Wheatley, 1992, p. 43)

Expertise, like intuition, is also sometimes misunderstood. The 'expert', for example, is regarded as possessing a greater amount of knowledge, skills and wisdom than most others. 'Experts' are invited to give lectures, advise on policy matters, make judgements on quality. Yet experts – as distinct from non-experts – far from accepting the status quo of knowledge and practice, continue to learn:

> The career of the expert is one of progressively advancing on the problem constituting a field of work, whereas the career of the non-expert is one of gradually constricting the field of work so that it more closely conforms to the routines the non-expert is prepared to execute. . . . There is something experts do over and above ordinary learning, which accounts for how they become experts and for how they remain experts, rather than settling into a rut of routine performance. . . . Experts . . . tackle problems that increase their

expertise, whereas non-experts tend to tackle problems for which they do not have to extend themselves. . . .

(Bereiter and Scardamalia, 1993, p. 78)

Neither intuition nor expertise is infallible. They are parts of teachers' repertoires and, like all the others, need to be revisited, reviewed and nurtured by new knowledge and new understandings.

As both van Manen, Eisner and others cited in this book recognize, good teaching depends not only upon knowledge of teaching approaches and skills, and of the part played by multiple, emotional, spiritual, and ethical intelligences in teaching and learning, but, crucially, upon passion, intuition and artistry, aesthetic considerations, pedagogical tact, and purpose. It therefore requires imagination and technique, intellect and emotion, heart, hand and head in the exercise of judgement about, 'the feel and significance of the particular' (Eisner, ibid., p. 382).

Artistry does not reduce complexity, it has a tendency to increase complexity by recognizing subtlety and emphasizing individuality. It does not search for the one best method. It puts a premium on productive idiosyncrasy. It is a crucial complement to getting it down to a science. In the vernacular, 'getting it down to a science' means, ideally, getting it down to errorless procedure. A procedure becomes errorless when there are no surprises. When there are no surprises, there is no problem. When there is no problem, there is neither challenge nor growth. Artistry in teaching as a pervasive concept goes beyond routine, invites risk, courts challenge, and fosters growth.

(Eisner, 1996, p. 18)

Looking beneath the surface: the challenge of pupils' learning needs

A teacher asked a class . . . what colour apples are. Most of the children answered, 'Red', a few said, 'Green'. But one child raised his hand with another answer: 'White'.

The teacher patiently EXPLAINED that apples were red or green, and sometimes yellow, but never white.

But the youngster insisted. Finally he said, 'Look inside'.

(Bennett-Goleman, 2001, p. 43)

Teachers with a passion for teaching take the trouble to look behind the 'front' each student presents in order to see things as they really are. This is the basis for building an authentic teacher–learner relationship and of planning to teach in ways that will touch each student's interest and imagination. Teachers with a passion for learning in a class that presents behavioural problems will seek first to understand rather than reach for an immediate short-term solution.

In writing about assessment as a form of learning, Earl and Le Mahieu (1997) write about the 'kid watching' of a teacher:

> As a teacher you have to be aware of your students' learning styles, of what they can do. And you have to do that very quickly and accept what a kid is doing. Then you can go from there. . . . At the beginning of the year, I use math activities, lots of visual activities. I take some of de Bono's ideas, things I picked up from Howard Gardner, and I make these activities into maths activities. I watch how the kids approach them and how they do them, and then I make decisions about the type of learning that each child did. . . . They are fun little games that the kids are doing. I do it with another purpose in mind. . . . It tells me a bit about their thinking.
>
> (Earl and LeMahieu, 1997, p. 154)

John Elliott, writing about experiences of teacher researchers in the Norwich Area Schools Consortium, which had as a focus for its inquiry 'pedagogical dimensions of student disaffection from learning', provides a good example of the need to and rewards of looking beneath the surface of a problem by collecting evidence from a number of sources to check out perceptions. In one example, Modern Foreign Language (MFL) teachers in a school believed that the significant number of disruptive students and absenteeism from lessons was due to negative parental attitudes. However, a survey of parents revealed that most had a positive attitude to their children learning a foreign language. The teachers then began to look inside their classrooms for reasons. Generalizing across the project's work, Elliott quotes a teacher researcher:

> I find every student is so different, and what one person is mani-festing can be a very obvious thing, just an attitude where they are not going to work . . . with other students it can be so different . . . even as simple as trying to get you into a conversation about some-thing completely outside the subject and in that sense trying to

distract you from teaching them because they are trying to avoid work.

(Elliott, 2004)

To be passionate about teaching means being passionate about engaging students in the kind of education that will provide them with opportunities to live a rich learning life – and a part of this is equipping them for the changing workplace. While educators cannot, of course, guarantee employment – that will always be down to the vagaries of the labour market – their prime role, as McLaughlin, Talbert and others recognize, is to inculcate a love of learning (or at least an understanding that learning is lifelong) and to ensure that they are able to problem-seek and problem-solve.

> The workforce that students will enter increasingly requires not only basic literacy and numeracy, but also problem-solving skills and the capacity to continue learning as technology and society changes.
>
> (McLaughlin and Talbert, 2001, p. 2)

This not only suggests that a particular range of teaching approaches that are fit for purpose must be used, but also that the learning culture of school and classroom encourages active participation, speculation, debate, and a sense of learning ownership by the students.

Like teachers, pupils will have different preferences for the ways they learn and may learn better in one way than another. These may be influenced by their learning histories, cognitive and emotional factors (e.g. dyslexia, dyspraxia, shyness) and, of course, the teaching approaches used. Galton and Simon (1980) identified four types of learner:

- Attention seekers
- Intermittent workers
- Solitary workers
- Quiet collaborators.

However, an attention seeker in one class may be a quiet collaborator in another. In other words, teachers can make a difference to learning by choosing the right approach and having the right relationship with pupils. Preferred ways of learning are likely to change over time according to circumstance and interest. Perhaps the best-known learning styles are those derived from Kolb's (1984) work:

- Reflector: learning by feeling and through experience
- Theorist: learning by watching and listening
- Pragmatist: enjoys problem solving
- Activist: learning by doing.

Awareness of these or other models enables teachers to plan for engagement based upon diagnosis of style and preference, and to work to extend pupils' learning repertoires. Passionate teachers are unlikely primarily to direct learners through the traditional transmission modes of learning, but rather are expert facilitators with students taking more proactive and active roles in their own learning. If mutual respect and trust are missing from the classroom, it is difficult for teachers to offer the kinds of freedom of choice such role changes imply. However, in such collaborative interactive contexts, teachers and students may exercise multiple roles. Bentley (1998) offers a generic list of capacities they entail:

Learner: the capacity to understand what it is to identify goals and learning needs, gain resources appropriate to achieving these, and evaluate learning

Worker: the capacity to understand how one's ability and energy can be employed in a productive activity

Teacher: the capacity to pass on appropriate knowledge and understanding, to facilitate the development of genuine understanding, to motivate and encourage the habits and disciplines of effective learning, and to evaluate progress

Citizen: the capacity to understand and enact responsibilities and opportunities entailed by membership of a civic and political community

Parent: the capacity to understand and fulfil the obligation of parenthood

Expert: the capacity to understand and develop the key components of expertise in a given realm (of knowledge)

Peer: the capacity to understand and perform the role of mentoring . . . including the establishment of trust and confidentiality

Leader: the capacity to recognize and formulate goals and challenges, to motivate people, to meet them in appropriate ways, and to reward and celebrate achievement, both individual and collective

Problem solver: the capacity to recognize, frame and analyse problems.

(From Bentley, 1998 pp. 131–2)

Bentley cites a report from the US National Center for Clinical Infant Programes that found that the seven most critical qualities needed for succeeding in school – confidence, curiosity, intentionality (the wish to have an impact), self-control, relatedness, the capacity to communicate, and cooperativeness – are directly concerned with relationships (Bentley, p. 159).

Being close to rather than distant from learning and the learner, contrary to received wisdom, increases the capacity of teachers to do their job well.

> Teachers may also at times wish for social distance from the complex, tangled and sometimes destructive lives of their students, but they cannot both teach well and ignore the many dimensions of the lives of their students. Teaching well requires as broad and deep an understanding of the learner as possible, a concern for how what is taught relates to the life experience of the learner, and a willingness to engage the learner in the context of the learner's own intentions, interests and desires. Social distance of the variety favoured by many physicians inhibits the capacity of teachers to do their job well. If teachers were to think of themselves professionally, they would be ill-served by adopting the same concept of social distance that characterizes much of the practice of law and medicine.
>
> (Fenstermacher, 1990, p. 137)

Two of the most influential writers on learner intelligences in recent decades have been Howard Gardner and Daniel Goleman.

Multiple intelligences

Gardner's (1983, 1996) theory of intelligence, based upon a range of studies and tests of the cognitive development of normal and gifted children, questions the old notions of intelligence as 'general' and 'fixed'. Instead, it recognizes that every individual possesses several kinds of intelligence, that within these some will be relatively stronger than others, and that context and environment influence their development. The theory has been criticized on the grounds that the different intelligences 'seem to reflect his own value judgements about what kind of questions are important' (White, 2000, p. 11) and that there are problems in identifying 'end-state performance' (ibid., p. 16), other than through subjective judgements about their importance. Nevertheless, this theory has significant implications for both the kinds of knowledge which are valued in school – traditionally the linguistic and logical – and the way they are examined. It also has implications for the way teachers may organize learning so that all, rather than a few, of these intelligences can be nurtured. Bentley (1998) draws attention to the recognition implicit in multiple intelligence theory that any occupation or task will involve a combination of these intelligences. Below are examples of some applications of Gardner's eight intelligences to student roles or characteristics.

Linguistic intelligence: the bookworm, the poet, the storyteller, the orator, the humorist, the test taker, the trivia expert . . . the super-speller, the playwright, the raconteur

Logical – mathematical intelligence: the computer programmer, the super-calculator, the math whiz, the scientist, the logician, the rationalist, the chess player

Spatial intelligence: the inventor, the artist, the cartoonist, the photographer, the mechanical wizard, the designer, the visualizer or daydreamer, the map-maker

Bodily – kinaesthetic intelligence: the athlete, the dancer, the actor, the craftsperson, the mime, the sculptor, the sports person, the hands-on learner

Musical intelligence: the singer, the songwriter, the guitarist (or player of any instrument), the rapper, the rhythm ace, the musical library (of songs), the acute listener

Interpersonal intelligence: the natural leader, the class mediator, the negotiator, the manipulator, the social director, the human barometer (of affective feelings in another person), the sympathetic friend, the highly moral or political student

Intrapersonal intelligence: the entrepreneur, the free-lancer, the different drummer, the independent spirit, the visionary, the goal setter, the reflective thinker, the futurist

Naturalist intelligence: the lizard expert (or expert on any specific fauna or flora), the nature enthusiast, the pet lover, the collector, the hunter, the scout.

(Armstrong, 1998, p. 67)

Table 5.3 Collecting classroom examples.

Intelligence	Examples of classroom activities	Examples from my classroom
Verbal – linguistic	Discussions, debates, journal-writing, conferences, essays, stories, poems, storytelling, listening activities, reading	
Logical – mathematical	Calculations, experiments, comparisons, number games, using evidence, formulating and testing hypotheses, deductive and inductive reasoning	
Spatial	Concept maps, graphs, charts, art projects, metaphorical thinking, visualization, videos, slides, visual presentations	
Bodily – kinaesthetic	Role-playing, dance, athletic activities, manipulatives, hands-on demonstrations, concept-miming	
Musical	Playing music, singing, rapping, whistling, clapping, analysing sounds and music	
Interpersonal	Community involvement projects, discussions, co-operative learning, team games, peer tutoring, conferences, social activities, sharing	
Intrapersonal	Student choice, journal writing, self-evaluation, personal instruction, independent study, discussing feelings, reflecting	
Naturalist	Ecological field trips, environmental study, caring for plants and animals, outdoor work, pattern recognition	

(Silver, Strong and Perini, 2000, p. 20)

These are not intended to be exhaustive. For teachers, recognition of these intelligences suggests that for each student there will be possibilities for development in many of these areas; and they pose huge challenges to the traditional limited structure of the curriculum in schools. Silver, Strong and Perini (2000) have provided a useful means of applying the intelligences to classroom teaching (Table 5.3).

Yet these examples still raise issues for the profile of learners in any one classroom and their response to such a planned diversity of pedagogical approaches. They also pose challenges for teachers' capacities to facilitate such kinds of learning. Much creativity and skill are required, and there are implications for both pre-service and in-service education.

Emotional intelligence

A research development that has major implications for teaching and learning has been the legitimization of the emotional component present in some form in all teaching–learning engagements. Daniel Goleman, in a synthesis of research, defined emotional intelligence as 'the ability to motivate oneself and persist in the face of frustrations; to control impulse and delay gratification, to regulate one's moods and keep distress from swamping the ability to think; to empathize and hope' (1995, p. 34). Using the original work of Salovey and Meyer (1990), he identifies five domains of emotional intelligence:

1   **Knowing one's emotions** . . . the ability to monitor feelings from moment to moment is crucial to psychological insight and self-understanding. . . . People with greater certainty about their feelings are better pilots of their lives, having a surer sense of how they really feel about personal decisions from whom to marry to what job to take.

2   **Managing emotions** . . . the capacity to soothe oneself, to shake off rampant anxiety, gloom, or irritability.

3   **Motivating oneself** . . . Emotional self-control – delaying gratification and stifling impulsiveness – underlies accomplishment of every sort.

4   **Recognizing emotions in others** . . . Empathy . . . the social cost of being emotionally tone-deaf, and the reasons empathy kindles altruism. . . . This makes them better at callings such as the caring professions, teaching, sales, and management

5   **Handling relationships** . . . The art of relationships is, in large part, skill in managing emotions in others. . . . These are the abilities that undergird popularity, leadership, and interpersonal effectiveness.

(Goleman, 1995, pp. 43–4)

Goleman has argued that *emotional literacy*, i.e. understanding and being able to apply emotional intelligence, is essential to success in life, and that emotional illiteracy, which makes coping with the tensions and dilemmas of life in schools difficult, and may be expressed through boredom, bad behaviour or withdrawal, is preventable. His work demonstrates the importance of the development of emotional competence in children, young people and adults. Students learn in different ways but their learning is almost always influenced by social and emotional factors (Wang, Haertel and Walberg, 1997). They need, therefore, to develop reflective skills that enable them to recognize, acknowledge, understand, and manage their emotions. This is the responsibility not only of parents but also teachers. The implications for teachers is that they need to have the confidence and skills to intervene and facilitate students' emotional literacy from a position of having a sense of their own.

Understanding and managing (not suppressing) one's own and others' emotions is a central part of all teachers' work. Yet it is important to distinguish between *negative* emotions which result from feelings of harm, loss or threat and can be productive, and *positive* emotions which result from progress towards or attainment of a goal and can be destructive (Lazarus, 1991). Take passion as an example. Although '. . . life without passion would be a dull wasteland of neutrality, cut off and isolated from the richness of life itself' (Goleman, 1995, p. 56), it is important to recognize, as I have noted earlier in this book, that when emotions grow in intensity they may 'shade over' into unmanageable, destructive extremes of rage, guilt, anxiety, shame, depression, melancholy, isolation, sleepless nights, and alienation (from self and others). It is also important to recognize first that emotional intelligence is not something teachers or students possess or do not possess; second, it is not isolated from the social context – cultures of collaboration, for example, are likely to nurture emotional intelligence; third, it may be affected by personal change contexts; and fourth, it can be learned. Regular engagement in forms of reflection, for instance, can assist in growth of one's emotional as well as cognitive self.

It is worth noting, also, that while this theory in one sense acknowledges the key role of emotion in teaching and learning for teachers and learners, it has also been criticized for failing to take into account historical, cultural and social differences and traditional power relationships in the workplace, which significantly affect the ways emotional intelligence is used. For example, those who are male and middle class and who occupy management roles may find emotional intelligence a more amenable construct as it is defined by Goleman than those with gendered, racial or social class histories (Boler, 1999).

Spiritual intelligence

It is difficult, if not impossible, to teach well over time, in different and sometimes adverse circumstances, without being passionate and having some sense of the spiritual and ethical. Even emotional and multiple intelligences are not enough to explain the rich complexities of the human heart and soul:

> [Spiritual intelligence] . . . gives us our ability to discriminate. It gives us our moral sense, an ability to temper rigid rules with understanding and compassion and an equal ability to see when compassion, and understanding have their limits. . . .
>
> (Zohar and Marshall, 2000, p. 5)

In the final chapter of their book *The Intelligent School* (1997), MacGilchrist, Myers and Reed identify and describe nine intelligences – contextual, strategic, academic, reflective, pedagogical, collegial, emotional, spiritual, and ethical. It is the last two that are of particular concern to those who are or would be passionate in their teaching.

Spiritual intelligence is characterized 'by a fundamental valuing of the lives and development of all members of a school community' (MacGilchrist *et al.*, 1997, p. 109) and is a key part of the passion in teaching that is fundamental to good teaching and learning. Yet it is not to be found in school improvement plans, policy documents or inspection reports.

> Spirituality is a source of creativity open to us all. It brings the quality of aliveness which sparks inquiry, ideas, observations, insights, empathy, artistic expression, earnest endeavours, and playfulness. It opens us to life and to each other. Spirituality is a thread that runs through our life, bringing hope, compassion, thankfulness, courage, peace, and a sense of purpose and meaning to the everyday, while reaching beyond the immediate world of the visible

and tangible. It drives us to seek and stay true to values not ruled by material success.

> (Burns and Lamont, 1995, p. xiii,
> cited in MacGilchrist *et al.*, 1997, p. 109)

Spiritual intelligence is closely related to the moral purposes of a teacher (see Chapter 2) and is different from emotional intelligence. Whereas the latter enables us to judge the situation – for instance, the emotional climate of the classroom – and then behave appropriately within it, the former enables each of us to ask if we want to be in this situation in the first place, or would we rather change it to create a better one. In this sense, we work *with* and not necessarily *within* the boundaries.

> Spiritual intelligence is the soul's intelligence. It is the intelligence with which we heal ourselves and with which we make ourselves whole. [It is] . . . the intelligence that rests in that deep part of the self that is connected to wisdom from beyond the ego, or conscious mind, it is the intelligence with which we not only recognize existing values, but with which we creatively discover new values.
>
> (Zohar and Marshall, 2000, p. 9)

To be spiritually intelligent is to integrate two of Gardner's multiple intelligences – the intra- and interpersonal – in order to understand more fully who we are, what we value, and how to develop care and concern for others in order to use this in teaching. To do so is to acknowledge that the teachers' roles in developing critically caring communities of learners and appreciating diversity as well as building students' learning capacities is as important as and interconnected with their 'academic' roles. The development of spiritual intelligence might involve forms of critical holistic reflection that focus upon the self. Zohar and Marshall (ibid.) suggest the following as being indicators of a highly developed spiritual intelligence:

- The capacity to be flexible (actively and spontaneously adaptive)
- A high degree of self-awareness
- A capacity to face and use suffering
- A capacity to face and transcend pain
- The quality of being inspired by vision and values
- A reluctance to cause unnecessary harm
- A tendency to see the connections between diverse things (being 'holistic')

- A marked tendency to ask 'Why?' or 'What if?' questions and to seek fundamental answers
- Being what psychologists call 'field-independent' – possessing a facility for working against convention.

(Ibid., p. 15)

It is not difficult to see the relevance and value of these indicators, or characteristics, to teachers who are passionate in their deep care and desire to provide the best opportunities for learning.

Ethical intelligence: the moral imperative

Ethical intelligence suggests the necessity for clear values and beliefs, a sense of moral purpose and principle, a commitment to access and entitlement for all, and high (but not complacent) self-esteem (MacGilchrist *et al.*, 1997, p. 112).

Taken together, the theory of multiple intelligence, models of teaching, emotional and spiritual intelligence all suggest a broad holistic, rather than narrow instrumental, view of teaching and learning, teacher and learner; and they suggest that teachers exercise clear moral and ethical responsibilities. It is essential that teachers develop students' capacities to act morally, i.e. working for the mutual benefit of all, engaging with moral issues. Always, and especially in contexts of disconnection and moral decline, teachers have a responsibility to actively encourage reflection upon moral values and principles.

Table 5.4 overleaf provides a salutary reminder of the relationship between the needs of children and young people, the 'virtuous responses' needed and the temptations which, if not resisted, work against the formation of the powerful interpersonal bonds that teachers who are passionate about their teaching forge with their students.

While there may be many teachers who will not associate their roles with helping students develop their moral selves because they feel it inappropriate, because they feel unqualified to do so, because they do not see this as part of their role, or because they have no time, there is much research to indicate that *in practice* classrooms are moral places (e.g. Jackson, Boostrom and Hansen, 1993; Cole, 1997), where students are constantly 'hearing' messages from teachers with regard to ideals and principles of equity, justice and ways of behaving with others, such as respect and honesty. Teachers with a passion for teaching will be aware of the implicit messages they communicate through expectations of codes of conduct, ways of working and relationships. They may also wish

Table 5.4 Needs of children, virtuous and negative responses.

Needs of children	Virtuous response	Temptations
To be loved	Unconditional love	Conditional love; emotional and sexual exploitation
To be led	Empowerment	Enslavement
To be vulnerable	Kindness	Cruelty
To make sense	Justice; fairness	Arbitrariness
To please others	Humility; patience	Anger; pride
To have hope	Hope	Despair
To be known	Respect	Contempt
To be safe	Responsibility	Indifference; dereliction
To make one's mark	Authentic work; autonomy	Narcissism; egocentrism

(Clark, 1995, p. 27)

to make some time for discussion of the social and moral contexts of life outside schools that are relevant to students. Time spent in this way – out of respect for their wider responsibilities to society – may also pay dividends through increased interest and motivation of students that result.

Brookfield suggests that adult moral learning focuses upon five interconnected processes:

> **Learning to be aware of the inevitable contextuality and situationality of moral reasoning**. This involves us realizing that what constitutes morally admirable or defensible behaviour is subjectively defined and experienced, and varies from person to person and time to time.
>
> **Learning that morality is collectively determined, transmitted and enforced**. This involves us in realizing that what passes for the dominant espoused moral code in any group of people is socially negotiated and invariably reflects the values of those in positions of power. It may also involve us realizing that subcultural codes that challenge the dominant code are evolved according to class, race and gender.
>
> **Learning to recognize the ambiguity of moral reasoning and behaviour**. This involves us understanding the limits to any attempt to apply universal moral rules to specific situations. We come

to understand the contradictions and disjunctions between our moral impulses and our actions. This learning entails the development of a reflective scepticism regarding claims of moral certainty, and a consequent tolerance for the multiplicity of views that can be taken regarding 'correct' moral choices.

Learning to accept one's own moral limitations. This is close to what some would call the attainment of personal wisdom. It involves us realizing the difficulties involved in our behaving morally (however we might define that) and our learning to live with a degree of moral inconsistency that falls short of the exact correspondence between our beliefs and actions that, ideally, we might desire.

Learning to be self-reflective about our own moral reasoning and claims to morality. This involves the application of critical reflection to our own moral decision-making. We come to realize that what we think are disinterested actions often end up as self-serving. We learn to recognize the dimensions of selfishness that attach themselves to moral action and come to distrust the pleasurable feelings we experience in acting 'morally'. Moral behaviour is scrutinized for the selfishness it sometimes represents.

(Brookfield, 1998, pp. 290–1)

If moral teaching is, as Brookfield (1998) suggests, 'a self-consciously moral dimension to educational practice' (p. 283), then it follows that moral learning for teachers must be taken seriously. Teachers need to extend their understandings of the moral choices that are made in classrooms and the part they play in influencing these, for instance in insisting on respect for all opinions as against a conformity with their own; or acknowledging or ignoring the ways in which worlds outside the classroom impinge upon attitudes, beliefs and behaviours within it. 'It is quite possible', Brookfield claims, 'for adults to live their years within a narrow moral universe in which values, assumptions and perspectives learned in childhood are constantly reinforced' (ibid., p. 286). Teachers, therefore, with their special responsibilities for educating children and young people, need to reflect regularly upon their own beliefs, meanings and values, those of the school, of the students they teach, and how these are played out in classrooms. To paraphrase Brookfield (ibid., p. 287), not to know anything about students' lives and experiences is pedagogically mistaken; not to think that these are important is disrespectful. These are important because they help teachers to take an integrated view of the often contradictory personal and social dynamics of their worlds, and the broader cultural and political contexts that influence them.

Time for reflection

Read the two columns below, plot what position you take in relation to the 'Then' statements and decide how in your teaching you will move forward to the 'Now' statements.

Raising the stakes

Then I wanted students to be:

- Curious, attentive, interested in what I was talking about
- Assured that I was interested in who they were and how well they could write
- Willing to talk, debate and share ideas, once I had provided them with the background I thought necessary for them to be able to contribute
- Open to the complexity of the subjects that we were covering on the course
- Making choices from topics I had prepared and presented them with
- Drawing on personal experiences in order to make their class participate and their written papers more interesting

- Able to accept, understand, practice, and adopt the suggestions I made on how to make their papers more literate
- Willing to complete their assignments on time, to be ready for quizzes or tests . . . and to work within the class rules and grading system that I had worked out and presented.

Now I want students to be:

- Curious, attentive, intrigued with what is taking place
- Assured that I am very interested in who they are and what they think
- Willing to talk, debate and share ideas as players, not spectators; getting right into an issue from the start
- Open to the complexity of the issue; curious about ideas and events that may shape their lives
- Thinking about and choosing what things are more important than others
- Drawing on expertise they themselves possess that might contribute to their classmates and tie 'school learning' to 'life experience'
- Reflecting upon and assessing their own and others' thoughts; ready to change their minds if it seems to make sense to do so
- Willing to contribute the power of their thoughts and feelings in creating something of value to society.

(Fried, 1995, pp. 150–1)

Chapter 6

A passion for learning and development

> Teaching and learning are interdependent, not separate functions. In this view, teachers are primarily learners. They are problem posers and problem solvers; they are researchers; and they are intellectuals engaged in unravelling the learning process both for themselves and for the young people in their charge. Learning is not consumption; it is knowledge production. Teaching is not performance; it is facilitative leadership. Curriculum is not given; it is constructed empirically, based on emergent needs and interests of learners. Assessment is not judgement; it documents progress over time. Instruction is not technocratic; it is inventive, craftlike, and above all an important human enterprise.
>
> (Lieberman and Miller, 1990, p. 12)

The maintenance of good teaching demands that teachers revisit and review regularly the ways they are applying principles of differentiation, coherence, progression and continuity, and balance, not only in the 'what' and the 'how' of their teaching but also in the 'why' in terms of their core 'moral' purposes. It demands also that teachers address issues of self-efficacy, identity, job satisfaction, commitment, and emotional intelligence discussed earlier in this book. Good teaching involves the head *and* the heart. To be a professional means a lifelong commitment to inquiry. There are both positive and negative reasons for making sure that teachers have access to a range of continuing professional development opportunities that are targeted at their intellectual and emotional health needs as well as the organizational needs of the school. We know, for example, that:

- Teachers' commitment to their work will increase student commitment (Bryk and Driscoll, 1988; Rosenholtz, 1989)

- Enthusiastic teachers (who are knowledgeable and skilled) work harder to make learning more meaningful for students, even those who may be difficult or unmotivated (Guskey and Passaro, 1994)
- Teachers who are able to understand and manage their own emotions are better able to understand and manage those of their pupils (Goleman, 1998). Teaching and learning are, by definition, not only cognitive but also emotional activities.

Yet for many teachers, the job of educator has become, 'more akin to blue-collar work than creative professional practice' (Sagor, 1997, p. 170). Research tells us that under normal circumstances, teachers' learning is limited by the development of routines; 'single-loop learning' (Argyris and Schon, 1974), school cultures that are inimical to teacher learning, and taken for granted assumptions that limit their capacity to engage in the different kinds of reflection necessary for learning and change (Day, 1999). We know also that there are some who work in contexts that are so challenging that they leave little time or energy for teacher learning. Much has been written about the development of 'routines' (Yinger, 1979). Routines are patterns of working, rapid intuitive responses to classroom situations and events, and taken for granted assumptions that frame normal practice and discourse in the classroom, staffroom and other school settings. While they are important for survival, their continual, often unconscious, uncritical use has been criticized as a limitation on their teaching (Schon, 1983). Pryer's description of the professional pedagogical encounter as 'erotic' illustrates the dangers of too much comfort and predictability.

> Pedagogy is a special kind of erotic encounter, a meeting of teacher and student. The student may find joy in learning something purely for its own sake. He/she may find pleasure in fulfilling his/her desire to become more knowledgeable or skilful or wise or powerful or competent. He/she may also enjoy successfully meeting the expectations of teachers, parents and community, thus becoming part of that wider community. But sometimes, teacher and student know all the steps of the erotic, pedagogical dance by heart, finding comfort and safety in its predictable order. Then the pedagogical process degenerates into mere routine. Too much comfort and predictability are anaesthetizing: you cannot sleepwalk through the pedagogical experience; the pedagogical dance is a wild and chaotic process, a struggle that is sometimes joyful, sometimes painful.
>
> (Pryer, 2001, p. 80)

It is not sufficient, then, to rely upon tried and tested teaching routines, since over-reliance on current expertise will not always produce the best teaching and learning. It is important to make time to breathe.

Making time to breathe

> . . . teachers have no time to wring their hands, reflect on complex theories of learning or of motivation, and make sophisticated choices between alternative courses of action. They have to act quickly, spontaneously and more or less automatically, immediacy is the essential characteristic of the situation, and any implicit theory the teacher may use must be such that it can swiftly produce the appropriate course of action.
>
> (Brown and McIntyre, 1993, p. 53)

This statement of what seems to be the obvious implicitly emphasizes the need for teachers who are passionate about their work to possess, prior to their entry into the classroom, considerable self-knowledge and clear sets of values and principles that will guide their actions. It also suggests, along with the work of many other researchers, that teaching is complex, requiring sustained amounts of intellectual, social and emotional energy. If it also seems to deny the possibilities of learning for teachers this is because it recognizes, also, the power that routines and the sheer intensity of the job have to limit learning.

> Look, I spend hours at home, preparing my lessons. The children keep me on the go all day – I barely have time to breathe, let alone reflect. The last thing I need is to spend yet more time at my job doing some kind of study no-one but me is going to see. . . . (Reaction of a primary school teacher attending a professional development seminar.)
>
> (Quoted in Mitchell and Weber, 1999, p. 1)

These words will be echoed by many teachers who see their own continuing learning as more of a luxury than a necessity. Yet the busier you are the less time you have to reflect upon what you do and how you do it; and to plan what you will teach next, it is necessary to evaluate your previous teaching (e.g. students' understandings, the effects of your teaching approaches). Therefore, to plan for progression and improvement, time is needed for critical reflection. There will also be times when teachers will want to 'take stock' of who they are, their broader purposes, motivations, attitudes, and values; to reflect upon the influence of their department and school culture on these; perhaps to consider how the broader social and political forces affect their work; maybe look back to examine personal influences on their life and work, at critical moments or phases in their development. To do this they may need the assistance of colleagues or critical friends from outside the school. They might even feel the need to share their own ideals and practices with colleagues from other schools through participating as a teacher-inquirer in a schools' consortium, such as a 'Networked Learning Community' where, with others, they can engage in a piece of sustained inquiry into practice that is relevant to their needs. Or, finally, they may decide that now is the time to undertake a period of sustained further study for the purpose of professional renewal.

None of these possibilities denies that teachers' in-school life will continue to be busy, or that to undertake any of them will not require additional energy. It will, and practical and moral support will be needed from colleagues and others closer to home. Yet, this is not *continuous* learning that is being proposed, but *time-limited* learning within an overall acknowledgement of the importance to sustaining and renewing the passion of commitment to *continuing* learning and development.

Learning from and alongside others is still relatively rare. Thus, because conditions dictate that the principal means of learning is through one's own experience, and because this will ultimately limit learning, it is not surprising that some teachers' passion becomes dimmed by routine and workload as they lose sight of why they came into teaching in the first place:

> We might also invent the concept of an 'at-risk' educator – 'any teacher or principal who leaves school at the end of the day or year with little possibility of continuing learning about the important work they do!' The perilous place of 'learning' in the life of school practitioners is confirmed by staff developers with whom I speak. Most observe that the voracious learners are the beginning, first-year teachers who care desperately to learn their new craft. The learning curve remains high for three or four years at which time of life the teacher becomes highly routinized and repetitive. . . . After perhaps ten years, many observers report that teachers, now beleaguered and depleted, become resistant to learning. The learning curve turns

downward. With twenty-five years of life in schools, many educators are described as 'burned out'. No learning curve!

(Barth, 1996, pp. 28–9)

A spirit of inquiry is a key part of maintaining and growing expertise, itself a part of the bedrock of good teaching. Passion, then, needs nurturing through continuing learning. Although research, school inspectors and government policy identify 'good' schools as those that have collegial cultures, engage in 'data-based' decision-making and place an emphasis upon the continuing professional development of the whole school community, there remain relatively few examples of systematic and sustained individual, whole-school and inter-school inquiry into practice.

The challenges of reflective practice

> The people who develop . . . are those who love to learn, who seek new challenges, who enjoy intellectually stimulating environments, who are reflective, who make plans and set goals, who take risks, who see themselves in the large social contexts of history and institutions and broad cultural trends, who take responsibility for themselves and their environs.
>
> (Rest, 1986, pp. 174–5)

Good teachers will not be content to reflect critically upon and examine their own teaching and its contexts, nor be satisfied only to plan for the next lesson on the basis of what they have learnt from the last. Rather, they will want to find ways of looking at the learning experience from different perspectives, engaging in the messy, frustrating and rewarding 'clay' of learning (Barth, 1990, p. 49). They will want to open up their classrooms to others in order to share and learn, and ensure that their thinking and practices are not always based solely upon their own experience. They will not be content only to comply with the institutional imperatives of performance-management processes or school-improvement planning, however well they are managed.

Planned or pre-meditated development can often be ineffective when it does not address teachers' personal–professional agendas and when it does not address affective issues of, for instance, sustaining enthusiasm, courage or love for teaching, or remaining clear about fundamental purposes. One simple way of learning is, from time to time, to do those tasks you are asking of the pupils:

> One pleasurable experience . . . was when I reversed the role of being a teacher to a learner. I did this in a variety of ways. I would sit with children and paint, or build, or cut and paste, but one particular session, I would sit on the carpet with the group and one student would sit on the teacher's chair and read us a story. . . . I found pleasure in allowing the students to feel the sense of power and importance. . . . The sharing, the laughter and the sense of closeness I felt was wonderful. . . .
>
> (Cited in McWilliam, 1999, pp. 65–6)

Reflective practice is based upon a particular notion of professionalism in which teachers have a responsibility for the education of students that goes beyond the instrumental, encompassing responsibilities to educate for citizenship and to imbue in their students a positive disposition towards lifelong learning. Such teachers must be 'knowledgeable, experienced, thoughtful, committed, and energetic workers' (Devaney and Sykes, 1988, p. 20) who care deeply for their work and their pupils, because:

> . . . complex organisms placed in complex environments require large repertoires of knowledge, the possibilities of choosing among many available responses, the ability to construct novel combinations of response, and the ability to plan ahead so as to avoid disastrous situations and instead propitiate favourable ones.
>
> (Damasio, 2000, p. 139)

Damasio is writing about the need for us as conscious beings to go beyond the here and now, to place ourselves and others in our contexts in order to be able to anticipate alternative futures. Yet time and circumstance dictate that this is not always a simple matter. Witness first the testimony of a newly qualified teacher:

> I used to think I'd be this great reflective teacher. I had visions of spending time at the end of each day replaying my classes to see what worked and what didn't, etc., but, quite honestly, by the end of the day I am so frazzled from just trying to keep up I can hardly even remember what took place only hours ago! And most of the time I am so worried about tomorrow I don't even want to think about

yesterday or today. . . . I've taken to doing things for myself in the evenings now in order to get my mind off [teaching].

(Cited in Cole, 1997, p. 9)

This illustrates the perils of taking the popular notion of conscious continuous learning too seriously. Certainly, reflection of different kinds is an essential part of teacher learning. However, it is important to remember that there will be times – perhaps in the early years of teaching, perhaps at moments of acute stress or at the end of a busy week – when reflection is either not appropriate or simply too difficult.

Brubacher and his colleagues, in answer to the question why should a teacher devote time and energy to becoming a reflective practitioner, suggest three principal benefits:

1   Reflective practice helps to free teachers from impulsive, routine behaviour;
2   Reflective practice allows teachers to act in a deliberate, intentional manner; and
3   Reflective practice distinguishes teachers as educated human beings since it is one of the hallmarks of intelligent action.

(Brubacher *et al.*, 1994, p. 25)

To these three, we might add:

4   Reflective practice enables teachers to assert their professional identity as change agents with moral purposes; and
5   Reflective practice is essential to self-knowledge.

Essentially, reflection involves a *critique* of practice; the values that are implicit in that practice; the personal, social, institutional and broad policy contexts in which practice takes place; and the implications of these for improvement of that practice. It is an essential means of re-examination and renewal of passion by those who care about their work, who are captivated by their pupils' potential for learning, and who, because of these, actively work against becoming isolated and apathetic. Reflection is about the past, the present and the future; it is about 'problem posing' as well as 'problem solving' (Mezirow, 1991, p. 105); and it is essential to building and maintaining the capacity and passionate commitment of all professionals whose work focuses upon the care and development of children, young people and adults. To engage in reflection is to create opportunities for choices that relate to values as well as purposes, practices, contexts, and change.

Various writers have coined the terms reflection-*in*-action, reflection-*on*-action, reflection-*about*-action, and reflection-*for*-action/anticipatory reflection that involves forward planning (Schon, 1983; Zeichner, 1993). There have been critiques of the notion of reflection-in-action which, it is claimed, is impossible in practice because there is insufficient time at a conscious level (Eraut, 1995; Leitch and Day, 2000). Reflection-on-action occurs in reviewing the action from outside its setting; reflection-about-action occurs in reviewing the broader personal, social, economic and political contexts in which the action occurs. It is often accompanied by a desire to achieve greater effectiveness and improvement, and at deeper levels, to consider issues such as social justice and emancipation. It has also been suggested by some that governments are now using 'reflective practice' as a means of promoting technical proficiency, thus developing a new 'technicist' teaching culture that further exacerbates the perceived theory–practice gap between the academy and schools, academics and school teachers; and, more importantly, diminishes the capacity of teachers to act effectively in using the discretionary judgement that is seen as central to their professionalism (Hargreaves and Goodson, 1996).

Kinds of reflection

Grimmett *et al.* (1990) propose three modes of reflection:

* *Technical*: as an instrument to direct or control practice. This may be used to improve the efficiency of the 'delivery' of existing prescribed curricula but not to question its value
* *Deliberative*: as a means of choosing from a range of alternative views and practices of teaching
* *Dialectical*: as a means of transforming by reconstructing practice within concepts of social justice and emancipation.

More recently, others have located learning through reflection within the context of fundamental values and beliefs about education. Five 'orientations' of reflective practice have been proposed: the immediate, the technical, the deliberative, the dialectic, and the transpersonal:

* *Immediate orientation*: emphasis on pleasant survival . . . tendency to focus upon immediate demands or task in hand, pedagogy often eclectic, but shallow

- *Technical orientation*: emphasis on development and perfection of teaching methodology and efficient delivery of prescribed results. Typically emphasizes behavioural techniques
- *Deliberative orientation*: emphasis on discovery, assignment and assessment of personal meaning within an educational setting. Accept given ends but negotiate process and content
- *Dialectic orientation*: emphasis upon political emancipation, questioning educational ends, content and means. Tendency to focus upon political and social issues. Pedagogy involves continual questioning, revision and internal validation, stressing empowerment and personal responsibility
- *Transpersonal orientation*: emphasis upon inner self-development and relationship of internal to external self.

(Wellington and Austin, 1996, pp. 309–11)

Teachers with a passion for and commitment to teaching will engage in each of these forms of reflection during their career lives at times that are appropriate to the maintenance and development of moral purposes, care, identity, knowledge, expertise, and emotional and professional health. This suggests a continuum rather than a hierarchy of reflective practice. The dilemma is which form to choose and when. No single form of reflection is necessarily 'better' than another. However, if teachers want to move beyond the limitations of bureaucratic and technical conceptions of their role, assert a broad vision of their work and its purposes, and not just look inwardly at the efficiency of their own practices within externally imposed agendas, then they:

> . . . cannot restrict their attention to the classroom alone, leaving the larger setting and purposes of schooling to be determined by others. They must take active responsibility for the goals to which they are committed, and for the social setting in which these goals may prosper. If they are not to be mere agents of others, of the state, of the military, of the media, of the experts and bureaucrats, they need to determine their own agency through a critical and continual evaluation of the purposes, the consequences, and the social context of their calling.
>
> (Zeichner and Liston, 1996, p. 11)

The problems in pursuing reflective practice on one's own have been well-documented in research on the busyness of classrooms, the pressures generated by increased bureaucracy associated with new forms of accountability, and the difficulties of self-confrontation that challenge beliefs and practices that have become valued routines and may lead to possibilities of potentially uncomfortable, temporarily disruptive change processes (Day, 1993). Schools themselves have long been characterized as lonely places for adults to work (Cole, 1997, p. 18). Conditions of service and the organizational cultures in many schools do not always allow for regular professional dialogues about teaching that go much beyond anecdotal exchange and the trading of techniques (Day, 1997). These effectively discourage teachers from improving their practice. Such conditions, and cultures in schools that often discourage disclosure, feedback and collaboration, act as potential barriers to participation in all forms of reflective practice. The problem with reflecting alone is that there is a limit to what can be disclosed and what information can be collected and received by an individual with a 'vested' interest in avoiding uncomfortable change processes. Others are needed in the process. Although this aspect has not always been made explicit, the concept of reflective practice has been linked with that of collaboration.

Peer partnerships and networks, discussions and dialogues between practitioners with common purposes, and periods of sustained intellectual challenge through programmes of study in universities, are needed, first, to move from routine to reflective practice in schools; and second, to combat the dangers of cultures that cut off teachers from opportunities to open up and review and renew core moral purposes, identity, and emotional commitments through interrogating their thinking and practices. Yet to understand the role of emotion in the formation, maintenance and negotiation of identity, and to create possibilities for change, requires a conscious examination of habit and routines, the beliefs and values that underpin these, and the broader personal, social, cultural, and ideological contexts in which they operate. Reflection, alone and with others, is necessary. Critically reflective teachers understand and respond to the connections between what they do in the classroom, alternatives to these, and the broader social, cultural and political contexts that interact with their students and their work, how they undertake their work and who they are. In other words, critically reflective teaching is informed by critical reflection.

In research with teachers (Leitch and Day, 2001), five influences upon learning and opportunities for reflective practice were identified:

1   **The paradox of productivity** (Handy, 1994) Because ever more and ever better work was being demanded from even fewer people, there is less and less time to engage in reflection that is other than

solution-seeking to immediately pressing problems. Whether in middle-management leadership roles or face-to-face teaching, participants perceived that they spent most of their time and energy in maintenance rather than development activities. By any definition, this was paradoxical because their roles were inherently developmental:

> In my world of work, the dilemma for me is that I want to spend time with the parents and children, talking with them, helping them to adjust, but efficiency (and that's how I'm appraised) demands that I intervene and leave, write the report and move on.

> All schools now have regular meetings for teachers, but this 'thinking time' is spent on 'housekeeping' with emphasis on the planning of subject progressions, and the establishment of systems to ensure each child touches an attainment target and is recorded as having done so.

2   **Isolation and contrived collegiality** Because of the 'busyness' culture in which teachers work, and increasing accountability demands, there is little time to be collaborative (collaboration is itself a means of providing opportunities for reflection). Most of the work of participants with other professionals consisted of meetings called to satisfy bureaucratic demands:

> Most of our contact however is now standardized and routinized by necessity.

> When we meet now, it's all agenda-driven, solutions to problems, next item please, AOB! Then individuals up and rush off to the next meeting. We hardly pass the time of day with colleagues any more and these are people we would have worked closely with in the past. It's a sad statement really.

Clearly, there is not time in such meetings – often called at the end of the day or attended 'on the hoof' between other tasks – for the kinds of reflection necessary:

> . . . we seem to have generated an inner psychological culture of speed, pressure and the need for control – mirroring the outer

culture of efficiency and productivity – in which access to the slower modes of mind have been lost. People are in a hurry to know, to have answers, to plan and to solve.

3   **Feelings of bereavement** These have been associated with the kinds of 'radical, social, economic, and legislative changes' (Nias, 1991, p. 139) in which many teachers have been involved. Participants wrote of the challenges to their professional status and self-concept, esteem, confidence, and some of the undermining of their professional identity:

> In our culture, there has been so much change since I joined, leaving me with an identity crisis. I could relate to Dante in *Inferno* when he said 'In the midst of our journey of life I came across a dark wood and the straight path was lost'.

These teachers were thus

> victims of a double paradox: the personal rewards found in their work come only from self-investment in it, yet when the cost of the latter is too high to be paid its rewards are also reduced.
>
> (Nias, 1991, p. 144)

Many teachers spoke of their guilt for not taking time to reflect upon anything. This often meant the physical and emotional disruption of personal and social lives.

4   **Time** Linked closely to feelings of guilt and sacrifice were problems (real and perceived) of time:

> Time is at a premium; whatever it is you decide to invest in, no matter how good your intentions at the outset, it's not long before your choice is simply one further demand competing for your attention.

Hargreaves (1994) has identified four interrelated dimensions of time

(a)   *Technical-rational*: the form within principles of technical-rationality which dominate current models of management;

(b) *Micropolitical*: which reflect dominant configurations of power and status within systems;

(c) *Phenomenological*: which reflect subjective perceptions of available time;

(d) *Socio-political*: in which time-frames are defined by the powerful.

5 **Habit**

> Habit reaches . . . down into the very structure of the self; it signifies a building up and solidifying of certain desires; an increased sensitiveness and responsiveness . . . or an improved capacity to attend to and think about certain things.
>
> (Dewey, 1932/1985, p. 171)

Habits or routines, as Argyris and Schon (1974) and later Clark and Yinger (1977) confirmed, can get in the way of growth because they are the expression of tacit knowledge (Polanyi, 1967) that is not easily examined for its validity or relevance to purpose and context. Teachers often, for example, develop an emotional dependence on routines since these may be the result of much investment and form an essential part of hard-won present identity.

Challenging the self: the emotional dimension

> As we study our teaching, we are studying the images we hold of ourselves as teachers. Where these established self-images are challenged, questioned and perhaps threatened in the learning process, we may experience feelings of instability, anxiety, negativity, even depression. This is especially so if the 'self' we come to see in self-study is not the 'self' we think we are, or the 'self' we would like to be.
>
> (Dadds, 1993, p. 287)

Much adult-learning theory promotes emotional detachment, physical distance and rationality. The recognition of the importance of other ways of knowing and learning that are non-rational is necessary. Though complicated because 'non-rational processes cannot easily be analysed and influenced' (Korthagen, 1993), professional development can be designed to address teachers' emotional growth. Thus, studying one's own professional work is not a straightforward matter and adopting the reflective mode is not simply a cerebral activity.

> The self is a citadel of one's own being and worth, and the stronghold from which one moves out to others . . . each teacher will seek as best he can to face himself and to find himself in order to further his own growth. . . . We must raise the question of personal significance in connection with everything we seek to learn and everything that is taught from the nursery school through postgraduate years.
>
> (Jersild, 1955, pp. 135–6)

Understanding the self is part of learning to grow personally and professionally as a teacher in changing and sometimes challenging circumstances. It is difficult to be clear about purposes and values in practice without such an understanding. It is difficult to improve without it. Purposeful passion requires it. Yet, according to Jersild (1955), feelings of anxiety, fear, helplessness, loneliness, meaninglessness, and hostility are often present in teaching environments. External reform and internal culture can threaten teachers' sense of identity, commitment and passionate vocation.

> The core capacity at work here is access to one's *own* feeling life – one's range of affects or emotions: the capacity instantly to effect discriminations among those feelings and eventually to label them, to enmesh them in symbolic codes, to draw upon them as a means of understanding and guiding one's behaviour.
>
> (Cited in Day *et al.*, 1998, p. 109)

Conceptualizing reflection at the centre of any of the processes of change inherent in, for example, action research and networked learning processes, not only acknowledges that teaching is an 'emotional practice' (Hargreaves, 1998, p. 139), but also that emotions are integral to organizational life (Fineman, 1993), frequently occurring as by-products of the socio-political circumstances in which teachers work. What this acknowledgement demands of teachers engaging in reflection, for whatever purpose and within whichever learning mode selected, is that they are committed to engaging with the emotional dimension of their context, whether at personal or system level. Arriving at emotional understanding through, for example, unravelling the relationship between current thinking, feeling and behaving, and how these link to our most basic emotional roots or, through unpicking the way in which the cultural value system of a school controls, inhibits or nurtures the emotions of its members, is central to developing flexible and rational approaches to change. To avoid a well-rehearsed but limited approach to reflection on feelings (i.e. intellectualizing that is usually self-serving and justificatory, and thereby defeats the goals of arriving at new insights or clear decision-making or problem-finding/solving), the approaches derived from the worlds of psychology or psychotherapy are those which by-pass the rational in the first instance, and find access to the emotional and imaginary substratas of the teacher. Thus, for example, the use of drawings or collage work with individuals or groups of teachers to represent the 'felt sense' of an organization, and perceived impediments to development, powerfully access emotional and symbolic dimensions that would not otherwise be available to exploration and reappraisal (Leitch and Day, 2001). Without access to these emotions, there is no opportunity to release feelings and without release there is little room for re-evaluation.

> Teaching, like any truly human activity, emerges from one's inwardness. . . . As I teach, I project the condition of my soul onto my students, my subject, and our way of being together. . . . Teaching holds a mirror to the soul. If I am willing to look in the mirror and not run from what I see, I have a chance to gain self-knowledge – and knowing myself is as crucial to good teaching as knowing my students and my subject. . . . When I do not know myself, I cannot know who my students are. I will see them through a glass darkly, in the shadows of my unexamined life – and when I cannot see them clearly, I cannot teach them well. When I do not know myself, I cannot know my subject – not at the deepest levels of embodied personal meaning.
>
> (Palmer, 1998, p. 2)

Four modes of reflective practice

A disposition to engage in reflection with the mind and heart will be part of the mindset of all teachers who are passionate about teaching. As we have seen, however, time and circumstance may prevent regular, systematic, data-driven reflection but allow the kind of reflection described by one New Zealand teacher and almost certainly experienced by many others across the world.

Reflective mode 1: preparation for what must be done to get by

> I'm reflecting all the time, even as I drive home from school – what
> happened there, where did I go wrong, what can I do? I spend at
> least an hour a day at different times reflecting. Even when I'm out
> on school duty I'm always one step ahead in my mind. I reflect in the
> middle of the night.
>
> (New Zealand teacher, in Ramsay, 1993, p. 58)

In a sense, this teacher is accepting that so much time is spent in
maintaining the system that reflection is enacted as an activity in which
vagueness is normal, and values are left unexamined in the preparation
for what must be done to get by today and tomorrow. Yet this will not be
enough to ensure growth, for it is limited to feedback of experience by self
on self.

Reflective mode 2: critical incidents

Professional growth is enhanced when teachers analyse events from
everyday teaching, make explicit the implicit assumptions that guide their
practice and locate their practice in micro-political, cultural, and broader
political and social contexts. One means of doing this within a busy
timetable is to examine *critical incidents*, i.e. those events that are indicative
of underlying trends, motives, structures, patterns, and values, which
occur at key moments in our lives and work, and result in significant
personal and professional change.

> Incidents happen, but critical incidents are produced by the way we
> look at a situation: a critical incident is an interpretation of the
> significance of an event.
>
> (Tripp, 1993, p. 8)

Kelchtermans (1993) argues that a 'teacher's professional behaviour
and its development can only be understood properly when it is situated
in the broader context of their career and their personal life history'
(p. 202). He defines 'critical incidents' or 'critical phases' as 'events
that challenge the professional self of the teacher' and predictably will
influence their 'further professional biography'. These range from the
questioning of underlying assumptions, opinions and espoused theories
through to the retrospective reconsideration of personal choice points,

decisions and priorities and how these may be linked to changes in patterns of professional behaviour. This can be achieved alone or with others.

Reflective mode 3: autobiographical reflection

One way of reclaiming, reconstructing and recapturing events and accomplishments, and of reaching into issues of purpose, identity, values, and commitment, is through diary or journal keeping and dialogue. The exploration of personal and professional life and work histories can act as a window through which teachers can track the origins of beliefs and practices in order to review their influences. Teachers also accumulate a store of knowledge – emotional and cognitive – that has been shaped by past experiences. For many years, Connelly and Clandinin have worked closely with teachers in Canada exploring their lives as educational wholes, encouraging them to draw upon their professional knowledge 'landscapes':

> What is missing in the classroom is a place for teachers to tell and retell their stories of teaching. The classroom can become a place for endless, repetitive, living out of stories without possibility for awakenings and transformations. . . . [But] . . . the possibilities for reflective awakenings and transformations are limited when one is alone. Teachers need others in order to engage in conversations where stories can be told, related back, heard in different ways, retold and relived in new ways. . . .
>
> (Connelly and Clandinin, 1995, p. 13)

Professional work contexts may not encourage such reflection, and making sense of experience is complex. Yet it is difficult to envisage teachers with a passion for learning not engaging in this mode of reflection at some points during their careers.

Reflective mode 4: action research

Action research has been defined as

> the study of a social situation, involving the participants themselves as researchers, with a view to improving the quality of action within it.
>
> (Somekh, 1989, p. 164)

Collaborative action research combines the quest for individual renewal with that of school improvement. Sagor (1997, p. 177) suggests that this form of individual and collective inquiry contains most of the findings from the literature on successful change:

- Action research projects are chosen based on a *felt need*
- Participants *adapt* their work to meet local conditions
- *Time* is provided for implementation
- *Consultants* are available to assist on demand
- Opportunities to *share and learn from one another in safety* are provided
- *Experimentation* is encouraged
- *Risk* is minimized
- Appropriate *pressure and support* are built into the system

There is a clear connection between conducting action research and the characteristics of creative individuals:

> [They] do not rush to define the nature of problems; they look at the situation from various angles first and leave the formulation undetermined for a long time. They consider different causes and reasons. They test their hunches about what is really going on, first in their own mind and then in reality. They try tentative solutions and check their success – and they are open to reformulating the problem if the evidence suggests they started out on the wrong path.
>
> (Csikszentmihalyi, 1996, p. 365)

Teaching is a highly complex activity and it is, therefore, in the interests of policy makers and managers who wish to recruit and retain teachers, and sustain them at their best, to ensure that they remain passionate, healthy, knowledgeable, and committed to providing the best-possible learning opportunities for students. Since the needs of society and students will change, it is necessary for teachers to be able to evaluate the part they play in meeting such needs. It follows that they need regular opportunities to exercise discretionary judgement; to reflect upon their moral and social purposes; to work collaboratively with colleagues in and outside school; to engage in a self-directed search; and to struggle for continuous learning related to their own needs for growth of expertise and maintenance of standards of practice. In short, they need to be educated to become and remain passionate practitioners at the heart of whose practice is reflection.

Teachers with a passion for teaching will, by definition, possess a passion for learning – about the subject or topic they teach, about the students (their backgrounds, histories, motivations, dispositions, learning styles, and preferences), about the different teaching approaches and tools available, about change (for they are in the business of change), about the contexts in which they teach and students learn, and *about themselves*. Without such understandings and continuing inquiry it will be difficult for initial passion to be sustained as circumstances, needs and students change. Such teachers will be aware that learning from their own experience of teaching, while valuable, will ultimately be limiting. They will wish to learn from others directly and indirectly or vicariously. They will have different learning needs, depending upon the contexts in which they work, personal circumstances and particular career phase. They will recognise that no one means of learning will in itself be sufficient but rather that a range of learning opportunities will need to be available – from the much maligned 'one-shot' workshop or lecture that may or may not inspire, to the sustained but difficult learning that is made possible through action research or membership of a school–university partnership or networked learning community.

Yet, unless carefully managed, the rush towards collaborative cultures and networked learning communities, much lauded in the school improvement/effective schools literatures, can leave in its wake individuals who are less passionate than they were before:

> In some school systems, the purge of individualism [a preferred work pattern not to be confused with individuality] has become unrestrained, and the eccentricity, independence, imagination, and initiative that we call individuality have become casualties in its wake. . . . If most teachers in a school prefer solitude, this is probably indicative of a problem with the system – of individualism representing a withdrawal from threatening, unpleasant, or unrewarding personal relationships.
>
> (Hargreaves A., 1993, pp. 71–3)

Just as it is a key challenge for the individual teacher to sustain a passion for teaching, so it is a key role of school professional develop-ment co-ordinators, in acknowledging that passionate teaching involves the head and the heart, to ensure that there are opportunities to reflect upon and inquire into the means of sustaining passionate involve-ment. Figure 6.1 analyses professional development needs in the context of the different selves of teachers, and the direct and indirect

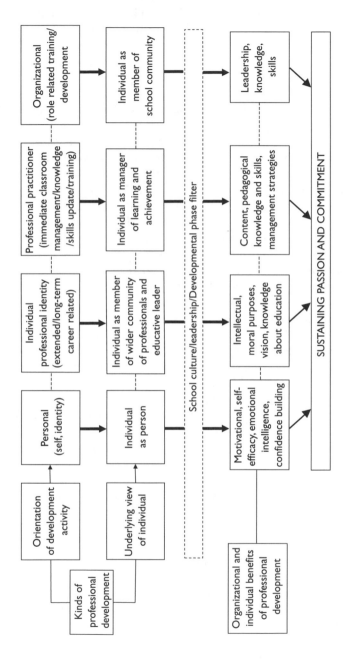

Figure 6.1 Direct and indirect benefits of career-long professional development planning oriented to teachers' different selves.

benefits to the individual and the school that flow from attending to these.

Teachers' career phases

In England (Ball and Goodson, 1985; Sikes *et al.*, 1985; Nias, 1989); the United States (Lightfoot, 1983); in Australia (Ingvarson and Greenway, 1984; Maclean, 1992); in Canada (Butt, 1984); and in Switzerland (Huberman, 1989, 1993), a number of key phases have been identified through which many teachers are perceived to move in their careers. Bolam (1990, p. 153) identified five 'job' stages: the preparatory stage; the appointment stage; the induction stage; the in-service stage (i.e. 3–5 years, 6–10 years, 11 years in post); and the transitional stage (i.e. promotion, re-employment, retirement). He reminds us that the needs of individuals will vary according to these and other factors, such as age, gender, school type. Kremer-Hayon and Fessler (1991) posited nine career-cycle stages: pre-service; induction; competency; building; enthusiasm and growth; career frustration; stability and stagnation; career wind-down; and career exit.

The most authoritative studies of teachers' career experiences and the most influential determinants of them within and outside the institution are those of Swiss secondary school teachers by Michael Huberman (Huberman 1989, 1993), of English teachers by Sikes *et al.* (1985), and of American teachers by Fessler and Christensen (1992). Their work suggests that teachers pass through five broad phases:

1 *Launching a career*: initial commitment; easy or painful beginnings
2 *Stabilization*: find commitment; consolidation, emancipation, integration into peer group
3 *New challenges*: new concerns; experimentation, responsibility, consternation
4 *Reaching a professional plateau*: sense of mortality, stop striving for promotion, enjoy or stagnate
5 *Final phase*: increased concern with pupil learning and increasing pursuit of outside interests; disenchantment; contraction of professional activity and interest.

Although many teachers begin their careers 'with a sense that their work is socially meaningful and will yield great satisfactions', this tends to be lost as:

- Career development is often accompanied by 'a sense of inconsequentiality' (Farber, 1991)
- Many teachers in mid- to late-career become disenchanted or marginalize themselves from learning, no longer holding the good of their pupils as a high priority
- Low self-esteem and shame (at not achieving desired results) are directly correlated with less variety of teaching approaches and thus less connection with students' learning needs.

Many of the 'short-burst' training opportunities do not fulfil the longer-term motivational and intellectual needs of teachers themselves. They fail to connect with the essential moral purposes that are at the heart of their professionalism, or to address directly the emotional commitments of teachers that are the glue of connection as they seek to improve the quality of pupils' learning in changing and challenging circumstances.

> Teaching 'involves immense amounts of emotional labour. . . . This kind of labour calls for a co-ordination of mind and feeling, and it sometimes draws on a source of self that we honour as deep and integral to our personality. . . .
>
> (Hochschild, 1983, p. 7)

Such emotional commitments are part of teachers' substantive, professional selves. Teacher development, then, must take account of these and the psychological and social settings which can encourage or discourage learning – for example, the teachers' own personal life histories, their professional learning experiences and expertise, and the school professional learning cultures that provide the day-to-day contexts for their work. If we are truly to engage in learning for teachers as well as students, then interventions in their working lives over a career must be based on an understanding of them.

Ralph Fessler (1995) has developed a descriptive multi-dimensional model of teachers' professional development over their working lives, which takes into account the interplay of organizational, personal (life) and career (professional) factors. This model eschews simplistic notions of linear trajectories of teacher growth and points clearly to the need for personalized, differentiated development opportunities that also take account of changes in the conditions of work. In this sense, it can be related to research on job satisfaction and teacher efficacy.

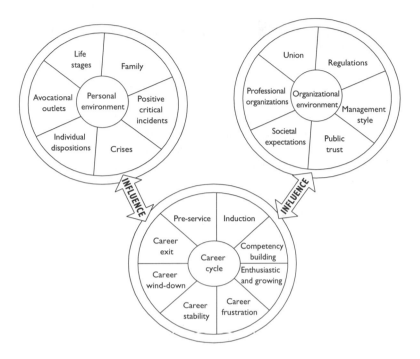

Figure 6.2 Dynamics of the teacher career cycle.
Source: Fessler and Christensen, 1992, p. 36

The principal career cycle components are:

- *Pre-service*: The period of initial preparation
- *Induction*: The first few years of employment (or the first period in a new job) when teachers are striving for acceptance and respect
- *Competency building*: When skills, competencies are being improved (or frustrated through lack of ability, support or extremes of student behaviour)
- *Enthusiastic and growing*: A period of recognized competence and acceptance into the school community in which there is a high degree of personal and organizational job satisfaction
- *Career frustration*: Tends to occur in the early years and at the midpoint of a career when, either through lack of support,

disillusionment with the difficulty of the challenges of classroom teaching, lack of recognition, or adverse personal circumstances, teachers no longer look forward to their work. *This is the phase when passion may die.*

- *Career stability*: A 'plateauing' as teachers meet the requirements of the job but are no longer committed to continuing growth. This period may mark the further erosion of passion and the beginning of disengagement.
- *Career wind-down*: Either a pleasant, positive period of enduring commitment with respect, or a bitter unrewarding ending to a no-longer passionate engagement with teaching and learning.

(Based on Fessler, 1995, pp. 185–6)

Towards an optimal mix of opportunities

Most teachers still work in isolation from their colleagues for most of the time; opportunities for the development of practice based upon observation and critique of that practice remain limited; and, despite the best efforts of many school leaders to promote collegial cultures, these are almost always at the level of planning or talking about teaching rather than at the level of examining practice itself.

Tom Guskey (1995) proposes that because such contexts are dynamic, there is a need for providing an 'optimal mix' of professional learning and development opportunities that will work best in any given setting:

> In the minds of many today there is a clear vision of what would be ideal in professional development. That ideal sees educators at all levels constantly in search of new and better ways to address the diverse learning needs of their students. It sees schools as learning communities where teachers and students are continually engaged in inquiry and stimulating discourse. It sees practitioners in education respected for their professional knowledge and pedagogic skill.
>
> (Guskey, 1995, p. 126)

Schools, therefore, need to be able to support a mix of professional learning opportunities within a range of on- and off-site activities that provide for on-going needs and take account of the influences upon teachers. Lieberman and Miller (1999) provide one way of conceptualizing what they call the 'multiple entry points' which provide support and challenge (see Figure 6.3).

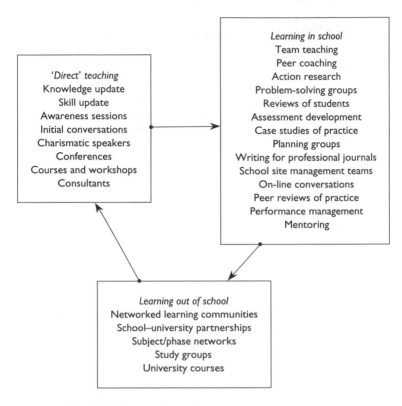

Figure 6.3 Organizing for professional development.
Source: Based on Lieberman and Miller, 1999, p. 73

In-service education and training

In-service education and training (INSET) as part of continuing professional development, is still the most widely used form of development intended to provide intensive learning over a limited period. Although it may be jointly planned, it usually has a designated leader(s) whose role is not only to facilitate but also actively to stimulate learning. Where it is timed to 'fit' the needs of teachers in relation to their phase of experience, career development, demands of the system, lifelong learning cycle, or systems needs, it is likely to succeed in *accelerating growth*, whether that growth is additive (taking knowledge, skills, understanding forward a step) or transformative (resulting in major changes in beliefs, knowledge, skills, or understandings). Over recent years, governments have realized, however, that successful change requires the active co-operation of teachers. Thus, they have reasoned that restructuring schools, providing nationally directed curriculum reform and targets for student achievement will not in themselves improve teaching practices or student learning and achievement (Elmore, 1992). These will be more likely to be implemented successfully if teachers' knowledge and skills are upgraded. However, in-service activities that have no immediate bearing on specific social policies and issues need also to be supported, because schools and individual teachers need to develop and maintain their capacity for renewal in order both to improve the quality of current services and to meet new demands.

The development of centrally promoted INSET has tended to be at the expense of, rather than complementary to, INSET opportunities chosen by the teachers themselves. Reporting on the findings of a Leverhulme-funded study of teachers' perceptions of the provision of Continuing Professional Development (CPD), conducted in four Local Education Authorities in England, McMahon (1999) found that tensions between the two overall purposes of CPD – to promote school improvement and individual teacher development – had not been resolved. The evidence was that 'teachers are keen to improve their knowledge and skills, although at any one time their learning priorities might differ from those of the school or government' (McMahon, 1999, p. 104). The introduction of site-based school management through which, in theory, 'need' and 'relevance' might be more accurately identified had not, the research revealed, proved to be a success. Because resources were more thinly and unevenly spread, choice of CPD mode had diminished (e.g. rural schools had less access to HE, school networking had largely ceased), and there were wide variations within schools. Few professional development co-ordinators were allocated time to do their job, commitments of headteachers to CPD varied and the bulk of the CPD budget was used for responding to external demands for curriculum reform and renewal. This meant that

> individual development needs were neglected unless they were in an area that was designated a school priority.
>
> (McMahon, 1999, p. 106)

The conclusion from McMahon's (1999) research on secondary school teachers' CPD clearly indicates the need to ensure that all teachers have opportunities to participate in a range of learning activities, that individual needs are an important focus and that school conditions must provide space for teacher development. It recognizes implicitly the importance to effective teaching of:

* Individual commitment
* High self efficacy
* A learning culture
* Self knowledge.

It follows that teachers need not only to be knowledgeable about learners, their needs and learning processes, they need also to be knowledgeable about themselves.

McMahon pointed to the limitations of the focus upon half-day programmes, concluding that:

> In a half-day programme the most that can be achieved is to make teachers aware of new information and ideas. If CPD provision is to become more effective, government and schools will need to strive to:
>
> * Ensure their CPD resources are available for teachers on a more equitable basis
> * Strengthen and expand the range of school-based CPD support mechanisms
> * Take greater account of the specific development needs of individuals
> * Clarify the purposes of particular CPD activities and select a form of provision that is likely to achieve the stated purpose
> * Strive to provide conditions at work which will give teachers the mental space to concentrate on professional development.
>
> (McMahon, 1997, p. 6)

Three propositions for professional development

Three propositions are at the core of teachers' professionalism:

1 To improve schools, one must be prepared to invest in professional development.

2   To improve teachers, their professional development must be set within the contexts of personal and institutional needs and these will not always coincide.

3   Teachers' hearts (passions, enthusiasms, personal identities, commitment, emotions) are as important a focus as their heads and hands.

It is . . . [a] . . . concern for the individual that is surely lacking in present professional development planning. Unlike other professions, education gives teachers few personal options when it comes to professional development. Too much of what we presently do is collective in-service, not personalized professional development. In-service education is oriented toward immediate collective training objectives, whereas professional development implies engagement in persistent and personally significant activities.

(Marczely, 1996, pp. 7–8)

School-provided INSET may support only systems-oriented needs and so, in emphasizing only concepts of practicality and relevance, 'contribute to the development of instrumentalist ideologies which emphasize a technical approach by both providers and consumers of in-service education' (Sachs and Logan, 1990, p. 477). Emphasis upon teachers' experiential knowledge and immediate needs reinforces the view that they need only to know how to manage teaching and that, by implication, understanding the broader purposes, processes and contexts of education is less important.

> Rather than developing reflective practitioners who are able to understand, challenge and transform their practice, in-service education in its current form encourages the development of teachers who see their world in terms of instrumental ends achievable through the recipes of 'tried and true' practices legitimated by unexamined experience or uncritically accepted research findings.
>
> (Sachs and Logan, 1990, p. 479)

There are five valuable lessons here for those whose responsibility it is to promote teacher development. First, any comprehensive programme must attend to the different selves of the teacher – the person, the professional, the classroom practitioner, and the member of the school community. Second, feedback and sustained support are essential components in the process of continuing but not continuous learning. Third, the disposition towards and commitment to learning must be nurtured in the teacher as lifelong learner. Fourth, the organizational culture must be supportive of collegial relationships. Finally, resources must be targeted at long-term as well as short-term development, taking into account a balanced portfolio of learning needs.

Teachers' professional development will be restricted rather than extended, fragmentary rather than coherent, while the breadth of their learning needs continues to be ignored. Professional learning will come to be associated not with capacity-building for the use of insightful judgement exercised in complex situations, but with one-shot events specifically targeted at immediate technically defined implementation needs as determined by others.

Time to reflect

> Probably nothing within a school has more impact on students in terms of skills development, self-confidence, or classroom behaviour than the personal and professional growth of their teachers. . . .
>
> (Barth, 1996, p. 49)

1   What have been the (a) informal, and (b) formal professional development experiences that have made a difference to your work?
2   Identify particular moments of personal and professional significance in your life and career that have caused you to change, positively or negatively. Consider the causes, and the short-, medium- and longer-term effects upon your work.
3   What is the learning now and in the future that is most appropriate to your

- Personal growth needs (e.g. self-efficacy, health, commitment, motivation)?
- Professional growth needs (e.g. role development, classroom management and teaching)?

4   What action steps do you need to take in order to get support for these needs to be met?
5   Who will assist you in this process?

Chapter 7

Passionate learning communities

> As emotional arenas, organizations bond and divide their members. Workaday frustrations and passions – boredom, envy, fear, love, anger, guilt, infatuation, embarrassment, nostalgia, anxiety – are deeply woven into the ways roles are enacted and learned, power is exercised, trust is held, commitment formed and decisions made. Emotions are not simply excisable from these, and many other, organizational processes; they both characterize and inform them.
>
> (Fineman, 2000, p. 1)

In recent years, there has been a proliferation of texts about school and teacher effectiveness. Yet each one has failed to acknowledge that effective teaching and learning relies, at its heart, on the exercise by teachers of sustained passion (as well as compassion) in the classroom and as part of a wider school learning community. A key influence upon teachers' capacity to do this is the part played by the school context.

Roland Barth presents assumptions about schools as a community of learners, according to which there is an implicit view of schools as places where students learn and adults teach, places that are 'fundamentally different' from those of the list makers:

- Schools have the capacity to improve themselves, if the conditions are right. A major responsibility of those outside the schools is to help provide these conditions for those inside
- When the need and the purpose is there, when the conditions are right, adults and students alike learn and each energizes and contributes to the learning of the other

- What needs to be improved about schools is their culture, the quality of interpersonal relationships, and the nature and quality of learning experiences
- School improvement is an effort to determine and provide, from without and within, conditions under which the adults and youngsters who inhabit schools will promote and sustain learning among themselves.

(Barth, 1990, p. 45)

Teachers' perceptions and experiences of their work conditions – leadership, physical plant, resources, organizational features, and relationships – inevitably will affect their attitudes to and practices of teaching and learning. For example, a shared sense of values will bind staff together:

People feel their parts in the life of the group. When welcomed in a safe, vital, active group, they feel secure, vital and active themselves, and take pleasure in these feelings. When confined in a moribund or passive group, they feel deadened and passive themselves, and take no pleasure in these feelings. And when excluded from the group, they feel worst of all – cut off, isolated, alone and unhappy. Feeling is how social life appears in consciousness.

(Sandelands and Boudens, 2000, p. 47)

Those who are passionate about teaching for the 'betterment' of the pupils they teach will also have a stake in the betterment of all pupils in the school – and this means that they, with their colleagues, will want to 'take charge of change' (Stoll, 1999, p. 32).

School effectiveness is about a great deal more than maximizing academic achievement. Learning and the love of learning; personal development and self-esteem; life skills, problem solving and learning how to learn; the development of independent thinkers and well-rounded CONFIDENT individuals; all rank as highly or more highly as the outcomes of effective schooling as success in a narrow range of academic disciplines.

(McGraw et al., 1992, p. 174)

Whatever the definition of school effectiveness, schools will change most effectively when improvement comes from within.

School cultures

Essentially culture is about the way people are with each other in the classroom, department or school. It is characterized by the ways values, beliefs, prejudices and behaviour are played out within the micro-political processes of school life. It is often described as the ethos or climate, 'the deeper level of basic assumptions and beliefs that are shared by members of our organization, that operate unconsciously, and that define in a basic 'taken-for-granted' fashion an organization's view of itself and its environment' (Schein, 1985, p. 6). Just as conditions in classrooms affect the ability of teachers to provide the best learning opportunities for students, so the school culture provides positive or negative support for its teachers' learning.

In reporting research on what matters most to teachers in their workplace context, McLaughlin emphasized the importance of the '*school as workplace community*'.

> The school workplace is a physical setting, a formal organization, an employer. It is also a social and psychological setting in which teachers construct a sense of practice, of professional efficacy, and of professional community. This aspect of the workplace – the nature of the professional community that exists there – appears more critical than any other factor to the character of teaching and learning for teachers and their students. . . .
>
> (McLaughlin, 1993, p. 99)

Jennifer Nias and colleagues (1989) have written extensively about forms of primary school culture that have different implications for teachers' work and professional development opportunities. Schools that are 'stuck' or 'moving' (Rosenholtz, 1989), 'cruising' or 'strolling' (Stoll and Fink, 1996), will inevitably affect teacher development. Norms for improving schools, identified by Stoll and Fink (1996) and summarized by Stoll (1999), clearly suggest the presence of a collective *passion for improvement* (see Figure 7.1).

Such a passion for establishing and sustaining these norms would reject, for example, the cultures of individualism (where autonomy, isolation and insulation rule); contrived collegiality (where working relationships are bureaucratically imposed); balkanization (where competition for resources and rewards exists and loyalties to 'phase', 'subject' or department come before those to the whole school) (Hargreaves, A., 1994). It would be likely to embrace collegial work

1 *Shared goals:* 'We know where we're going'
2 *Responsibility for success:* 'We must succeed'
3 *Collegiality:* 'We're working on this together'
4 *Continuous improvement:*[1] 'We can get better'
5 *Lifelong learning:* 'Learning is for everyone'
6 *Risk taking:* 'We learn by trying something new'
7 *Support:* 'There's always someone there to help'
8 *Mutual respect:* 'Everyone has something to offer'
9 *Openness:* 'We can discuss our differences'
10 *Celebration and humour:* 'We feel good about ourselves'.
(Stoll, 1999, p. 37)

Figure 7.1 Norms for improving schools.

relations in which the 'person' is as important as the 'professional' (the one nests within the other); where there is joint work through, for instance, critical friendships in classroom-based inquiry, mentoring, monitoring, and review; where values and visions for the school match values and visions in the classroom; and where there is *emotional* understanding:

> . . . an intersubjective process requiring that one person enter into the field of experience of another and experience for herself the same or similar experiences experienced by another. The subjective interpretation of another's emotional experience from one's own standpoint is central to emotional understanding. Shared and sharable emotionality lie at the core of what it means to understand and meaningfully enter into the emotional experiences of another.
> (Denzin, 1984, p. 137)

Collegiality

Cultures of collegiality rely for their success upon the emotional understandings by all members of their own motivations, purposes,

---

1 I have a difficulty with the word 'continuous'. It implies that we never rest and this is clearly impossible. For this reason, a much better word is *continuing*.

commitments and identities, and those of their colleagues. Judith
Warren-Little (1981) provides both an operational definition of collegiality and a protocol for recognizing its presence in schools related to
behaviours of the headteacher. There is collegiality when:

- Adults talk about practice
- Observe each other in practice
- Work together on planning, assessing, evaluating and researching
  teaching and learning
- Teach each other what they know about teaching, learning and
  leading.

To these might be added

- Adults share emotional understandings of and commitments to each
  other.

Cultures of collegiality should not suffocate teachers' individuality
or mute their continuing passion to exercise responsibility in their
classrooms:

> The press for teachers to work together as colleagues is strong, but
> so also is the desire or perhaps necessity for teachers to feel that
> they have the freedom and autonomy as individuals to construct
> classrooms that make sense to them and their students.
>
> (Little and McLaughlin, 1993, p. vii)

In recent years, reforms have ensured that teachers work more closely
in planning the curriculum and assessing pupil progress. And yet, passion
for teaching remains principally an individual endeavour. There are few
planning meetings called for the purpose of discussing and enhancing
passion. Indeed it may be that too much collegiality takes much-needed
personal energy away from classroom teaching, and that too much
detailed collective planning denies the reality of classroom life, which
requires of the teacher the ability to improvise in response to the
immediate learning needs of students. Nevertheless, the emotions of
teaching may be shared in collaborative cultures:

> in the small gestures, jokes and glances that signal sympathy and
> understanding; in kind words and personal interest shown in
> corridors or outside classroom doors; in birthdays, treat days and

other little ceremonies; in the acceptance and intermixture of personal lives with professional ones; in overt praise, recognition and gratitude; and in sharing and discussion of ideas and resources.

(Hargreaves, A., 1989, p.14)

Learning communities: classrooms and schools

> As helpers, we should only be pleasured by what is in the students' best interest. Laughing in public at another's misfortune may be enjoyable if we are not interested in a relationship with that person and take no responsibility for their welfare. Good teachers, however, would take no pleasure in such behaviour if one of their students was the object of ridicule, because of how they feel about the teaching/learning relationship and the student as an individual.
>
> (McWilliam, 1999, pp. 58–9)

Characteristic of outstanding teachers is that they respect and like their students, and are 'committed to and skilled at connecting the two things they care deeply about – their subject matter and their students' (Harrell, 1996, p. 12). It is the intimacy of the teacher–learner relationship that is an essential part of the teaching–learning relationship. It results in the 'pedagogical tact' that involves and invokes, simultaneously, perceptiveness, insight and feeling (van Manen, 1995, p. 41); and because teaching is, essentially, an interpersonal activity, such tact must in itself – at least in the moment of the connection – minimize status or power differentials between teacher, context and learner. That the result of this will be enjoyment and satisfaction for the teacher and the learner is undeniable.

Louis, Kruse and Associates (1995) suggest that professional school communities share five core characteristics:

- Shared norms and values
- Reflective dialogue
- Sharing of practice
- Focus on student learning
- Inclusivity.

Passionate teachers do not work in isolation. They are part of a complex web of social and interpersonal relationships that make up the

Table 7.1 Patterns of teaching practice in contemporary classrooms.

Patterns of practice	Dimensions of classroom practice			
	Students	Content	Pedagogy	Education outcomes
Enact traditions of practice	Passive learner role	Subject static; knowledge given	Routine, teacher-centred	Success with traditional students only
Lower expectations and standards	Passive learner role	Watered-down subject matter	Routine, teacher-centred	Limited success with all students
Innovate to engage learners	Active learner role	Subject dynamic; knowledge constructed	Non-routine, student-centred	Increased success with non-traditional students

(McLaughlin and Talbert, 2001, p. 19)

culture of the school and department and will inevitably affect their work and lives. Research was conducted over a four-year period, aimed at understanding how teachers in a range of sixteen American high schools in two contrasting states were constructing their classroom practices in order to meet the challenges of preparing students for their lives beyond school. Milbrey McLaughlin and Joan Talbert found that:

> Even the best teacher attitudes and responses have trouble enduring without a professional community to support, endorse and validate them. Every teacher we encountered who was engaged in a high level of pedagogy belonged to such a community.
>
> (McLaughlin and Talbert, 1993, p. 17)

They observed that school and departmental cultures had a significant influence upon the kinds of teaching approaches used, and identified three broad patterns of practice which, in terms of the subject of this book, imply much about the different degrees of passion which teachers communicate to their students.

It is clear from this that for teachers to be effective, they need to break out of predominantly transmission modes of teaching to those that are more dynamic and take students' learning needs seriously (Table 7.1 sets out the outcomes of some practices). Passion is not only about how teachers present themselves but also how students see their substantive (whole) selves valued in the approaches to teaching and learning. The kinds of 'reflexive conservatism' (Lortie, 1975, p. 240) in which teaching routines never change is the enemy of all who are passionate about teaching that connects with learners' immediate and longer-term needs.

Having a passion for teaching means working

> . . . to establish an active role for students in developing new, deeper subject knowledge that builds upon their interests, skills and prior knowledge . . . [moving] towards teaching for understanding – emphasizing depth in students' content knowledge over coverage of many topics and skills, and problem-solving skills over mastery of the kinds of routines emphasized in traditional instruction.
>
> (McLaughlin and Talbert, 2001, p. 25)

Yet to achieve this means seeking to understand the classroom from students' perspectives, focusing in the process of teaching upon building self-esteem through the knowledge and understanding of the student. The challenge of teaching the student as well as the subject is likely to result in higher levels of satisfaction, the intrinsic reward that helps to maintain teacher commitment.

The cultures of those schools in which teacher learning communities – and thus it might be assumed a climate for passionate teaching – were found, were described as opening each year with discussions of values, norms and practices:

> Teachers become committed or recommitted to working within these schools' structures for collective problem solving . . . [they] learn how to participate as partners in constructing school success . . . trusting the community as a vehicle for teaching success and professional growth.
>
> (McLaughlin and Talbert, 2001, p. 85)

Teachers felt that, although their work demanded an enormous investment of energy, 'the shared struggle' sustained their personal commitment and effort and professional growth (ibid., p. 88). In the concluding chapter of the research report, the authors point unequivocally to the importance of teacher learning communities:

> Principles for professional development policy, practice, and initiative that come from nearly two decades of US education reform underscore our conclusion that teacher learning communities constitute the best context for professional growth and change.
>
> (McLaughlin and Talbert, 2001, p. 35)

Connecting teachers to development: promoting teacher learning

While by definition individual teachers are responsible for the quality of their work in the classroom, schools that espouse the ideals and practices of *community*, exercise a collective responsibility for the conditions in which teachers and students work, recognizing that the learning health of both is fundamental to their growth and development. To claim that a school is a learning community suggests the presence of a number of relational qualities.

- *Respect*: Teachers and students treat each other with respect and authentic courtesy.
- *Caring*: Encompassing but going beyond respect, caring is more particularistic and pro-active in that it acknowledges the uniqueness of each individual and reaches out to initiate positive interaction, rather than being expressed only as a response to another.
- *Inclusiveness*: There are continual attempts to ensure that all participants are drawn into the whole range of interactions throughout the school, and none are left as outsiders. What is different about a school as a community is that teachers and students are typically not separated by physical division; for example, they might share a lunch room or students might be invited to participate in teachers' meetings, and, perhaps more importantly, they share a common culture of assumptions and values in the school so that students and teachers are not pitted against each other.
- *Trust*: Members of a genuine community trust one another to the point where they are prepared to disclose themselves and their work to their colleagues because they know that such disclosure will be beneficial to their relationships and improve their work as teachers and learners.

- *Empowerment*: Both students and teachers feel empowered in a community because they know their voice will be heard and their feelings will count when it comes to expressing their concerns. This is especially important for students, who are often locked out of decision-making processes in schools and denied opportunities for influencing policy and practice.
- *Commitment*: A strong sense of attachment and a high level of investment of energy are features of a community; the school may be described as 'like a family' and there is particular attachment to the goals and values of the school which motivate members to achieve the best possible outcomes for all concerned.

(Raywid, 1993, pp. 32–9)

The challenge for teachers and their leaders is to sustain the passion as the needs of the students and society change and as teachers themselves grow older. McLaughlin and Talbert's (op. cit.) research suggests that meeting this challenge is vital to the maintenance of healthy patterns in teachers' work lives and careers. Table 7.2 summarizes the importance of school and department cultures to the patterns of teachers' professional relations and careers they identified in the schools and departments they studied.

Yet passion for teaching is difficult to sustain in schools and departments that themselves do not promote the continuing professional development of all who work in them through, for example, mentoring schemes, regular peer observation, dialogue about teaching and learning, inquiries into practice for the purposes of further understanding and improvement, as well as the more traditional forms of 'in-service' activity.

Lieberman and Miller (1999) suggest ways transitions may be made from the more traditional views of teaching and learning that are no longer appropriate for the needs of schooling in the twenty-first century, to 'new understandings of the social realities' (p. 20):

1 *From individualism to professional community*: Working jointly to decide on common goals, develop programmes, deal with problems, and manage tensions between individuality and collegiality.
2 *From teaching at the centre to learning at the centre*: planning based on outcomes and assessments of students and how they learn.

Table 7.2 Patterns of teachers' work lives and careers.

	Dimensions of teachers' work lives		
Patterns of teaching careers	*Colleague relations*	*Assignment to courses and students*	*Professional rewards*
Stagnant or declining careers (weak community)	Professional isolation; social relations enforce privacy norms	Seniority logic: prerogatives of tenure	Intrinsic rewards vary by students taught; esteem based on social standing of students and the profession
Divergent career trends (traditional community)	Co-ordination around course tracking and student testing	Expertise logic; teacher tracking by credentials	Intrinsic rewards vary by teaching credentials and assignments; prestige based on certified expertise.
Shared career progress (teacher learning community)	Collaboration around teaching and learning	Equity logic: teacher rotation across course levels	Intrinsic rewards grow with collective success; pride based on professional growth

(MacLaughlin and Talbert, 2001, p. 78)

3   *From technical work to inquiry*: Putting research, reflection and systematic inquiry into their own practice at the heart of their teaching, demonstrating that they too are continuing to learn.

4   *From control to accountability*: Each teacher assumes responsibility for creating a classroom where students can master school knowledge at an appropriate pace and with an appropriately high degree of challenge. Instead of working to establish norms of control, teachers work to establish norms of learning.

5 *From managed work to leadership*: Teachers relinquish 'power over' students in exchange for 'power to' affect student performance. This form of 'distributed leadership', which recognizes that everyone has a stake in success, is modelled throughout the school.

6 *From classroom concerns to whole-school concerns and beyond*: Teachers recognize that their work extends beyond the walls of their class-room, that they have an essential part to play in defining the school culture. They form partnerships and networks with other schools in order to extend their thinking and practices. They become 'activist professionals' (Sachs, 2003).

7 *From a weak knowledge base to a broad knowledge base*: Teachers base their teaching on new as well as old understandings of the way students learn and use the tools that best relate to this.

(Lieberman and Miller, 1999, pp. 21–3)

Networks for learning

Writing in a school improvement context, Michael Huberman (1995) proposed research-based, cross-school networks, 'with a focus on bridging the gap between peer exchanges, the interventions of external resource people, and the greater likelihood of actual change at the classroom level' (p. 193). Their aim is almost always systemic change and they consist of a number of schools that work together over extended periods of time with the support of staff from universities and other organizations with an interest in supporting improvement efforts. Because they meet over time, this creates opportunities for a wide variety of agreed intervention strategies by university staff and others, and for changes in the focus of their work together.

In a review of the American literature, Hord (1997) explored the concept and uses of professional learning networks, focusing primarily upon those in which whole schools or departments were involved. While recognizing that such communities of continuous inquiry and improve-ment are 'embryonic and scattered' (Darling-Hammond, 1996, p. 10), she identified several factors necessary for their development: (i) significant contributions made by school principals to provide supportive environ-ments (Leithwood *et al.*, 1997); (ii) staff involvement in decision-making, reflective dialogue through shared practice and peer review, and inquiry; and (iii) 'undeviating' focus upon student and staff learning (Louis and Kruse, 1995; Sarason, 1990). Although building collaborative learning networks takes time, the literature suggests that there are significant benefits for both staff and students. Among these are:

- Reduction in the isolation of teachers
- Increased commitment to the mission and goals of the school, and increased vigour in working to strengthen the mission
- Higher likelihood that teachers will be well-informed, professionally renewed, and inspired to inspire students
- Significant advances into making teaching adaptations for students, and changes for learners made more quickly than in traditional schools
- Higher likelihood of undertaking fundamental, systemic change.

(Hord, 1997, pp. 27–8)

Teachers' learning – two examples

Here is how two experienced teachers in America responded to the opportunity for the first time in many years, to engage in supported systematic inquiry into the consequences of different kinds of practice:

> [It] opened my mind to certain strategies – and I have been teaching for more than a quarter of a century . . . but I didn't realise there were other outlets – that I could use much better strategies. So I became a strategy seeker . . . I was open to the fact that it's not my way or the highway anymore. I am opening up new approaches to my students. . . .

(Quoted in McLaughlin, 2002, p. 100)

> I could never see what a good school this is because I was into my own classroom. I never had the broad picture. And until I saw that, when I could really sit down and see the whole school, that's when the light went on. You know, we have some holes, we have some gaps, but boy, we're okay!

(Quoted in McLaughlin, 2002, p. 102)

In Australia, involvement in a school consortium involving collaborative inquiry with support from a small group of academics had similar effects:

> It's other teachers going through the same things as you. You find out what's important to your colleagues and it makes you ready to reflect.

(Quoted in Loughran, 2002, p. 149)

and

> I've come to know that people learn in different ways . . . I now know
> what is happening when someone is a good 'swatter' for exams while
> others need connections between ideas, or relevance to their life. . . .
> So increasing experiences for students really matters and you need a
> wide range and use of questioning techniques . . . there's a difference
> between knowing and understanding.
>
> (Quoted in Loughran, 2002, p. 152)

Only by doing things together over time are the conditions for people
to develop shared meanings, values and goals created. There is no
substitute for what Michael Huberman (1995) calls 'sustained inter-
activity' of the kind to be found in collegial school cultures and school
learning networks.

The leadership role

> Organizations are not solely concerned with outcomes, processes and
> resources. They are also concerned with the human spirit and their
> values and relationships. Authentic leaders breathe the life force into
> the workplace and keep the people feeling energized and focused. As
> stewards and guides they build people and their self-esteem. They
> derive their credibility from personal integrity and 'walking' their
> values.
>
> (Bhindi and Duignan, 1996, p. 29)

Headteachers have the prime responsibility for building, sustaining,
storing, and communicating the schools' culture. Recently, leadership
studies have focused upon values – the 'moral purposes' and moral
craft of leadership (Sergiovanni, 1992); the roles of leaders in creating a
'community of learners' (Barth, 1990; Senge, 1990); and the capacities
of leaders to 'make a difference' through their ability to 'transform'
(Sergiovanni, 1995) or 'liberate' (Tampoe, 1998) rather than simply
'transact'. The most popular theories are located in the 'transactional'
and 'transformational' models identified more than twenty years
ago (Burns, 1978), and lately re-invented through such terms as
'liberation' (Tampoe, 1998), 'educative' (Duignan and MacPherson,
1992), 'invitational' (Stoll and Fink, 1996), and 'moral' leadership

(Sergiovanni, 1992). What is clear from these, and the effective schools literature, is that successful leaders not only set direction, organize and monitor, build relationships with the school community, and are people-centred; but they also model values and practices consistent with those of the school so that 'purposes which may have initially seemed to be separate, become fused' (Sergiovanni, 1995, p. 119). However:

> Organizational culture only exists if the members of an organization share common experiences and encounters. It is precisely through such encounters that a culture is created.
>
> (Schein, 1985, p. 7)

For these to happen requires leadership that enables regular time to discuss, critically reflect upon and share ideals, ideas and practices within as well as outside the school day. There need to be opportunities for teachers to engage in different kinds of learning and development, through a range of formal and informal activities, some class-based (e.g. action research, co-teaching), some role-focused (e.g. mentoring, coaching), others off-site, through in-service courses, and others through networked learning communities that bring groups of schools together to collaborate on inquiries over a sustained period of time. Such emphasis upon continuing professional development will inevitably lead to and be underpinned by values of autonomy, openness to improvement and trust and respect.

Successful teachers have come to understand the importance of and are able to work with the intellectual capital embedded in all members of the school community, the social capital embedded in the relationships between individuals and groups, and the organizational capital embedded in the school's structure and cultures (Hargreaves, D., 1999). Most importantly, they ensure that teachers are at the heart of the creation of such learning communities (Day, 1999). There is a tension between focusing effort upon building capacity in such communities that distribute power and decision-making, and the bureaucratic model of leadership suggested by the pressures of achieving success in the current results-orientated policy environment. Successful heads, it seems, ensure that one supports the other, despite the tensions evident between their purposes. Multiple rather than single forms of leadership seem to be what are required, then, in today's English policy context. As Hayes *et al.* (2001) note in their empirical study of 'productive' leadership in Australian schools:

... style is not as important as the willingness of ... principals to contribute to the development of broad-based learning communities within their schools. ...

(Hayes *et al.*, 2001, p. 15)

They found, like Louis, Kruse and Associates (1995) in America before them that

... the most effective administration leaders delegated authority, developed collaborative decision-making processes, and stepped back from being the central problem solver.

(Louis *et al.*, 1996, p. 193)

'Moving' (learning-enriched) rather than 'stuck' (learning-impoverished) schools (Rosenholtz, 1989) are places in which there are commonly held core values and purposes, regular and frequent opportunities for the sharing of experience, exchange of ideas, norms of collegiality, peer observation and review, experimentation. There will be on- and off-site sustained professional development activities ranging from *knowledge for practice* (formal knowledge made available for teachers' use); *knowledge in practice* (expert teachers' practical knowledge made explicit and shared); *knowledge of practice* (teachers inquiring into their own and others' knowledge of practice) (Cochran-Smith and Lytle, 2001, p. 46); and most importantly, *knowledge of self* (teachers reflecting critically on their motivations, emotions, commitment, identities). In such schools, self-efficacy will be high. Such schools do not just make space for, but positively encourage, all in their individual and collective passion for teaching and learning. Collaboration tends to reduce teachers' sense of powerlessness, and increase their individual and collective self-efficacy. Networked learning communities have this effect too.

Collective efficacy and relational trust

Schools where teachers' conversations dwell on the insurmountable difficulties of educating their students are likely to undermine teachers' sense of efficacy. Schools where teachers work together find ways to address the learning, motivation, and behaviour problems of their students are likely to enhance teachers' sense of efficacy.

(Tschannen-Moran *et al.*, 1998, p. 221)

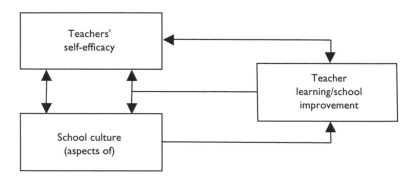

Figure 7.2 The dynamic relations between (a) teacher learning and school improvement, (b) teachers' self-efficacy, and (c) school culture. Source: Adapted from Imants *et al.*, 1993, p. 118

In Chapter 4, efficacy was defined as the extent to which teachers *believe* that they can make a difference in the learning and achievement of all pupils (Bandura, 1997). It is linked to feelings of personal and professional self-worth, confidence, and professional identity and commitment, and it will vary according to situation, task and phase of development (Ashton and Webb, 1986). It is influenced by both individual histories and school or departmental work contexts (Goddard, 2000). It follows that whereas a teacher working in one set of circumstances may have low self-efficacy, that same teacher working in a different set of circumstances, or indeed at a different phase of their life, may have high levels of self-efficacy. We know from other research, also, that the complex interaction between the personal and the professional, and the external and internal environments in which they work, significantly affect teachers' sense of well-being, confidence and, ultimately, their classroom effectiveness (Acker, 1999; Troman and Woods, 2001; Lortie, 1975). Thus efficacy may be affected by relationships with colleagues and by the culture of the school as a whole.

Research in The Netherlands suggests a strong dynamic between self-efficacy, school culture and teacher learning and school improvement (Imants *et al.*, 1993) (see Figure 7.2).

Learning communities need leaders who understand the importance of building learning communities for all staff and students that are physically, emotionally, intellectually, and spiritually healthy; that depend upon integrity, sense of moral purpose, are trusting and trustworthy; and hold to an ethic of service and are 'genuinely respectful of the intelligence and contributions of their constituents' (Kouzes and Posner, 1993, p. xvii).

A study of the successful building of professional community in schools concluded that:

> Human resources – such as openness to improvement, trust and respect, teachers having knowledge and skills, supportive leadership, and socialization – are more critical to the development of professional community than structural conditions. . . . The need to improve the culture, climate and interpersonal relationships in schools has received too little attention.
>
> (Kruse, Louis and Bryk, 1994, p. 8)

In a longitudinal, intensive study of different elementary school communities in Chicago, Bryk and Schneider (2003) identified relational trust – an interrelated set of agreed mutual dependencies in all social relationships and interaction – as a core indicator of success, where, '[e]ach party in a relationship maintains an understanding of his or her role's obligations and holds some expectations about the obligations of the other parties' (Bryk and Schneider, 2003, p. 41). They suggest that relational trust is dependent upon the understanding and application to relationships (between teacher–teacher, teacher–student, teacher–parents, all groups–principal) of four qualities:

- *Respect*: Marked by genuine listening and taking others' views into account
- *Personal regard*: The willingness of individuals to extend themselves beyond the formal requirements of job definitions to 'go the extra mile' to reach out to students, colleagues and parents in an open way
- *Competence in core role responsibilities*: Reliance upon a concerted effort by all to create, maintain and where appropriate, work to improve work conditions (the head), community relations (all), and professional ethics and skills (individuals and teams of teachers)
- *Personal integrity*: Collective trust in moral and ethical commitment by all to the education and welfare of students is a primary concern.

(Adapted from Bryk and Schneider, ibid., pp. 41–2)

This cluster of qualities make up relational trust that itself fosters learning, reduces the sense of risk often associated with change, enables individual and organizational tensions to be resolved. According to Bryk and Schneider's (2003) research, this is 'much more likely to demonstrate marked improvements in students' learning' (ibid., p. 43).

> Community does not emerge spontaneously from some relational reflex, especially not in the complex and often conflicted institutions where most teachers work. If we are to have communities of discourse about teaching and learning . . . we need leaders who can call people toward that vision.
>
> (Palmer, 1998, p. 156)

In short, schools need leaders who are passionate about their calling. Even in those moving schools where continuous learning is an organic part of school culture, change is not always easy and must be led by principals who are clear in their vision and committed to promoting learning for teachers as well as students.

Responsibility for the professional learning culture of the school is at the centre of the cultural and educative leadership roles of headteachers. It is pivotal to enabling teacher development and, through this, school improvement. Indeed:

> In a community of learners, the most important role of teacher *and principal* is that . . . of leading learner. One who engages in the central enterprise of the schoolhouse by displaying and modelling the behaviour we expect and hope students . . . (and teachers) . . . will acquire. As one bumper sticker puts so well: 'You can't lead where you won't go'.
>
> (Barth, 1996, p. 29)

The role that the principal takes in supporting passionate teaching is a critical variable in determining whether it is seen as an '*add on*' to the policy-implementation roles of teachers, or whether it is an integral part of the conception of school as a dynamic community of learning for adults as well as for students. I will highlight just two pieces of recent research that provide empirical data on the importance of leaders in this respect.

The first took place in non-educational settings, and focused upon the development of knowledge and skills in employment with workers at different levels in the engineering, business and health care sectors of twelve medium to large organizations in England. It confirms that

> a manager's indirect impact on learning through the allocation of work, as a role model and by creating/sustaining a micro-culture which supports learning from peers, subordinates and outsiders, is no less important than his or her direct impact through advice and encouragement, appraisal and feedback. . . .
>
> (Eraut, Alderton, Cole, and Senker, 1997a, p. 109)

The second was a 360° study of successful school headteachers commissioned by the National Association of Headteachers, the UK's largest association. Analysis of all the data revealed a surprising consensus among the different constituencies in each school and between them. All held similar constructions of why the head in their school was successful. Their heads were:

- Values-led
- People-centred
- Achievement-oriented
- Inwards- and outwards-facing
- Able to manage a number of ongoing tensions and dilemmas.

All emphasized the sets of core personal values of the heads, based upon care, equity, high expectations, and achievement, which were clear to and shared by the overwhelming majority of the school constituencies and were the drivers of the life of the school. All emphasized the importance attached by the heads to monitoring standards in the school, to keeping 'ahead of the game' so that their schools responded rather than reacted to new external demands, testing them against their own standards, minimizing bureaucratic demands on staff. All spoke of the improvement-oriented collaborative school cultures that the heads promoted, and the emphasis upon continuing professional development that met both organizational and individual needs. All spoke too of the time and care the heads gave enthusiastically to their work, of the way the heads modelled their values. The heads themselves were clearly strategic, 'reflective practitioners', exercising a range of inter and intrapersonal skills, able to analyse, evaluate, articulate and communicate with a range of agencies locally and nationally (Day *et al.*, 2000).

A passion for change

The characteristics of successful leaders and their ability to be simultaneously people-centred while managing a number of tensions and dilemmas highlight the complexity of the kinds of values-led contingency leadership exercised by these successful heads. These and other studies illustrate that there are no neat solutions to situations that hold within them so many variables; and that successful leadership is defined and driven by individual and collective value systems rather than instrumental, bureaucratic, managerial concerns. For example, in her research on disadvantaged schools in Australia, Thomson (2002) suggests that while there is some evidence that policies of devolution have (indirectly) led to improved student attainment, she also sees evidence of growing inequalities among students and schools, particularly those in disadvantaged contexts. Furthermore:

> Principals in competitively developed schools must try to balance central requirements and local needs and interests, must run schools like multinational corporations but offer a family-like experience to students, and must answer the often uncoordinated and ever increasing flow of faxes, letters, forms, and e-mails, at the same time as 'manage by walking around'. Diminishing resources, rapidly intensifying workloads and escalating policy churn (the rapid replacement of one policy after another) is a moving stairway on which principals often struggle to maintain balance.
>
> (Thomson, 2002, p. 134)

Successful leaders placed a high premium upon personal values and were concerned more with cultural than structural change. They had all moved beyond a narrow, rational, managerial view of their role to a more holistic, values-led approach guided by personal experience and preference, in which they recognized the intimate link in successful leadership between the personal and the professional, and between the development of the individual and the organization. Here is a description of one such headteacher, drawn from a four-country study of passionate leadership. She is:

> passionate about her work, is very committed, and underlines how she experiences many moments of pride. She has a clear focus on the purpose of schooling and is driven by her wish to make a difference in the students' life. She invests herself as a person in her job, and her story

shows how professional knowledge is both about cognition and about emotions. She must do what she feels is right. Unlike many of her colleagues she does not look upon managerial accountability as a problem. As a matter of fact she misses external affirmation. She is willing to play with power, but she does not problematize the emphasis on hierarchical structure in the school system. That is taken for granted.

(Moller, 2004)

There can be no doubt that headteachers are in the front line of the change agenda, responsible for mediating external agendas and leading in the building of the school as a learning community. Michael Fullan (1997) offers eight lessons for change that expose its complexity. Implicit in many of these is an acknowledgement of the importance of passion:

Lesson 1   Moral purpose is complex and problematic

Here, Fullan suggests that top–down initiatives that do not connect with teachers' moral purposes and demand only compliance are unlikely to gain teachers' commitment. There is need, therefore, for change to be driven by bottom–up energies as well as top–down mandates.

Lesson 2   Theories of change and theories of education need each other

Schools are different, so theory can only serve as a guide. Change leaders must recognize that there is no blueprint that will be appropriate to all situations and so be prepared to adapt.

Lesson 3   Conflict and diversity are our friends

The process of successful change will inevitably involve working through discomforts, tensions and uncertainties. It is important to acknowledge differences at the outset and, in doing so, address the emotional dimension of change from the start.

Lesson 4   Understand the meaning of operating on the edge of chaos

Because uncertainty is a constant feature of life in the twenty-first century, a key element of successful change is the willingness to take risks and learn from experience, to be prepared to identify key situation-related priorities while trusting in the learning journey.

Lesson 5   Emotional intelligence is anxiety provoking and anxiety containing

An understanding of the power of emotion when facing the unknown is necessary, to manage one's own and others' emotions is vital.

Lesson 6   Collaborative cultures are anxiety provoking and anxiety containing

This is a recognition that for collaboration to be effective, all involved must accept and celebrate a degree of diversity. Acknowledging individuality within collaboration is an expression of trust, empathy and connectivity.

Lesson 7   Attack incoherence: connectedness and knowledge creation are critical

While teachers will spend much of their time in individual learning journeys, the moral purposes of the organization need to be agreed, understood, articulated, and communicated if growth is to be sustained.

Lesson 8   There is no single solution: craft your own theories and actions by being a critical consumer

Fullan's final lesson acknowledges that in the end it is the teachers who will change the world of the classroom. It recognizes the importance to change of the 'activist' professional, someone who is part of a critically reflective community of activist professionals who are emotionally intelligent, committed to students and their own learning and achievement – in short, passionate about their calling (Fullan, 1999, pp. 19–29).

Time to reflect

Emotional geographies

Andy Hargreaves coined the term 'emotional geographies' of schooling and human interaction to assist in the identification of what supports and what threatens basic emotional bonds in teaching. He and his colleagues found five forms of 'emotional distance and closeness that can threaten emotional understanding among teachers, students, colleagues, and parents' (Hargreaves, A., 2000, p. 815):

- *Sociocultural geographies*: Where differences of culture and class can make teachers on the one hand, and parents and students on the other, alien and unknowable to each other.
  Question: What are you and your colleagues doing to make sure that this is not happening?
- *Moral geographies*: Where teachers' purposes are at odds with those they serve and where there are no mechanisms to discuss or resolve these differences.
  Question: What are your moral purposes? How do you discuss them with colleagues, students, parents?
- *Professional geographies*: Where teacher professionalism is defined . . . [in a way which] . . . creates a distance between teachers and the clients they serve, and that is especially prejudicial to feminine, 'caring' ethics of teaching.
  Question: How is 'care' expressed by you through teacher and learner relationships and teacher–parent interactions?
- *Political geographies*: Where hierarchical power relationships distort emotional and cognitive aspects of communication between teachers and those around them.
  Question: How is leadership enacted in your classroom and in the school?
- *Physical geographies*: Where fragmented, infrequent, formalized, and episodic encounters replace the possibility of relationships between teachers and students, or teachers and parents with strings of disconnected interactions.
  Question: How does your school manage the learning community so as to develop it?

(Based on Hargreaves, 2000, p. 816)

Chapter 8

Sustaining the passion

> There's never a time when one can say, 'well, I've done all that can be
> done'. There is always something else. A child you haven't done quite
> right for; a family that is in unnecessary distress because of school
> issues; a teacher you haven't been a help to; a book, a game, an idea
> that might turn the tide.
>
> (Meier, 1995, p. 180)

Inevitably, there will be times over the course of a career, whether for
personal reasons (illness, lack of promotion, critical phases in life), as
a consequence of changes in policy, or as a result of the emotional
drive that committed, caring teachers put into their teaching, when
initial passion turns to frustration, fatigue, routine, and cynicism or
even burn-out. Without commitment and passion, teaching, in Chris
Clark's words, 'loses its heart' (ibid., p. 3). Witness the account of Kerrie,
a committed teacher who, after nine years, left teaching for another
job:

> [It] . . . was propitious because Kerrie did not have to face her
> changing feelings about teaching and seek ways of rekindling
> her passion. She was feeling, 'older', 'less tolerant' and increasingly
> 'frustrated', even while she pushed herself to remain engaged. She
> wrote, 'I found my ability to cope with daily occurrences in an
> accepting, loving manner was dwindling rapidly. I was losing not
> only my composure but my inner peace.' Without commitment and
> passion, teaching becomes drudgery, the kind of work that produced
> the complaining and irritating teachers Kerrie encountered in that
> in-service course on stress management a decade ago.
>
> (Bullough and Baughman, 1997, p. 177)

Such phases may be temporary, and if recognized, acknowledged, understood, and supported, they may be addressed through appropriate formal and informal life adjustment, formal and informal professional development, counselling (or a change of job). Some research has found that professional development plateaux at between five and seven years where there are unsatisfactory policies for continuing professional development (McLaughlin and Marsh, 1978; Sikes *et al.*, 1985). Other studies have found that disillusionment of teachers (and headteachers) in mid- to late-career is often in response to unwelcomed changes in national policies or to the way they are managed (Poppleton, 1988; Troman, 1996).

If teachers' personal lives and identities closely interact with their professional lives in a symbiotic relationship, as the overwhelming research and anecdotal evidence suggests, and if it can be predicted that almost all teachers will face a time when the well of passion runs dry, then it would seem reasonable for schools to plan to meet this eventuality. Certainly it would be in the interests of 'standards', the well-being of staff, and, ultimately, of pupils. This implies a managerial and leadership commitment to the continuing professional development of all staff.

Reaching a professional plateau: reorientation or continued development

It is likely that *trajectories in the middle phases of the career cycle (7–18 years) are more diverse than earlier or later ones* (Huberman, 1995, pp. 196–7). This diversity will relate to career advancement, school culture and the way teachers respond to the now well-established annual cycle of repetition of students and colleagues, which provides security but may, paradoxically, lack the variety, challenge and discovery of earlier years. It is a time when many teachers are likely to seek new challenges, either by taking new responsibilities in the same school or by moving schools for the purposes of promotion. It is a time, also, when responsibilities outside the school may begin to grow, whether it be ageing parents, growing families, or deepening relationships. While the workplace may remain the epicentre of their lives, other demands may create tensions as they compete for time. Some teachers may begin to *re-orientate* themselves, scaling down the time they give to their profession outside working hours. There may be a tension between this and increasing workloads. Research into teacher workload indicates that for most teachers the working week is between 55 and 70 hours (UNESCO, 1996).

This phase may also witness midlife crises and the beginnings of increasing levels of disenchantment caused by lack of promotion or role change, or diminishing levels of energy and enthusiasm. On the other hand, the phase may lead to a 're-energizing' (Vonk, 1995), in terms of classroom teaching, together with a 'mellowing characterized by less drive but also less restlessness, a lesser need to control others or to drive oneself, a greater tolerance for one's limits or weaknesses, a greater acceptance of the 'inevitability' of one's life course' (Huberman, 1995, p. 200). It is during this phase, also, when some teachers may seek opportunities to re-examine the basis upon which their assumptions and beliefs about teaching are founded, to question the purposes and contexts of their work, to review and renew their intellectual commitments through further study, either by participating in school, LEA or district networks or in further degree work.

The final ten to fifteen years of a career is, theoretically, the phase of greatest expertise in teaching, albeit accompanied by the potential for increased personal-health and family concerns. Yet it may also be the time of greatest 'conservatism'. Teachers in this phase complain more about the behaviour, commitment and values of students 'these days' (Day and Bakioglu, 1996), and are sceptical about the virtues of change. This is not surprising, given the huge investment of time, effort and expertise these teachers are likely to have already made in their work. They are unlikely to be looking to further promotion and may either be serenely moving towards a 'satisfactory' career end, or having to survive, dissatisfied, in an alien climate. These teachers may feel marginalized within the institution and embittered towards those whom they see as responsible for the condition of education, schooling and the declining standards of the students they must teach. They may work hard in their core acts of teaching, but this may not be accompanied by the levels of enthusiasm, emotional and intellectual commitment necessary for achieving excellence.

Although it is not always possible to predict the turning points or critical phases in teachers' work and lives when intervention is needed to nurture, maintain or re-ignite passions for teaching, here are some examples that might be considered important:

- A particular year group or sub-set of students whose attitudes and behaviour will stimulate (leading to growth) or alienate (leading to disillusionment)
- The quality of staff-room relationships will enervate or discourage

- Leadership that is transactional (concerned principally with systems and system maintenance) or transformational (concerned with fostering learning communities through participation and dialogue)
- External policy decisions that affect perceptions of professionalism, pay or conditions of work
- Parental attitudes
- Life events outside the school
- Personal health (spiritual, physical, emotional, intellectual).

If a passion for teaching is to be sustained throughout a career, then such influences must be considered. To act on them, however, requires first, an understanding of self (an ability to be reflective), second, empathic leadership, third, cultures of openness and collegiality among staff, and fourth, professional learning and development opportunities which are integral to the progress of the lives and work of individuals as well as organizations. It requires, also, an acknowledgement that there is no single answer that will meet everyone's learning needs: contextual differences of location, culture, pupils, and life simply do not permit it!

Fostering self-esteem

In acknowledging that teachers, like students, have different needs, learning preferences and motivations, Hertzberg's (1968) and Dinham and Scott's (1996) empirical studies of job satisfaction and dissatisfaction found that intrinsic factors outweighed extrinsic factors (see Chapter 4 for a discussion of self-efficacy). Both conclude that simply to reduce or remove a 'dissatisfier' (e.g. bureaucratic tasks) did not necessarily lead to more job satisfaction. The enhancement of both 'satisfiers' and 'dissatisfiers' is necessary. Nias' (1989) empirical work with primary school teachers identified a sense of competence, affective rewards (the pleasure derived from children's progress), working with colleagues, intellectual satisfaction and continuing personal challenge through the unpredictability and variety of the job, and feeling autonomous as satisfiers. The felt strength of each differed in different phases of teachers' careers. For example, she found that working conditions featured less as a source of job satisfaction for teachers in their second decade of teaching than for those in their first, and that a sense of autonomy and extension of personal skills and qualities through other responsibilities mainly involving colleagues was a much greater satisfier for those in their second decade. In terms of dissatisfiers, a greater proportion of teachers in their second decade of teaching cited stress and fatigue, conditions of work, and lack of autonomy. For teachers in their first decade, the bigger sources of dissatisfaction were factors outside the classroom, stress and fatigue, uncongenial colleagues and conflict with individual principals (Nias, 1989, pp. 100, 133). An important finding was the identification of a crisis of identity in the lives of some mid-career teachers:

> committed mid-career teachers work hard, to a high standard and, as a result, get very tired. At the same time, they are conscious of being publicly undervalued, underestimated and under-resourced, all of which adds to the strain upon them. The harder they work to maintain the values, principles and standards they believe in, the more fatigued they become and the greater the discrepancy between their own perception of what they achieve and the public image they experience.
>
> (Nias, 1989, pp. 133–4)

This is particularly worrying, since these now form the 'largest' single cohort of practising teachers in many countries. Yet fifteen years later it seems that little has changed. Recruitment and retention at every level remain big issues for managers. In England, there continues to be evidence that many teachers who remain are dissatisfied with their conditions of work and levels of classroom autonomy, which themselves are far lower now than in 1989 when Nias published her study. Here is a sample of responses from teachers that illustrate the continuing erosion of passion:

> Anna reported feelings of deep frustration in her job as a Home Economics teacher . . . saying repeatedly that her face 'didn't fit'. She worked very hard, and put in a lot of time organizing the catering for staff and public events. But she felt undervalued and personally slighted by senior management, and that her contributions were overlooked. . . .
>
> (Reported in MacLure, 1993, p. 317)

> Roger had been in at the start of the middle-management movement, and had taken part as a young teacher-researcher in a prestigious national curriculum research project in the 1970s. But Roger had now been in the same school since it opened twelve years ago. The profession, he said, no longer offered him the chance to realize those personal values and ideals with which he started out.
>
> (Reported in MacLure, 1993, p. 318)

In the first few years of my teaching I worked with enthusiasm and motivation . . . and the most valuable reward was the love and respect I gained from the students. [Later] . . . I became stagnant and cynical. I stopped striving for improvement.

(Rosanne)

Even though the school was one of the worst in the area I enjoyed myself because the children were wonderful. However, things gradually wore me down. I became bored with teaching. There was nothing wrong with the school or the students. I just felt that I went through a very dull routine every day . . . every year. Sometimes, waking up in the morning to go to school was dreadful. My self-esteem declined. I became a different person. I got angry over trivial things, especially at home. I became very moody and ill-tempered. I felt guilty.

(Sharon)

After teaching for fourteen years, I became physically and mentally fatigued.

(Karen)

Passionate teachers can be found at any age in any school, through all developmental phases. Yet for every passionate teacher, there will be others who are not. Among them will be those who once were passionate but no longer are. For most of us at some time or other, initial passion dies or mutates: as a result of circumstance, such as a school culture that frowns upon the communication of excitement about learning; or as the physical, emotional and intellectual challenges of 'being the best' every day, every week, every year with children and young people who are not always appreciative become too wearing; because of personal circumstances; or, quite simply, as the ageing process begins to take its toll.

Long ago, Farber and Miller (1981) found that emotionally exhausted teachers are less sympathetic to their students and that their teaching effectiveness is adversely affected. Once fun or playfulness goes out of teaching, the passion begins to die:

I don't think there is a much [fun]. It's still there but its artificial. Everything seems much more artificial than it used to be. As a staff we don't really discuss the deep-seated issues as far as education is concerned, but a lot of my time is spent chivvying along, calming people down, trying to make things sound a bit more positive, just generally humouring people.

(Sandra, quoted in Woods and Jeffrey 1996, p. 46)

Yet if passion for teaching cannot always be sustained, if we accept that it can die, then, knowing its importance to good teaching, we must identify 'what went wrong' and find ways of rekindling the passion.

Pigge and Marso (1997) studied sixty teachers in America over a seven-year period, from the beginning of their two-year pre-service training course through the first five years of their teaching. They investigated 'possible relationships between selected personal, family and academic ability' (p. 226). Not surprisingly, they found that initial concerns about survival in the classroom gave way to concerns about the task of teaching and their impact upon pupils. Interestingly, they also differentiated between 'less' and 'more' capable teachers, and found that 'more capable, successful teachers feel more concern about impact upon pupils much further through their career' (p. 233).

Leadership issues

We cannot afford to underestimate the debilitating effects upon teachers' commitments not only of changes in the external environments that may alienate teachers but also through the influence of internal school cultures that discourage initiative, collaboration and trust. Take, for example, leadership and management of a hierarchical kind. When people are over-controlled and over-supervised, they feel mistrusted. The effects are often that individuals withhold energy, enthusiasm and commitment to their work, and this in turn may result in a loss of pride and loyalty to the school (Rowan, 1988). Some of the effects of hierarchical school leadership on colleagues are:

- Feelings of inadequacy
- Inability to express oneself
- Inability to influence anyone
- Feelings of being shut out
- Increase in cynicism
- Increase in destructive feelings
- Feelings that one has either to dominate or be dominated
- Feeling that to conform is the safest way forward
- Feeling that intolerance and exploitation have to be accepted
- Feeling that new ideas must only come from the top

- Feeling that those at the top are not interested in these feelings and that there are no easy ways of communicating with them.

(Day *et al.*, 1998, p. 48)

School leaders may help or hinder in the business of supporting a passion for teaching and providing opportunities for re-stimulating it where appropriate. For example, it is important to prevent too much isolation of staff:

> If you're feeling ill and can't cope, that's the very time you want someone to come in and help you, isn't it? But if you say you're run down and tired and can't cope, it's not a good thing [in this school], it's a reflection on you.

(Quoted in Nias, 1989, p. 142)

It is important, also, for staff to feel a sense of involvement:

> It was impossible to disagree with our last headteacher. But I'm happier now. There's more open discussion, and people are more involved in the school.

(Quoted in Nias, 1989, p. 156)

and to feel valued:

> I find it very hard to cope with messages sent from heads and deputies, where they're asking you to implement things but there's been no discussion and no feedback . . . basically they're treating you as a second-rate citizen, using you but not listening to you. And the other thing I don't like is in staff meetings . . . where, if you're asked your opinion, the head seems to be listening, but then it has no effect on the ultimate outcome. You know – 'Yes, but this is how we're going to do it'.

(Quoted in Nias, 1989, p. 157)

Nias found that experienced teachers wanted to 'be themselves', 'be whole' (in combining the personal with the professional), 'be natural', establish relationships with their students, to feel in control within the uncertainty and unpredictability of their classrooms in what they regarded, accurately, as an emotionally dangerous occupation.

Staying healthy: balancing life and work

> I realized I was human; that there were things that were very important to me in my own life as well as life here. So that you can't do a good job if you're not a happy person, so you have to maintain some sort of level of sanity, whether it's through not taking your briefcase home one night a week and not feeling guilty about it. . . . You just can't do it. . . .
>
> (Canadian teacher, quoted in Hargreaves, A., 1994, p. 154)

Because successful teaching demands sustained personal as well as professional investment, the boundaries between the two are often blurred. Such blurring is exacerbated because most teachers bring work home with them – either in marking pupils' work, planning for the next series of lessons, or in retrospective and anticipatory reflection. The effects of this will be felt differently by different teachers.

Here are the responses of five teachers when asked to talk about the interaction between 'life' and 'work'. One who has been teaching for thirteen years said:

> The workload is far greater than it ever was. I never go out in the week. I couldn't do it, 'cos I'd be tired the next day. . . . You have to be on top of it all the time, which is I suppose why so many people have problems with health . . . and people have decided that they really don't want to do the job any more because of that . . . they get tired of thinking . . . 'I'm going away for the weekend, but I can't because I've got my planning to do'. . . . It's about getting a bit of balance . . . but it's hard because you have to work quite hard for it.
>
> (Primary school teacher, Day *et al.*, 2003)

> I've spent years feeling guilty about not wanting to take work home but . . . it is more than a job . . . and I do go home and shout. . . .
>
> (Primary school teacher, ten years' experience, Day *et al.*, 2003)

> I don't do that much extra work in school. I take it home . . . I have many nights I'll be working quite late up till midnight. . . .
>
> (Primary teacher, fifteen years' experience, Day *et al.*, 2003)

I don't have a family and I don't know how anybody who has a family manages to do it. Because the evenings are all taken up with work, the Sundays are taken up with work. . . . I would say it takes up the majority of your existence . . . and it's difficult to make the division between . . . [work and life]. . . . I have tried to think, 'Right . . . I'm going to stop there' and tried to switch off but it's very difficult. . . . You've always got your stack of coursework to mark and it takes over.

(Secondary teacher, two years' experience, ibid., 2003)

I'm struggling more and more against . . . this incredible investment of time outside the job. And it takes over before you know it. You even enjoy it . . . but then your [child] is sitting in front of the video or my partner is taking her out because I have to work at home. . . . We had several rows at home about me not doing things with [my child]. . . . I have to deal with my job. If I've not done it, then you feel a failure professionally as well . . . at the end of the day I just get home and I just don't want to talk. . . .

(Secondary teacher, eighteen years' experience, ibid., 2003)

These quotes from a research project involving 300 teachers in 100 primary and secondary schools in England are not untypical. They demonstrate both positive and negative aspects of the passionate teacher: positive, because these teachers, like many others, are willing to work beyond the formally allocated hours; negative, because in neglecting their own health, they are jeopardizing their ability to be at their best in the classroom.

In writing about intensification and stress in teaching, Peter Woods provides an example of a response from one teacher with thirty years experience to the then-new performativity culture, in which strong, centrally prescribed directives on all matters relating to schools, teachers and teaching are the key characteristics:

'One of the main reasons I threw in the towel (i.e. resigned) was that the job was no longer the one for which I had trained and which I had enjoyed. When the praise changes almost overnight to criticism, when you are told that what you are doing and know works is all wrong, but are not told how or why or even given any hints as to how you should improve, demoralization swiftly follows. . . .

(Hawes, 1995, quoted in Woods, 1999, p. 119)

A Canadian teacher tells a similar story:

> When I first started teaching, I was excited about how students came to math and how they made discoveries. . . .The first year the department head was a great mentor . . . and the principal was supportive of my initiatives. But things have changed. Now I feel all that is wanted of me is a quiet classroom, with no problems that go beyond my realm as math teacher. . . . It is difficult to get recharged in the face of cynicism about my profession. I get upset by the teacher-bashing articles in the news and the teacher union's latest fight with the school board.
>
> I've been teaching for three years. Most of my teacher friends see themselves teaching for one or two more. I still love to teach math. I wish I could spend more time doing it. I wish I had more time for reflection, and preparation, for research and sharing. . . . I want less time to defend my teaching environment, to defend it from those teachers who have already given up and lost their respect for them-selves and their students. . . .
>
> (Ford and Ford, 1994, p. 22,
> cited in Cole, 1997, pp. 21–2)

While government reform may take little notice of teachers' views, and while most teachers will adjust if they feel that it is in the interests and to the benefit of their students, they will not always find it easy to do so. Indeed, Nias suggests that, 'an underlying cause of burn-out among English teachers . . . is a deep-seated, passionately felt sense that the moral, person-related basis of their work is being eroded, to be replaced by formal accountability and the accountancy of cost effectiveness' (1999, p. 227).

Moreover as bureaucratic tasks associated with contractual account-ability increase, so the *time to care* for the whole student inside and outside the classroom (as distinct from that part of her/him that can be enabled to succeed in national tests and examinations) decreases.

Nias (1999) traced a connection between notions of vocational and professional commitment, values, identity, and interests, and linked these with teachers' moral purposes and ethic of care. They willingly 'allocate scarce personal resources (time, energy, money) to the day-to-day performance' of their job, and in doing so invest in it a personal sense of identity (Nias, 1999, p. 224). Thus, anything that appears to threaten such occupational identity, and the values and practices that are an expression and manifestation of it, is likely to cause emotional turmoil and a sense of rejection of their hard won professional identities (van Veen *et al.*, 2004). For example, in the UK numerous surveys and research reports point to the negative effects of educational policies upon teachers' workload (Campbell and Neill, 1994), morale (*Guardian*, 2002), motivation (Travers and Cooper, 1996; Evans, 1997), and health (Macleod and Meikle, 1994).

Most teachers, however, do adapt as workload and work pressures increase because they care and are conscientious in their moral purposes. Informal conversations with many teachers suggest that the length of their working week, the number of roles they perform, and the complexity of classroom have all increased over the last twenty years. Even reform-enthusiastic teachers, however, sometimes find themselves emotionally exhausted because of the increased work pressures that often accompany innovative practices which leave no room or time for discretionary judgements:

> . . . there is a conflict between teachers' desire to have authentic relationships with children and the exhaustion which results. It is very tiring, physically and emotionally, to attempt to sustain individual and sometimes intense relationships with many people throughout a working day; teachers' chronic fatigue is legendary, as their partners and children testify . . . they engage in thousands of individual interactions during a working day . . . many involving considerable self-control. It is small wonder that a large number of practitioners feel that their job has an adverse impact upon their domestic lives. . . .
>
> (Nias, 1999, p. 72)

Although Nias is writing about primary school teachers, all those who are passionate about their work and who care for their students will experience fatigue. Fatigue is predictable not only because of the conditions under which teachers work – class size, resources, 'performativity' cultures in which great store is placed by those outside the school upon teachers' individual and collective answerability for raising standards of pupil achievement – but also because teaching is emotional work. Moreover, there is a tension in the promotion of collegial, collaborative cultures such as those constantly espoused both in the school improvement literature and, more recently, through the government-backed initiative of the National College for School Leadership, in its promotion of 'Networked Learning Communities' where groups of schools work together on inquiry-led action research projects. Paradoxically, such cultures of learning place a greater burden upon those teachers who are often the most committed, passionate and altruistic.

All the more important then, for teachers, headteachers and others to ensure that teaching remains a healthy profession. The literature on the working of the brain itself shows that '. . . stress and anxiety are in opposition to learning. The term "down-shifting" describes the process when the brain experiences threat or fear and down shifts to the primitive state of fight or flight where learning is much less possible' (McNeil, 1999, p. 8).

Nias (1999) offers three reasons for the negative effects of increased pressure on teachers:

- Teachers are socialized into a service ethic that encourages them to ignore their own needs
- The greater teachers' sense of responsibility to their colleagues and the more they care for them, the less likely they are to heed their own early warning signals (of stress)
- Women (the majority of teachers) are less likely than men to look after themselves as long as they feel that there are others who need to be cared for.

To these should be added

- The increase in the social and emotional intensity of work in classrooms as external reference points for pupils become fragmented
- The increase in stress caused by the need to meet externally imposed targets for pupil achievement that may not always be appropriate to their pupils' needs.

To remain passionate about teaching, it is vital to recognize the need for personal and professional renewal. Indeed, there are some who would conclude that the expectations of self and others of the conscientiousness that characterizes the work of the best teachers may be a form of actual or potential, exploitation in which they themselves tacitly collude.

Re-examination of the self and the context in which the self lives and works is an essential part of reviewing a passion for teaching. There are five ways in which the particular aspects of collegial relations in schools strengthen moral purposes and values-based teacher identity:

1   Strong interpersonal relationships based upon sustained, regular, informal and formal face-to-face contacts

2   People-centred leadership (see also Day *et al.*, 2000)
3   Collaborative cultures that are characterized by mutual respect, openness, praise, interdependence, and emotional understandings, in which teachers and students feel a sense of community
4   An emphasis upon professional growth that contributes to high self-esteem and encourages critical reflection
5   A passionate commitment to providing the highest quality of teaching and learning for all pupils.

Self-fulfilling prophecies

> *Interviewer:* Are you getting less satisfaction from teaching as the years go by?
>
> *Karen:* The kids are changing . . . people always tend to look back and say, 'Well, when I was in school, we would never do this or we would never do that', but I'm not that old . . . .What I'm saying is, you always hear people talking about young people and how awful they are . . . but the truth of the matter is that the kids are not the same as they were. I've been teaching for nine years, and I don't like what I'm seeing.'
>
> (Cohn and Kottkamp, 1993, p. 85)

Often what is missing in discussions of teacher morale, commitment, efficacy, and job satisfaction is consideration of changes in students' attitudes and behaviour, those of their parents, and the broader communities and cultures in which they work. All these are beyond their control and that of government. Yet the negative consequences for teaching and learning, for recruitment and retention, and for the satisfaction levels of teachers are enormous. In England and many other countries, a range of initiatives have been designed to counter pupil absenteeism, alienation, disruptive classroom behaviour, and lack of motivation to learn school subjects. In America, Cohn and Kottkamp (1993) noted that a number of teachers reported that unmotivated students 'continually need to be given a reason for coming to school' (ibid., p. 90). Others complained that normal sanctions (e.g. detention, supervision) seemed to have no effect, that drug use and part-time paid work took precedence over homework, that changing family structures made life more problematic for many children; also that parents, many of whom were in full-time work, were less involved and only took an interest when things went wrong. It is not so much that teachers are 'victims' of such changes (though some are), but more that they make their job harder to do well. Their lessons are more vulnerable to disruption than previously. They are more frequently and publicly judged on pupils' achievement as measured by tests and examinations. They have less control over what they do in their classrooms.

In circumstances such as these it is easy to blame others, if only to retain an element of self-esteem. In her classic study of 'stuck' and 'moving' elementary schools in Tennessee, Susan Rosenholtz pointed to the dangers of teachers becoming the victims of a self-fulfilling prophecy:

> And the more teachers complain about uncooperative parents, the more they tend to believe there is little they can do. There is something of a self-fulfilling prophecy in all of this: Teachers who view parents adversarily often reduce or altogether cease communicating with them, substantially diminishing their opportunities for successful instruction.
>
> (Rosenholtz, 1989, pp. 109–10)

Stay connected

> We lose heart, in part, because teaching is a daily exercise in vulnerability. . . . [It] is always done at the intersection of personal and public life. . . . To reduce our vulnerability, we disconnect from students, from subjects, even from ourselves. We build a wall between inner truth and outer performance, and we play-act the teacher's part.
>
> (Palmer, 1998, p. 17)

In some cultures, such objective 'disconnection' is encouraged as a virtue. The self is seen as an obstacle to good teaching. Yet to accept this is to invite cynicism and to deliberately limit the potential benefits of our teaching to students. Disconnection achieves the opposite of what it is said to be intended: it constrains dialogue, discourages participation, alienates the student and the self:

> . . . when we distance ourselves from something, it becomes an object; when it becomes an object it no longer has life; when it is lifeless, it cannot touch or transform us, so our knowledge of the thing remains pure.
>
> (Palmer, 1998, p. 52)

It is vital to avoid being isolated from other adults as a teacher. Since conditions for most teachers continue to place them in classrooms for most of the time, becoming collegial is not always easy unless the culture of the school positively encourages it.

A reference group or groups will be important not only for teachers new to the school – in relation to establishing 'norms' of teaching and relationships, for example – but to all teachers, in order to:

- Formulate, revisit and review individual and collective values and vision
- Regularly consider social, moral and political issues that affect teaching and learning
- Share experiences and maintain contact with the world of ideas about education outside the school
- Engage with others in collaborative practitioner inquiry
- Provide moral and practical support in times of self-doubt and celebrate successes as they occur.

Sustaining passion over time and in challenging circumstances requires that it be nurtured in different ways. Many of the 2718 teachers surveyed and 73 teachers interviewed by Cohn and Kottkamp (1993) believed that teaching then was more difficult and less rewarding than in the past, but nevertheless coped. Within them, however, was a smaller group who displayed consistently a high degree of enthusiasm for their work. They had:

- *A deep sense of mission*: 'We're dealing with the minds of all these children. We're with them all day in the formative years; what could be more important?' (ibid., p. 162).
- *Young people: they give the mission its meaning*: 'I really am interested in teaching them literature and getting them interested in wanting to read. Having . . . a curiosity for the rest of their lives and having the ability to satiate that curiosity' (ibid., p. 164)
- *The teacher as 'origin' and motivator of others*: 'You can make your bad days good days. You are dealing with a spontaneity that's there all the time. It's almost like a volcano. You never know when it's going to erupt, and when it erupts, how high it is going to go and which direction the lava is going to pour. Here you are as the guiding force, and you can create this and you can generate it or you can just let it lie there' (ibid., p. 166). . . . 'You have to stimulate them to the point that they look forward to coming to your class' (ibid., p. 167).

- *Investment in self: giving in order to get*: 'It's a two-way thing. You're going to get as much as you put in. Sometimes you get more back' (ibid., p. 168). Enthusiastic (passionate) teachers thrive on psychic rewards from reaching students and invest heavily of their time and energy in giving themselves (ibid., p. 167).
- *Change of pace: striking a balance*: Enthusiastic teachers will always be looking for new ways of teaching in order to strike a balance between routine and variety and devising a work–life balance through which burnout can be avoided.
- *Coping with the external pressures: closing the classroom door*: 'If you are really serious and energetic about your job, then you wake up every morning . . . with a positive attitude: "No matter what bombards me today, it's not going to get to me. I'm not going to fail. I'm going to come through with it". . . . My job is in the classroom . . . [where] . . . I have to help these youngsters' (ibid., pp. 170–1). Often it is better to focus upon the core business of teaching and learning, teacher and learner, because this is where most teachers find success and satisfaction.

Being passionate in challenging circumstances

> We saw more teachers who had withdrawn into cynicism or venial passing of time in class at the low-SES schools than at the middle-SES schools, and more at the middle-SES schools than at the high-SES schools. Teachers who did not withdraw often switched their goals, seeking success in the passing of competency tests that tested low-level skills, in the mere face of graduation even with a tenuous record, or in a few students' return to class attendance and reasonably steady classroom effort as a result of teachers' intense personal relationships with them.
>
> (Metz, 1993, p. 121)

Students play a significant part in defining teachers' realities at work. Who they are, their backgrounds, attitudes and how they behave, inevitably affect the ways teachers conceive of their work, their approaches to it, their professional identities, commitment and sense of self-worth. For example, it is important to note that in many schools in socio-economically deprived areas, teachers spend considerably more time and energy in managing behaviour than do those in the traditionally populated school. Acquiring the qualifications to become a teacher has always been a necessary but insufficient condition to succeed as a professional over a career span. Inevitably, subject knowledge will need to be regularly updated, teaching organization and methods and skills revisited as on the one hand information becomes more accessible through advances in technology, while on the other, teaching pupils who are less socially compliant in conditions that are less conducive to promoting learning becomes more challenging, particularly for teachers who work in schools located in socio-economically deprived areas. As Thomson (2002) observes in her recent and authoritative research on disadvantaged secondary schools in Australia, dealing with children and young people who exhibit considerable insecurity and anxiety requires regular time away from the business of task-focused instruction in the classroom. For teachers in these schools:

> Dealing with children and young people exhibiting evidence of considerable insecurity and anxiety requires regular time away from instruction and involves teachers and administrators alike. The time-order economy of schools in neighbourhoods where this becomes a dominant feature is inevitably distorted, becoming overwhelmingly about the daily management of welfare issues. . . .
>
> (Thomson, 2002, p. 78)

Significantly, in terms of government 'one size fits all' policies or national curricula, teaching and assessment standards,

> It is little wonder that those who spend large amounts of their time simply policing recalcitrant young people find their patience and endurance running thin. Being the literal face of authority, engaged in numerous face-offs every day, takes considerable personal energy. . . .
>
> (Thomson, 2002, p. 53).

It is one thing to be passionate about teaching and quite another to be a passionate teacher in all kinds of working conditions. For example, it is a well-known phenomenon that many teachers lose their passion when their conditions of service change. Such was the case – now well documented – with reforms over the last twenty years in England. For example, the introduction of a national curriculum and national pupil testing at age 7, 11, 14, 16, 17, and 18 had the effect of limiting teachers' ability to make significant decisions with regard to curriculum content in those areas of the curriculum. Annual school development planning and target-setting through performance management (otherwise known as 'appraisal') against which progress is judged created a 'surveillance' culture that caused a crisis in recruitment and retention. Increased bureaucracy associated with these and public 'league tables' of schools also had their effects upon teachers' self-confidence. Closer to home, those who work in inner-city and other schools in socio-economically deprived areas have to survive against the odds in schools which often have high levels of teacher and pupil mobility, poor attendance rates and pupils who do not wish to be taught.

There are those who would argue that however skilled, knowledgeable and passionate teachers are, they can never influence the lives of more than a few of their pupils, particularly those from economically and emotionally deprived home backgrounds:

> It relies on the myth that individuals can buck the system and transform their destiny, but ignores the fact that these individuals are the exception. They leave many others, with similar potentials for achievement, behind.
>
> (Bentley, 1998, p. 77)

Bentley argues, like Thrupp (1999) and Thomson (2002), that however good teachers are, they can help only a minority of pupils from deprived socio-economic, emotional backgrounds to escape them. Yet, powerful though these arguments are, they represent a rationalist, means–ends driven perspective. Passionate teaching does not claim to affect the historical constraints imposed by social, economic and political, or indeed, emotional orders. Its emancipatory function, however, is to tap into the capacity of pupils to become excited by learning, to help them raise their eyes beyond the immediate and to learn more about themselves, to build an identity grounded in new self-images. In short, the 'ultimate' aim of passionate teachers may be to provide opportunities of the kind envisioned by Bentley and others, but they do not rely upon these being achieved in order to sustain their core purposes and commitments.

Sustaining the passion

The temptation is for teachers who are hard-pressed on all sides – whether by pupils, parents, the media, league tables, or new curricula initiatives – to become enmeshed in a downward spiral of expectation and practice. The imperative, despite the difficulties, is to resist a drift

towards cynicism, to look for and find incentives and rewards within
the changing realities of teaching; to accept that while they might
wish to work with creative, respectful, hardworking, and intellectually
demanding students, this will not always be the case.

> Teachers with high self-esteem know how to value both themselves
> and others. . . . This basic sense of self-worth is internalized, deeply
> embedded, so it is not easily susceptible to any gross distortion by life
> events, however calamitious. . . .
>
> (Day *et al.*, 1998, p. 116)

To find such incentives and rewards requires that teachers revisit core
values and beliefs, regularly engage in reflection upon the contexts that
influence their work and lives, engage in collaborative dialogue with
colleagues about improvement, visit other schools and teachers, and join
inter-school learning networks so that the isolation and hopelessness that
sometimes erodes passion may be broken.

Teachers with a passion for teaching are driven by hope rather than
optimism. They are hard-working, practical people who know their craft
and like their pupils. They are sustained as active learners by their own
sense of moral purposes to do the best they can under all circumstances,
and by the sense of common purposes shared with colleagues. Their
commitment is to their pupils, and to the subjects and topics they teach.
The kinds of reflective practice and continuing professional development
in which they engage individually and collectively will be undertaken in
order to improve these. They understand that teaching is emotional as
well as intellectual and practical work. They are not heroes and heroines
but they are heroic.

Teaching is a courageous activity that tests energy, commitment and
resolve. This book acknowledges this. Passion is not an add-on but is
at the heart of teaching at its best. It must, therefore, be nurtured and
sustained. Because it is at the heart, its understanding and nurturing
must not be ignored by teacher educators in pre-service or in-service
educators, nor by policy makers in their continuing quest to raise
standards and to promote life-long learning.

References

Acker, S. (1999) *The Realities of Teachers' Work: Never a Dull Moment.* London: Cassell.

Altet, M. (1993) *La qualité des enseignants, seminaires d'enseignants. Rapport final de l'étude française demandée par la Direction de l'Evaluation et de la Prospective.* Centre de recherches en éducation, Université de Nantes.

Apple, M. W. and Beane, J. (1995) *Democratic Schools.* Alexandra, VA: Association for Supervision and Curriculum Development.

Argyris, C. and Schon, D. A. (1976) *Theory in Practice: Increasing Professional Effectiveness*, New York: Jossey-Bass.

Argyris, C. and Schon, D. A. (1978) *Organizational Learning: A Theory in Action Perspective.* Reading, Mass.; Addison-Wesley Clark and Yinger.

Armstrong, T. (1998) *Awakening Genius in the Classroom.* Alexandra, VA: Association for Supervision and Curriculum Development.

Arnold, C. L. (1993) *Modelling Teacher Supply and Demand. Schools and Staffing Survey.* Berkeley, CA: MPR Associates.

Ashton, P. T. and Webb, R. B. (1986) *Making a Difference. Teachers' Sense of Efficacy and Student Achievement.* New York: Longman.

Ball, S. J. (1972) Self and Identity in the Context of Deviance: The Case of Criminal Abortion. In R. Scott and J. Douglas (eds) *Theoretical Perspectives on Deviance.* New York, Basic Books.

Ball, S. J. (1994) *Education Reform: A Critical and Post-Structural Approach.* Buckingham: Open University Press.

Ball, S. J. (2000) Performativities and Fabrications in the Education Economy: Towards the Performative State. *The Australian Educational Researcher*, Vol. 27, 2, pp. 1–23.

Ball, S. J. (2001) *The Teachers' Soul and the Terrors of Performativity.* Research Students' Society, Issue 38, University of London, Institute of Education, England, November 2001.

Ball, S. J. and Goodson, I. (1985) *Teachers' Lives and Careers.* Lewes: Falmer Press.

Bandura, A. (1997) *Self-Efficacy: the Exercise of Control.* New York: W. H. Freeman.

Barbalet J. (2002) Introduction: Why Emotions are Crucial. In J. Barbalet (ed.) *Emotional Sociology*. London: Blackwell Publishing, pp. 1–9.

Barth, R. S. (1990) *Improving Schools from Within: Teachers, Parents and Principals Can Make the Difference*. San Francisco: Jossey-Bass.

Barth, R. S. (1996) Building a Community of Learners. *Conversation 96*. CA: California School Leadership Center – South Bay School Leadership Team Development Seminar Series; Seminar 10.

Batson, C. D. (1994) Why Act for the Public Good: Four Answers. *Personality and Social Psychological Bulletin*, Vol. 20, 5, pp. 603–10.

Beijaard, D. (1995) Teachers' Prior Experiences and Actual Perceptions of Professional Identity. *Teachers and Teaching: Theory and Practice*, Vol. 1, 2, pp. 281–94.

Bendelow, G. and Mayall, B. (2000) How Children Manage Emotion in Schools. In S. Fineman (ed.) op. cit., pp. 241–54.

Bennett-Goleman, T. (2001) *Emotional Alchemy: How the Mind Can Heal the Heart*. London: Harmony Books.

Bentley, T. (1998) *Learning Beyond the Classroom: Education for a Changing World*. London: Routledge.

Bereiter, C. and Scardamalia, M. (1993) *Surpassing Ourselves: An Inquiry into the Nature and Implications of Expertise*. Chicago: Open Court.

Beynon, J. (1985) *Initial Encounters in the Secondary School*. Lewes: Falmer Press.

Bhindi, N. and Duignan, P. (1996) *Leadership 2020: A Visionary Paradigm*. Paper presented at Commonwealth Council for Educational Administration International Conference, Kuala Lumpur.

Biggs, S. (1999) *The Mature Imagination: Dynamics of Identity in Midlife and Beyond*. Buckingham: Open University Press.

Blishen, E. (1969) *The School that I'd Like*. London: Penguin Education.

Bolam, R. (1990) Recent Developments in England and Wales. In B. Joyce (ed.) *Changing School Culture through Staff Development: An International Survey*. Beckenham: Croom Helm, pp. 147–67.

Boler, M. (1999) *Feeling Power: Emotions and Education*. New York: Routledge.

Bottery, M. (1996) The Challenge to Professionals from the New Public Management: Implications for the Teaching Profession. *Oxford Review of Education*, 22 (2), pp. 179–97.

Bottery, M. and Wright, N. (2000) *Teachers and the State*. London: Routledge.

Brighouse, T. (1994) The Magicians of the Inner City. *Times Educational Supplement*, 22 April, pp. 29–30.

Brookfield, S. (1998) Understanding and Facilitating Moral Learning in Adults. *Journal of Moral Education*, Vol. 27, 3, pp. 283–300.

Brown, L. and Coles, A. (2000) Complex Decision-making in the Classroom: The Teacher as an Intuitive Practitioner. In K. Atkinson and G. Claxton (eds) (2000) *The Intuitive Practitioner: On the Value of Not Always Knowing What One is Doing*. Buckingham: Open University Press, pp. 165–81.

Brown, S. and McIntyre, D. (1993) *Making Sense of Teaching.* Buckingham: Open University Press.

Brubacher, J. W., Case, C. W. and Reagan, T. G. (1994) *Becoming a Reflective Educator: How to Build a Culture of Inquiry in the Schools.* California: Corwin Press.

Bryk, A. S. and Schneider, B. (2003) Trust in Schools: A Core Resource for School Reform. In *Educational Leadership*, 6 (60), March 2003, pp. 40–4.

Bryk, A. S. and Driscoll, M. E. (1988) *The High School as Community: Contextual Influences and Consequences for Students and Teachers.* Washington Office of Educational Research and Improvement.

Buber, M. (1965) *Knowledge of Man.* New York: Harper and Row.

Bullough, R. V., Jr and Baughman, K. (1997) *First Year Teacher Eight Years Later: An Inquiry into Teacher Development.* New York: Teachers College Press.

Burns, J. M. (1978) *Leadership.* New York: Harper and Row

Burns, S. and Lamont, G. (1995) *Values and Visions, Handbook for Spiritual Development and Global Awareness.* London: Hodder & Stoughton.

Butt, R. (1984) Arguments for Using Biography in Understanding Teacher Thinking. In R. Halkes and J. K. Olson (eds) *Teacher Thinking: A New Perspective on Persisting Problems in Education*, Lisse: Swets and Zeitlinger, pp. 95–102.

Campbell, R. and Neill, S. (1994) *Primary Teachers at Work.* London: Routledge.

Campbell, S. (1997) *Interpreting the Personal: Expression and the Formation of Feelings.* Ithaca, New York: Cornell University Press.

Castells, M. (1997) *The Power of Identity.* Oxford: Basil Blackwell.

Clark, C. M. (1995) *Thoughtful Teaching.* London: Cassell.

Clark, C. M. and Yinger, R. J. (1977) Research on Teacher Thinking. *Curriculum Enquiry*, Vol. 7, 4, pp. 279–305.

Cochran-Smith, M. and Lytle, S. (2001) Beyond Certainty: Taking an Inquiry Stance on Practice. In A. Lieberman and L. Miller (eds) (2001) *Teachers Caught in the Action: Professional Development that Matters.* New York: Teachers College Press.

Cockburn, A. D. (2000) Elementary Teachers' Needs: Issues of Retention and Recruitment. *Teaching and Teacher Education*, 16 (2), pp. 223–38.

Cohn, M. M. and Kottkamp, R. B (1993) *Teachers: The Missing Voice in Education.* Albany: SUNY Press.

Coldron, J. and Smith, R. (1997) *Active Location in the Construction of the Professional Self.* Paper presented at the European Conference on Educational Research, Frankfurt am Main, September 1997.

Cole, A. L. (1997) Impediments to Reflective Practice: Toward a New Agenda for Research for Teaching. *Teachers and Teaching: Theory and Practice.* Vol. 3, 1, pp. 7–27.

Connelly, F. M. and Clandinin, D. J. (1995) Teachers' Professional Knowledge Landscapes: Secret, Sacred and Cover Stories. In D. J. Clandinin and F. M. Connelly (eds) *Teachers' Professional Knowledge Landscapes.* New York: Teachers College Press, pp. 3–15.

Cotton, T. (1998) *Thinking About Teaching.* Abingdon: Bookpoint Ltd.

Csikszentmihalyi, M. (1990) *Flow and the Psychology of Discovery and Invention.* New York: Harper and Row.

Csikszentmihalyi, M. (1996) *Creativity.* New York: Harper and Collins.

Csikszentmihalyi, M. (1997) *Living Well: The Psychology of Everyday Life.* London: Weidenfeld and Nicolson.

Dadds, M. (1993) The Feeling of Thinking in Professional Self-Study. *Educational Action Research Journal,* Vol. 1 (2), pp. 287–303.

Damasio, A. (1994) *Descartes' Error: Emotion, Reason and the Human Brain.* New York: Grosser/Putnan, 1994.

Damasio, A. R. (2000) *The Feeling of What Happens: Body and Emotion in the Making of Consciousness.* New York: Harcourt Brace.

Darling-Hammond, L. (1996a) The Quiet Revolution: Rethinking Teacher Development. *Educational Leadership,* Vol. 53, 6, pp. 4–10.

Darling-Hammond, L. (1996b) The Right to Learn and the Advancement of Teaching: Research, Policy, and Practice for Democratic Education. *Educational Researcher,* Vol. 25, 6, pp. 5–17.

Day, C. (1993) Reflection: A Necessary But Not Sufficient Condition for Professional Development. *British Educational Research Journal,* Vol. 19, 1, pp. 83–93.

Day, C. (1997) Being a Professional in Schools and Universities: Limits, Purposes and Possibilities for Development. *British Educational Research Journal,* Vol. 23, 2, pp. 192–208.

Day, C. (1998) Working with Different Selves of Teachers: Beyond Comfortable Collaboration. *Educational Action Research,* Vol. 6, 2, pp. 255–74.

Day, C. (1999) *Developing Teachers: The Challenges of Lifelong Learning.* London: Falmer Press.

Day, C. (2000) Stories of Change and Professional Development: The Costs of Commitment. In C. Day, A. Fernandez, T. Hauge and J. Moller (eds) *The Life and Work of Teachers: International Perspectives in Changing Times.* London: Falmer Press, pp. 109–29.

Day, C. W. (2001) Experienced Teachers: an Enduring Commitment. Paper presented at the Annual Conference of the European Educational Research Association, 4–7 September, Lille, France.

Day, C. and Bakioglu, A. (1996) Development and Disenchantment in the Professional Lives of Headteachers. In I. F. Goodson and A. Hargreaves (eds) *Teachers Professional Lives.* London: Falmer Press, pp. 205–27.

Day, C. and Hadfield, M. (1996) Metaphors for Movement: Accounts of Professional Development. In M. Kompf, R. T. Boak, W. R. Bond and D. H. Dworek (eds) *Changing Research and Practice: Teachers' Professionalism, Identities and Knowledge.* London: Falmer Press, pp. 149–66.

Day C., Hall C. and Whitaker P. (1998) *Developing Leadership in Primary Schools.* London: Paul Chapman Publishing Ltd.

Day, C. and Leitch, R. (2001) Teachers' and Teacher Educators' Lives: The Role of Emotion. *Teaching and Teacher Education,* Vol. 17, 4, pp. 403–15.

Day, C., van Veen, D. and Walraven, G. (eds) (1997) *Children and Youth at Risk and Urban Education: Research, Policy and Practice.* Appledoorn: Garant.

Day, C., Harris, A., Hadfield, M., Tolley, H. and Beresford, J. (2000) *Leading Schools in Times of Change.* Buckingham: Open University Press.

Day, C., Stobart, G., Kington, A., Sammons, P. and Last, J. (2003) Variations in Teachers' Lives, Work and the Impact on Pupils. Paper presented to the 11th Biennial Conference of the International Study Association on Teachers and Teaching (ISATT), 27 June to 1 July 2003, Leiden, The Netherlands.

Denzin, N. (1984) *On Understanding Emotion.* San Francisco: Jossey-Bass.

DES (1990) *Statistics of Education, Teachers, England and Wales*, 1998 edition. London: The Stationery Office.

Devaney, K. and Sykes, G. (1988) Making the Case for Professionalism. In A. Lieberman (ed.) *Building a Professional Culture in Schools.* New York: Teachers College Press.

Dewey, J. (1932/1985) Ethics. In J. A. Boydston (ed.) *John Dewey: the Later Works.* Vol. 7, Carbondale, IL: Southern Illinois University Press.

DfEE (1998) *Statistics of Education: Teachers, England and Wales*, 1998 edition. London: The Stationery Office.

Dinham, C. and Scott, C. (1996) *The Teacher 2000 Project: A Study of Teacher Satisfaction, Motivation and Health.* Penrith, University of Western Sydney, Nepean: Faculty of Education.

Doyle, W. (1997) Heard Any Really Good Stories Lately? A Critique of the Critics of Narrative in Educational Research. *Teaching and Teacher Education*, Vol. 13, 1, pp. 93–9.

Duignan, P. A. and Macpherson, R. J. S. (1992) *Educative Leadership: A Practical Theory for New Administrators and Managers.* London: Falmer Press.

Earl, L. M. and LeMahieu, P. G. (1997) Rethinking Assessment and Accountability. In A. Hargreaves (ed.), op. cit., pp. 149–68.

Einstein, A. (1950) Out of My Later Life, Ch. 51 *Columbia Encyclopaedia, The Columbia World of Quotations*, 1996.

Eisner, E. (1979) *The Educational Imagination.* West Drayton: Collier-Macmillan.

Eisner, E. (1996) Is 'The Art of Teaching' a Metaphor? In M. Kompf, W. Richard Bond, D. Dworet and R. Terrance Boak (eds) *Changing Research and Practice: Teachers' Professionalism, Identities and Knowledge.* London: Falmer Press, pp. 9–19.

Eisner, E. W. (2002) From Episteme to Phronesis to Artistry in the Study and Improvement of Teaching. *Teaching and Teacher Education*, Vol. 18, pp. 375–85.

Elias, M. J., Zins, J. E., Weissberg, R. P., Frey, K. S., Greenberg, M. T., Haynes, N. M., Kessler, R., Schwab-Stone, M. E. and Shriver, T. P. (1997) *Promoting Social and Emotional Learning.* Alexandra, VA: Association for Supervision and Curriculum Development.

Elliott, J. (1991) *Action Research for Educational Change.* Buckingham: Open University Press.

Elliott, J. (2004) Using Research to Improve Practice: The Notion of Evidence-Based Practice. In C. Day and J. Sachs (eds) *International Handbook of Continuing Professional Development of Teachers*. Buckingham: Open University Press (in press).

Elmore, R. (1992) Why Restructuring Alone Won't Improve Teaching. *Educational Leadership*, April 1992, pp. 44–9.

Epstein, A. (1978) *Ethos and Identity*. London: Tavistock.

Epstein, H. (1986) Stages in Human Brain Development. *Developmental Brain Research*, 30, pp. 114–19.

Eraut, M. E. (1995) Schon Shock: A Case Study for Reframing Reflection-in-action? *Teachers and Teaching: Theory and Practice*, Vol. 1, 1, pp. 9–22.

Eraut, M., Alderton, J., Cole, G. and Senker, P. (1997a) Learning from Other People at Work'. In F. Coffield (ed.) *Skill Formation*, Polity Press.

Eraut, M., Alderton, J., Cole, G. and Senker, P. (1997b) The Impact of the Manager on Learning in the Workplace. Paper presented at BERA Conference, York, England, September, 1997.

Esteve, J. (1989) Teacher Burnout and Teacher Stress. In M. Cole and S. Walker (eds) *Teaching and Stress*. Oxford: Aldern Press, pp. 4–25.

Evans, L. (1997) Understanding Teacher Morale and Job Satisfaction. *Teaching and Teacher Education*, 31 (8), pp. 831–45.

Evans, L. (1998) *Teacher Morale, Job Satisfaction and Motivation*. London: Paul Chapman Publishing.

Evison, R. and Horobin, R. (1988) Co-counselling. In J. Rowan and W. Dryden, *Innovative Therapy in Britain*. Milton Keynes: Open University Press.

Farber, B. (1991) *Crisis in Education*. San Francisco: Jossey-Bass

Farber, B. and Miller, J. (1981) Teacher Burnout. A Psychoeducational Perspective. *Teachers' College Record*, Vol. 83, 2, pp. 235–43.

Fensham, P. J. and Marton, F. (1992) What Has Happened to Intuition in Science Education? *Research in Science Education*, 22, pp. 114–22.

Fenstermacher, G. D. (1990) Some Moral Considerations on Teaching as a Profession. In J. I. Goodlad, R. Soder and K. A. Sirotnik (eds) *The Moral Dimensions of Teaching*. San Francisco: Jossey-Bass, pp. 130–51.

Fessler, R. (1995) Dynamics of Teacher Career Stages. In T. R. Guskey and M. Huberman (eds) *Professional Development in Education: New Paradigms and Practices*. New York: Teachers College Press, pp. 171–92

Fessler, R. and Christensen J. (1992) *The Teacher's Career Cycle: Understanding and Guiding the Professional Development of Teachers*. Boston: Allyn and Bacon.

Figley, C. R. (ed.) (1995) *Compassion Fatigue: Secondary Traumatic Stress Disorders from Treating the Traumatized*. New York: Bruner/Matzel.

Fineman, S. (2000a) (ed.) *Emotions in Organizations*. London: Sage Publications Ltd.

Fineman, S. (2000b) Emotional Arenas Revisited. In S. Fineman (ed.), op. cit., pp. 1–24.

Firestone, W. A. (1996) Images of Teaching and Proposals for Reform: A Comparison of Ideas from Cognitive and Organizational Research. *Educational Administration Quarterly*, 32 (2), pp. 209–35.

Fletcher-Campbell, F. (1995) Caring about Caring? *Pastoral Care*, Sept., pp. 26–8.

Flores, M. A. (2002) Learning, Development and Change in the Early Years of Teaching: A Two-Year Empirical Study, PhD Dissertation, University of Nottingham, England.

Ford, L. and Ford, L. B. (1994) Our Schools Our Selves: The Story of a New Teacher. *Orbit*, 25, pp. 21–2.

Francis, L. J. and Grindle, Z. (1998) Whatever Happened to Progressive Education? A Comparison of Primary School Teachers' Attitudes in 1982 and 1996. *Educational Studies*, 24 (3), pp. 269–79.

Fraser, H., Draper, J. and Taylor, W. (1998) The Quality of Teachers' Professional Lives: Teachers and Job Satisfaction. *Evaluation and Research in Education*, 12 (2), pp. 61–71.

Fried, R. L. (1995) *The Passionate Teacher: A Practical Guide*. Boston, Mass.: Beacon Press.

Fukuyama, F. (1999) *The Great Disruption: Human Nature and the Reconstitution of Social Order*. London: Profile Books Ltd.

Fullan, M. (1997) Emotion and Hope: Constructive Concepts for Complex Times. In A. Hargreaves (ed.) op. cit., pp. 216–33.

Fullan, M. (1999) *Change Forces: The Sequel*. London: Falmer Press.

GTCE (2003) *Commitment. The Teachers' Professional Learning Framework*. General Teaching Council for England, March 2003, London. www.gtce.org.uk, pp. 1–16.

Galton, M. and Simon, B. (1980) *Progress and Performance in the Primary Classroom*. London: Routledge.

Gardner, H. (1983) *Frames of Mind: The Theory of Multiple Intelligence*. New York: Basic Books.

Gardner, H. (1996) Are There Additional Intelligences? The Case for Naturalist, Spiritual and Existential Intelligences. In J. Kane (ed.) *Education, Information, and Transformation*. Englewood Cliffs, NJ: Prentice-Hall.

Giddens, A. (1991) *Modernity and Self Identity*. Stanford: Stanford University Press.

Glickman, C. and Tamashiro, R. (1982) A Comparison of First Year, Fifth Year and Former Teachers on Efficacy, Ego Development and Problem Solving. *Psychology in Schools*, Vol. 19, pp. 558–62.

Goddard, R. D. (2000) Collective Teacher Efficacy: Its Meaning, Measure, and Impact on Student Achievement. *American Educational Research Journal*, Vol. 37, pp. 479–507.

Godfrey, J. J. (1987) *A Philosophy of Human Hope*. Dordrecht, The Netherlands: Martinns Nijhoff.

Goleman, D. (1995) *Emotional Intelligence: Why IT Can Matter More than IQ*. London: Bloomsbury.

Goleman, D. (1998) *Working with Emotional Intelligence*. New York: Bantam Books.

Goodlad, J. I. (1984) *A Place Called School*. New York: McGraw-Hill.

Goodson, I. F. and Hargreaves, A. (eds) (1996) *Teachers' Professional Lives*. London: Falmer Press.

Graham, K. C. (1996) Running Ahead: Enhancing Teaching Commitment, *Journal of Physical Education, Recreation and Dance*, 67 (1), pp. 45–7.

Grimmett, P. P., MacKinnon, A. M., Erickson, G. L. and Riecken T. J. (1990) Reflective Practice in Teacher Education. In R. T. Clift, W. R. Houston and M. C. Pugach (eds) *Encouraging Reflective Practice in Education: An Analysis of Issues and Programs.* New York: Teachers College Press.

Guardian (2003) Workload Hits Teacher Morale. Tuesday, 7 Jan. 2003 p. 8 (GTC/Guardian/Mori Teacher Survey).

Guskey, T. R. (1995) Professional Development in Education. In Search of the Optimal Mix. In T. R. Guskey and M. Huberman (eds), op. cit., pp. 114–32.

Guskey, T. R. and Huberman, M. (eds) (1995) *Professional Development in Education: New Paradigms and Practices.* Columbia University: Teachers College Press.

Guskey, T. R. and Passaro, P. D. (1994) Teacher Efficacy: A Study of Construct Dimensions. *American Educational Research Journal*, Vol. 31, 3, pp. 627–43.

Haavio, (1969), cited in E. Estola, R. Erkkila and L. Syrjala, Caring in Teachers' Thinking: Three Stories. Paper presented to the 8th Biennial Conference of the International Study Association on Teachers' Thinking, Kiel, Germany, 1–5 October 1997.

Hall, B. W., Pearso, L. C. and Carroll, A. (1992) Teachers' Long-range Teaching Plans: A Discriminant Analysis. *Journal of Educational Research*, 85 (4), pp. 221–5.

Halpin, D. (2003) *Hope and Education: The Role of the Utopian Imagination.* London: RoutledgeFalmer.

Handy, C. (1994) *The Age of Paradox.* Columbia, MA: Harvard Business Press.

Hansen, D. T. (1995) *The Call to Teach.* New York: Teachers College Press.

Hansen, D. T. (1998) The Moral is in the Practice. *Teaching and Teacher Education*, Vol. 14, 6, pp. 643–55.

Hansen, D. T. (1999) Conceptions of Teaching and their Consequences. In M. Lang, J. Olson, H. Hansen and J. W. Bünder (eds) *Changing Schools/Changing Practices: Perspectives on Educational Reform and Teacher Professionalism.* Louvain: Garant, pp. 91–8.

Hansen, D. T. (2001) *The Moral Heart of Teaching: Towards a Teacher's Creed.* New York: Teachers College Press.

Hargreaves, A. (1989) *Contrived Collegiality and the Culture of Teaching.* Paper presented at a meeting of the Canadian Society for Studies in Education Conference, Laval, Quebec, Canada.

Hargreaves, A. (1993) Individualism and Individuality: Reinterpreting the Teacher Culture. In J. W. Little and M. W. McLaughlin (eds) *Teachers' Work: Individuals, Colleagues, and Contexts.* New York: Teachers College Press, pp. 51–76.

Hargreaves, A. (1994) *Changing Teachers, Changing Times – Teachers' Work and Culture in the Postmodern Age.* London: Cassell.

Hargreaves, A. (1997) Rethinking Educational Change: Going Deeper and Wider in the Quest for Success. In A. Hargreaves (ed.) *Rethinking Educational Change with Heart and Mind.* Alexandra, VA: Association for Supervision and Curriculum Development, pp. 1–26.

Hargreaves, A. (1998) The Emotional Practice of Teaching. *Teaching and Teacher Education*, Vol. 14, 8, pp. 835–54.

Hargreaves, A. (2000) Mixed Emotions: Teachers' Perceptions of Their Interactions with Students. *Teaching and Teacher Education*, Vol. 16 (8), pp. 811–26.

Hargreaves, A. (2002) Teaching in a Box: Emotional Geographies of Teaching. In C. Sugrue and C. Day (eds) *Developing Teachers and Teaching Practice: International Research Perspectives*. London: RoutledgeFalmer, pp. 3–25.

Hargreaves, A. and Fullan, M. (1998) *What's Worth Fighting for Out There*. New York: Teachers College Press.

Hargreaves, A. and Goodson, I. (1996) Teachers Professional Lives: Aspirations and Actualities. In I. Goodson and A. Hargreaves (eds), 1996, op. cit., pp. 1–27.

Hargreaves, A., Shaw, P. and Fink, D. (1997). Change Frames: The Creation of Learning Communities. Unpublished paper, International Centre for Educational Change, OISE/UToronto, Canada.

Hargreaves, D. (1972) *Interpersonal Relations and Education*. London: Routledge and Kegan Paul Ltd.

Hargreaves, D. (1998) *Creative Professionalism: The Role of Teachers in the Knowledge Society*. London: Demos.

Hargreaves, D. (1999) The Knowledge Creating School. *British Journal of Educational Studies*, Vol. 47 (2), pp. 122–44.

Harrell, Carson B. (1996) Thirty Years of Stories: The Professor's Place in Student Memories. *Change*, 28 (6), pp. 11–17.

Hayes, D., Mills, M., Lingard, B. and Christie, P. (2001) Production Leaders and Productive Leadership: Schools as Learning Organisations. Paper presented to AERA Conference, Seattle, 10–14 April 2002.

Helsby, G. and McCulloch, G. (1996) Teacher Professionalism and Curriculum Control. In I. Goodson and A. Hargreaves (eds), op. cit., pp. 56–74.

Helsby, G., Knight P., McCulloch G., Saunders M. and Warburton T. (1997) *Professionalism in Crisis*. A Report to Participants on the Professional Cultures of Teachers Project, Lancaster University, January 1997.

Herman J. L. (1992) *Trauma and Recovery*. NY: Basic Books.

Hertzberg, F. (1968) *Work and the Nature of Man*. London: Staples Press.

Hochschild, A. R. (1983) *The Managed Heart: Commercialisation of Human Feeling*. London: University of California Press Ltd.

Hopkins, D. (2001) *School Improvement for Real*. London: RoutledgeFalmer.

Hopkins, D. and Stern, D. (1996) Quality Teachers, Quality Schools: International Perspectives and Policy Implications. *Teaching and Teacher Education*, Vol. 12, 5, pp. 501–17.

Hord, S. M. (1997) *Professional Learning Communities: Communities of Continuous Inquiry and Improvement*. Austin, Texas: Southwest Educational Development Laboratory.

Huberman, M. (1989) The Professional Life Cycle of Teachers. *Teachers' College Record*, 91, 1, Fall 1989, pp. 31–57.

Huberman, M. (1993a) *The Model of the Independent Artisan in Teachers' Professional Relations*. In J. W. Little and M. W. McLaughlin (eds), op. cit.

Huberman, M. (1993b) *The Lives of Teachers*. London: Cassell.

Huberman, M. (1995) Networks that Alter Teaching. *Teachers and Teaching: Theory and Practice*. Vol. 1, 2, pp. 193–221.

Imants, J., Tillema, H. H. and de Brabander, C. J. (1993) A Dynamic View of Teacher Learning and School Improvement. In F. K. Kieviev and R. Vandenberghe (eds) (1993) *School Culture, School Improvement and Teacher Development*. Leiden University, DSWO Press.

Ingvarson, L. and Greenway, P. A. (1984) Portrayal of Teacher Development. *Australian Journal of Education*, 28, 1, pp. 45–65.

Jackins, H. (1965) *The Human Side of Human Beings*. Seattle: Rational Island Publications.

Jackins, H. (1973) *The Human Situation*. Seattle: Rational Island Publications.

Jackins, H. (1989) *The Upward Trend*. Seattle: Rational Island Publications.

Jackson, P. W. (1968) *Life in Classrooms*. New York: Teachers College Press.

Jackson, P. W. (1999) *Teaching as a Moral Enterprise*. In M. Lang *et al.* (eds), op. cit., pp. 81–90.

Jackson, P. W., Boostrom, R. E. and Hansen, D. T. (1993) *The Moral Life of Schools*. San Francisco: Jossey-Bass.

James-Wilson, S. (2001) The Influence of Ethnocultural Identity on Emotions and Teaching. Paper presented at the Annual Meeting of the American Educational Research Association, New Orleans, April 2000.

Jeffrey, B. and Woods, P. (1996) Feeling Deprofessionalised. *Cambridge Journal of Education*, Vol. 26, 3, pp. 325–43.

Jersild, A. (1955) *When Teachers Face Themselves*. New York: Teachers College Press.

Jesus, S. N. (2000) *Motivacao e Formacio de Professores*. Coimbra: Quarteto Editora.

Joyce, B., Calhoun, E. and Hopkins, D. (1997) *Models of Learning – Tools for Teaching*. Buckingham: Open University Press.

Kelchtermans, G. (1993) Getting the Story, Understanding the Lives: From Career Stories to Teachers' Professional Development. *Teaching and Teacher Education*, Vol. 9, 5/6, pp. 443–56.

Kelchtermans, G. (1996) Teacher Vulnerability: Understanding its Moral and Political Roots. *Cambridge Journal of Education*, Vol. 26, 3, pp. 307–24.

Kelchtermans, G. (1999) Teacher Education for Teacher Development: Reflective Learning from Bbiography and Context. Keynote lecture at TD TR4 Teachers Develop Research: Fourth Conference on Reflective Learning, 2–4 Sept 1999, Leuven, Belgium.

Kelchtermans, G. and Vandenberghe, R. (1994) Teachers' Professional Development: A Biographical Perspective. *Journal of Curriculum Studies*, 26 (1), pp. 45–62.

Klette, K. (2000) Working-Time Blues: How Norwegian Teachers Experience Restructuring in Education. In C. Day, A. Fernandez, T. E. Hauge and

J. Moller (eds) *The Life and Work of Teachers: International Perspectives in Changing Times*. London: Falmer Press, pp. 146–58.

Kohn, A. (1996) *Beyond Discipline: From Compliance to Community*. Alexandra, VA: Association for Supervision and Curriculum Development.

Kolb, D. A. (1984) *Experiential Learning*. Englewood Cliffs, NJ: Prentice-Hall Inc.

Korthagen, F. A. J. (1993) Two Modes of Reflection. *Teaching and Teacher Education*, 9, pp. 317–26.

Kouzes, J. M. and Posner, B. Z. (1993) *Credibility*. San Francisco: Jossey-Bass.

Kremer-Hayon, L. and Fessler, R. (1991) The Inner World of School Principals: Reflections on Career Life Stages. Paper presented at the Fourth International Conference of the International Study Association on Teacher Thinking, 23–27 September, University of Surrey, England.

Kruse, S., Louis, K. S. and Bryk, A. S. (1994) *Building Professional Community in Schools*. Madison, WI: Center on Organization and Restructuring of Schools.

Lacey, C. (1977) *The Socialisation of Teachers*. London: Methuen.

Lander, R. (1993) *Repertoires of Teaching Quality: A Contribution to the OECD/CERI Project, Teacher Quality from Case Studies of Six Swedish Comprehensive Schools*. University of Goteborg, Department of Education and Science.

Laskey, S. (2000) The Cultural and Emotional Politics of Teacher–Parent Interactions. *Teaching and Teacher Education*, Vol. 16 (8), pp. 843–60.

Lawn, M. (1995) Restructuring Teaching in the USA and England: Moving Towards the Differentiated, Flexible Teacher. *Journal of Education Policy*, 10 (4), pp. 347–60.

Lazarus, R. S. (1991) *Emotion and Adaptation*. New York: Oxford University Press.

Lazarus, R. S., Kanner, A. D. and Folkman, S. (1980) Emotions: A Cognitive–Phenomenological Analysis. In R. Pluckik and H. Kellerman (eds) *Theories of Emotions, Vol. 1: Emotion, Theory, Research and Experience*. New York: Academic Press, pp. 189–217.

Le Doux, J. (1998) *The Emotional Brain*. London: Weidenfeld and Nicholson.

Leitch, R. and Day, C. (2000) Action Research and Reflective Practice: Towards an Holistic View. *Educational Action Research*, Vol. 8, 1, pp. 179–93.

Leitch, R. and Day, C. (2001) Reflective Processes in Action: Mapping Personal and Professional Contexts for Learning and Change. *Journal of In-Service Education*, Vol. 27, 2, pp. 237–59.

Leitch, R., Mitchell, S. and Kilpatrick, R. (2003) *A Study into Potential Models for the Successful Teaching of Personal Development in the Northern Ireland Curriculum*. Report to the Department of Education.

Leithwood, K., Leonard, L. and Sharratt, L. (1997) Conditions Fostering Organisational Learning in Schools. Paper presented at the annual Meeting of the International Congress on School Effectiveness and Improvement, Memphis, Tennessee.

Lieberman, A. and Miller, C. (1999) *Teachers – Transforming Their World and Their Work*. Columbia University: Teachers College Press

Lieberman, A. and Miller, L. (1990) Teacher Development in Professional Practice Schools. *Teachers College Record*, 92 (1), pp. 105–22.

Lightfoot, S. L. (1983) The Lives of Teachers. In L. S. Shulman and G. Sykes (eds) *Handbook of Teaching and Policy*. New York: Longman.

Little, J. W. (1981) *School Success and Staff Development in Urban Desegrated? Schools: A Summary of Recently Completed Research*. Boulder, CO: Centre for Action Research, April 1981.

Little, J. W. (1993) *Professional Community in Comprehensive High Schools: The Two Worlds of Academic and Vocational Teachers*. In J. W. Little and M. W. McLaughlin (eds), op. cit.

Little, J. W. and McLaughlin, M. W. (eds) (1993) *Teachers' Work: Individuals, Colleagues and Contexts*. New York: Teachers College Press.

Lortie, D. (1975) *The Schoolteacher: A Sociological Study*. Chicago: University of Chicago Press.

Loughran, J. (2002) Understanding and Articulating Teacher Knowledge. In C. Sugrue and C. Day (eds), op. cit., pp. 146–61.

Louis, K. S. (1998) Effects of Teacher Quality Worklife in Secondary Schools on Commitment and Sense of Efficacy. *School Effectiveness and School Improvement*, Vol. 9, No. 1, March, pp. 1–27.

Louis, K. S. and Miles, M. B. (1992) *Improving the Urban High School: What Works and Why*. New York: Teachers College Press.

Louis, K. S. and Kruse, S. D. (1995) *Professionalism and Community: Perspectives on Reforming Urban Schools*. Thousand Oaks, CA: Corwin Press.

Lyotard, J. (1979) *The Postmodern Condition: A Report on Knowledge*. Manchester: Manchester University Press.

Macconi, C. (1993) *Teacher Quality Project: Italian Case Study*. Rome: Ministero Pubblica Istruzione, Direzione Generale Scambi Culturali.

MacGilchrist, B., Myers, K. and Reed, J. (1997) *The Intelligent School*. London: Paul Chapman Publishing Ltd.

MacIntyre, A. (1981) *After Virtue*. Notre Dame, IN: University of Notre Dame Press.

Maclean, R. (1992) *Teachers' Careers and Promotion Patterns: A Sociological Analysis*. London: Falmer Press.

Macleod, D. and Meikle, J. (1994) Education Changes: 'Making Heads Quit'. *Guardian*, 1 Sept., p. 6.

MacLure, M. (1993) Arguing for Your Self: Identity as an Organising Principle in Teachers' Jobs and Lives. *British Educational Research Journal*, Vol. 19, 4, pp. 311–22.

Marczely, B. (1996) *Personalizing Professional Growth: Staff Development That Works*. California: Corwin Press Inc.

McCormack, S. (2001) Teachers Seem to Work Flat Out All the Time. *Independent*, Thursday, 19 April 2001, pp. 6–7.

McGaugh, J. L. (1989) Dissociating Learning and Performance: Drug and Hornmone Enhancement of Memory Storage. *Brain Research Bulletin*, 23, 4–5, pp. 339–45.

McGraw, B., Piper, K., Banks, D. and Evans, B. (1992) *Making Schools More Effective.* Hawthorn, Victoria: ACER.

McLaughlin, M. W. (1993) What Matters Most in Teachers' Workplace Context? In J. W. Little and M. W. McLaughlin (eds) *Teachers' Work: Individuals, Colleagues and Contexts.* New York: Teachers College Press, pp. 73–103.

McLaughlin, M. W. (2002) Sites and Sources of Teachers' Learning. In C. Sugrue and C. Day (eds), op. cit., pp. 95–115.

McLaughlin, M. W. and Marsh, D. (1978) Staff Development and School Change. *Teachers College Record,* 80, pp. 69–94.

McLaughlin, M. W. and Talbert, J. (1993) *Contexts that Matter for Teaching and Learning.* Stanford, CA: Center for Research on the Context of Secondary School Teaching.

McLaughlin, M. W. and Talbert, J. (2001) *Professional Communities and the Work of High School Teaching.* London: University of Chicago Press.

McMahon, A. (1997) Continuing Professional Development for Secondary School Teachers: Challenges and Opportunities. Paper presented at the European Conference on Educational Research, Frankfurt, Germany, 24–27 September.

McMahon, A. (1999) Promoting Continuing Professional Development for Teachers: An Achievable Target for School Leaders? In T. Bush, L. Bell, R. Bolam, R. Glatter and P. Ribbens (eds) *Educational Management: Refining Theory, Policy and Practice.* London: Paul Chapman Ltd, pp. 102–13.

McNeil, F. (1999) Brain Research and Learning: An Introduction. In *Research Matters, School Improvement Network No. 10,* Spring/Summer. University of London, Institute of Education, pp. 1–12.

McWilliam, E. (1999) *Pedagogical Pleasures.* New York: Peter Lang Publishing Inc.

Meier, D. (1995) *The Power of Their Ideas: Lessons for America from a Small School in Harlem.* Boston: Beacon.

Meighan, R. (1977) Pupils' Perceptions of the Classroom Techniques of Post-graduate Student Teachers. *British Journal of Teacher Education,* 3 (2), pp. 139–48.

Meijer, C. and Foster, S. (1988) The Effect of Teacher Efficacy on Referral Chance. *Journal of Special Education,* Vol. 22, pp. 378–85.

Metz, M. H. (1993) *Teachers' Ultimate Dependence on Their Students.* In J. W. Little and M. W. McLaughlin (eds), op. cit., pp. 104–36.

Metzger, R. *et al.* (1990) Worry, Changes, Decision-Making: The Effects of Negative Thoughts on Cognitive Processing. *Journal of Clinical Psychology,* Jan. 1990.

Meyerson, D. E. (2000) If Emotions Were Honoured: A Cultural Analysis. In S. Fineman (ed.), op. cit., pp. 167–83.

Mezirow, J. (1991) *Transformative Dimensions of Adult Learning.* San Francisco: Jossey-Bass.

Mitchell, C. and Weber, S. (1999) *Reinventing Ourselves as Teachers: Beyond Nostalgia.* London: Falmer Press.

Moller, J. (2000) School Principals in Transition: Conflicting Expectations, Remands and Desires. In C. Day, A. Fernandez, T. E. Hange and J. Moller (eds) *The Life and Work of Teachers: International Perspectives in Changing Times*. London: Falmer Press, pp. 210–23.

Moller, J. (2004) Old Metaphors, New Meanings: Being a Woman Principal. In C. Sugrue (ed.) *Passionate Principalship: Learning from Life Histories of School Leaders*. London: RoutledgeFalmer (in press).

Moore, W. and Esselman, M. (1992) Teacher Efficacy, Power, School Climate and Achievement: A Desegregating District's Experience. Paper presented at the Annual Conference of the American Educational Research Association, San Francisco, April 1992.

Morgan, C. and Morris, G. (1999) *Good Teaching and Learning: Pupils and Teachers Speak*. Buckingham: Open University Press.

Nash, R. (1973) *Classrooms Observed*. London: Routledge and Kegan Paul.

NCES (1997) Job Satisfaction Among America's Teachers: Effects of Workplace Conditions, Background Characteristics, and Teacher Compensation. Washington, DC: Office of Educational Research and Improvement, US Dept. of Education.

Nias, J. (1989) *Primary Teachers Talking: A Study of Teaching as Work*. London: Routledge.

Nias, J. (1991) Changing Times, Changing Identities: Grieving for a Lost Self. In R. G. Burgess (ed.) *Educational Research and Evaluation: For Policy and Practice*. London: Falmer Press.

Nias, J. (1996) Thinking about Feeling: The Emotions in Teaching. *Cambridge Journal of Education*, Vol. 26, 3, pp. 293–306.

Nias, J. (1999a) *Primary Teaching as a Culture of Care*. In J. Prosser (ed.), op. cit., pp. 66–81.

Nias, J. (1999b) Teachers' Moral Purposes: Stress, Vulnerability and Strength. In R. Vandenberghe and A. M. Huberman (eds) *Understanding and Preventing Teacher Burnout: A Source Book of International Research and Practice*. New York: Cambridge University Press, pp. 223–37.

Nias, J., Southworth, G. W. and Yeomans, R. (1989) *Staff Relationships in the Primary School: A Study of School Culture*. London: Cassell.

Nieto, S., Gordon, S. and Yearwood, J. (2002) Teachers' Experiences in a Critical Inquiry Group: A Conversation in Three Voices. *Teaching Education*, Vol. 13, 3, pp. 341–55.

Noddings, N. (1984) *Caring: A Feminine Approach to Ethics and Moral Education*. Berkeley, CA: University of California Press.

Noddings, N. (1992) *The Challenge to Care in Schools*. New York: Teachers College Press.

Noddings, N. (1996) Stories and Affect in Teacher Education. *Cambridge Journal of Education*, 26 (3), pp. 435–47.

OECD (1994) *Quality in Education*. Paris: OECD.

Oatley, K. and Nundy, S. (1996) Rethinking the Role of Emotions in Education. In D. R. Olson and N. Torrance (eds) *The Handbook of Education and Human*

Development: New Models of Learning, Teaching and Schooling. Cambridge, MA: Blackwell, pp. 202–24.

Oxford English Dictionary. Second edn. 1989 (eds J. A. Simpson and E. S. C. Weiner), Additions 1993–7 (ed John Simpson and Edmund Weiner; Michael Proffitt), and third edn. (in progress) Mar. 2000– (ed. John Simpson). OED Online. Oxford University Press. http://dictionary.oed.com.

Palmer, P. J. (1998) *The Courage to Teach: Exploring the Inner Landscape of a Teacher's Life.* San Francisco: Jossey-Bass.

Parkay, F. W., Greenwood, G., Olejnik, S. and Proller, N. (1998) A Study of the Relationship Between Teacher Efficacy, Locus of Control and Stress. *Journal of Research and Development in Education,* Vol. 21, 4, pp. 13–22.

Parker, R. (2002) *Passion and Intuition: The Impact of Life History on Leadership.* NCSL Practitioner Enquiry Report, National College for School Leadership, Nottingham, England, p. 3.

Peshkin, A. (1984) Odd Man Out: The Participant Observer in an Absolutist Setting. *Sociology of Education,* Vol. 57, pp. 254–64.

Peterson, W. (1964) Age, Teacher's Role and the Institutional Setting. In B. Biddle and W. Elena (eds) *Contemporary Research on Teacher Effectiveness.* New York: Holt, Rinehart and Winston, pp. 264–315.

Pigge, F. L. and Marso, R. N. (1997) A Seven Year Longitudinal Multi-Factor Assessment of Teaching Concerns Development Through Preparation and Early Years of Teaching. *Teaching and Teacher Education,* Vol. 13, 2, pp. 225–35.

Polanyi, M. (1967) *The Tacit Dimension.* Garden City, New York: Doubleday.

Poppleton, P. (1988) Teacher Professional Satisfaction. *Cambridge Journal of Education,* 1, pp. 5–16.

PriceWaterhouseCoopers (2001) *Teacher Workload Study.* London: Department for Education and Skills.

Prosser, J. (ed.) (1999) *School Culture.* London: Paul Chapman Publishing Ltd.

Pryer, A. (2001) 'What Spring Does with the Cherry Trees': The Eros of Teaching and Learning. *Teachers and Teaching: Theory and Practice.* Vol. 7, 1, pp. 75–88.

Ramsay, P. (1993) *Teacher Quality: A Case Study Prepared for the Ministry of Education as Part of the OECD Study on Teacher Quality.* Hamilton, New Zealand, University of Waikato.

Raudenbush, S., Rowen, B. and Cheong, Y. (1992) Contextual Effects on the Self-perceived Efficacy of High School Teachers. *Sociology of Education,* Vol. 65, pp. 150–67.

Raywid, M. A. (1993) Community: An Alternative School Accomplishment. In G. A. Smith (ed.) *Public Schools That Work: Creating Community.* New York: Routledge, pp. 23–44.

Rest, J. (1986) *Moral Development: Advances in Research and Theory.* New York: Praeger.

Riehl, C. and Sipple, J. W. (1996) Making the Most of Time Taken and Talent. Secondary School Organizational Climates, Teaching Tasks Environments, and Teacher Commitment. *American Educational Research Journal*, 33 (4), pp. 873–901.

Robertson, S. (1996) Teachers' Work, Restructuring and Postfordism: Constructing the New 'Professionalism'. In I. Goodson and A. Hargreaves (eds) *Teachers' Professional Lives*. London: The Falmer Press, pp. 28–55.

Rosenholtz, S. J. (1989) *Teachers' Workplace. The Social Organization of Schools*. New York: Longman.

Ross, J. A. (1992) Teacher Efficacy and the Effect of Coaching on Student Achievement. *Canadian Journal of Education*, Vol. 17, 1, pp. 51–65.

Ross, J. A. (1998) Antecedents and Consequences of Teacher Efficacy. In J. Brophy (ed.) *Advances in Research on Teaching*. Vol. 17, 1, pp. 51–65.

Rowan J. (1988) *Ordinary Ecstasy*. London: Routledge.

Rudduck, J., Chaplain, R. and Wallace, G. (1996) *School Improvement. What Can Pupils Tell Us?* London: David Fulton.

Rudow, B. (1999) Stress and Burnout in the Teaching Profession: European Studies, Issues, and Research Perpectives. In R. Vandenberghe and A. M. Huberman (eds.), op. cit., pp. 38–58.

Sachs, J. (2000) The Activist Professional. *Journal of Educational Change*, 1, pp. 77–95.

Sachs, J. (2003) *The Activist Teaching Profession*. Buckingham: Open University Press.

Sachs, J. and Logan, L. (1990) Control or Development? A Study of Inservice Education, *Journal of Curriculum Studies*, 22, 5, pp. 473–81.

Sagor, R. (1997) Collaborative Action Research for Educational Change. In A. Hargreaves (ed.), op. cit., pp. 169–91.

Salovey, P. and Mayer, J. D. (1990) Emotional Intelligence. *Imagination, Cognition, & Personality*, 9, pp. 185–211.

Salzberger-Wittenberg, I. (1996) The Emotional Climate in the Classroom. In G. Alfred and M. Fleming (eds) *Priorities in Education*. Durham: University of Durham, Fieldhouse Press.

Sandelands, L. E. and Boudens, C. J. (2000) Feeling at Work. In S. Fineman (ed.), op. cit., pp. 46–63.

Sarason, S. B. (1990) *The Predictable Failure of Educational Reform*. San Francisco: Jossey-Bass.

Saunders, L. (2002) What is Research Good For? Supporting Integrity, Intuition and Improvisation in Teaching. Paper presented to the Canternet Conference, 6 July 2002.

Schein, E. H. (1985) *Organizational Culture and Leadership*. San Francisco: Jossey-Bass.

Scherer, M. (2002) Do Students Care About Learning? A Conversation with Mihaly Csikszentmihalyi. *Educational Leadership*, 60 (1), September 2002, pp. 12–17.

Schon, D. A. (1983) *The Reflective Practitioner: How Professionals Think in Action*. London: Temple Smith.

Seltzer, K. and Bentley, T. (1999) *The Creative Age: Knowledge and Skills for the New Economy*. London: Demos.

Senge, P (1990) *The Fifth Discipline*. New York: Doubleday.

Sergiovanni, T. J. (1992) *Moral Leadership: Getting to the Heart of School Improvement*. San Francisco: Jossey-Bass.

Sergiovanni, T. J. (1995) *The Principalship: A Reflective Practice Perspective*. Boston: Allyn and Bacon.

Sergiovanni, T. J. and Starratt, R. J. (1993) *Supervision: A Redefinition*. Singapore: McGraw-Hill.

Shulman, L. (1997) Professional Development: Learning from Experience. In B. S. Kogan (ed.) *Common Schools, Uncommon Futures: A Working Consensus For School Renewal*. New York: Teachers College Press, pp. 89–106.

Sikes, P., Measor, L. and Woods, P. (1985) *Teachers' Careers: Crises and Continuities*. Lewes: Falmer Press.

Silver, H. F., Strong, R. W. and Perini, M. J. (2000) *So Each May Learn: Integrating Learning Styles and Multiple Intelligences*. Alexandria, VA: Association for Supervision and Curriculum Development.

Simecka, M. (1984) A World with Utopias or Without Them? In P. Alexander, and R. Gill (eds) *Utopias*. London: Duckworth.

Sleegers, P. and Kelchtermans, G. (1999) Inleiding op het themanummer: professionele identiteit van leraren (Professional Identity of Teachers). *Pedagogisch Tijdschrift*, 24, pp. 369–74.

Sockett, H. (1993) *The Moral Base for Teacher Professionalism*. Columbia University: Teachers College Press.

Somekh, B. (1989) Action Research and Collaborative School Development. In R. McBride (ed.) *The In-Service Training of Teachers*. London: The Falmer Press, pp. 160–76.

Stanislavski, C. (1965) *An Actor Prepares*. Trans. E. Reynolds Hapgood. New York: Theatre Arts Books, p. 22.

Stoll, L. (1999) *School Culture: Black Hole or Fertile Garden for School Improvement?* In J. Prosser (ed.), op. cit., pp. 30–47

Stoll, L. and Fink, D. (1996) *Changing Our Schools: Linking School Effectiveness and School Improvement*. Buckingham: Open University Press.

Stronach, I., Corbin, B., McNamara, O., Stark, S. and Warne, T. (2002) Towards an Uncertain Politics of Professionalism: Teacher and Nurse Identities in Flux. *Journal of Educational Policy*, Vol. 17, 1, pp. 109–38.

Stronge, J. H. (2002) *Qualities of Effective Teachers*. Alexandra, VA: Association for Supervision and Curriculum Development.

Sugrue, C. and Day, C. (eds) (2002) *Developing Teachers and Teaching Practice: International Research Perspectives*. London: RoutledgeFalmer.

Sumsion, J. (2002) Becoming, Being and Unbecoming an Early Childhood Educator: A Phenomenological Case Study of Teacher Attrition. *Teaching and Teacher Education*, Vol. 18, pp. 869–85.

Sutton, R. E. (2000) The Emotional Experiences of Teachers. Paper presented at the Annual Meeting of the American Educational Research Association, New Orleans, April 2000.

Sylwester, B. (1995) *A Celebration of Neurons: An Educator's Guide to the Human Brain*, Alexandra, VA: ASCD.

Talbert, J. E. (1993) *Constructing a Schoolwide Professional Community: The Negotiated Order of a Performing Arts School*. In J. W. Little and M. W. McLaughlin (eds), op. cit., pp. 164–84.

Tampoe, M. (1998) *Liberating Leadership: Releasing Leadership Potential Throughout the Organisation*. London: The Industrial Society.

Guardian, 29 February 2000, p. 79.

Thomson, P. (2002) *Schooling the Rust Belt Kids: Making the Difference in Changing Times*. London: Allen and Unwin.

Thrupp, M. (1999) *Schools Making a Difference: Let's be Realistic! School Mix, School Effectiveness and the Social Limits of Reform*. Buckingham: Open University Press.

Tickle, L. (1991) New Teachers and the Emotions of Learning Teaching. *Cambridge Journal of Education*, Vol. 21, 93, pp. 319–29.

Travers, C. J. and Cooper, C. L. (1993) Mental Health, Job Satisfaction and Occupational Stress among UK Teachers. *Work and Stress*, 7, pp. 203–19.

Travers, C. J. and Cooper, C. L. (1996) *Teachers under Pressure: Stress in the Teaching Profession*. London: Routledge.

Tripp, D. H. (1993) *Critical Incidents in Teaching: Developing Professional Judgement*. London: Routledge.

Troman, G. (1996) The Rise of the New Professionals? The Restructuring of Primary Teachers' Work and Professionalism. *British Journal of Sociology of Education*, 17(4), pp. 473–87.

Troman, G. and Woods, P. (2001) *Primary Teachers' Stress*. London: Routledge Falmer.

Tschannen-Moran, M., Woolfolk, Hoy, A. and Hoy, W. K. (1998) Teacher Efficacy: Its Meaning and Measure. *Review of Educational Research*, Vol. 68, 2, pp. 202–48.

Tsui, K. T. and Cheng, Y. C. (1999) School Organizational Health and Teacher Commitment: A Contingency Study with Multi-level Analysis. *Educational Research and Evaluation*, 5(3), pp. 249–65.

UNESCO (1996) Enhancing the Role of Teachers in a Changing World, ED/BIE/CONFINTED 45/Info 10. Paper presented by Educational International to UNESCO, International Conference on Education, 45th session, Geneva, 30 Sept.–5 Oct.

Valli, L. (1990) Moral Approaches to Reflective Practice. In R. T. Clift, W. R. Houston and M. C. Pugachi (eds) *Encouraging Reflective Practice in Education*. New York: Teachers College Press, pp. 39–56.

van der Kolk (1994) The Body Keeps the Score: Memory and the Evolving Psychobiology of Post-traumatic Stress. *Harvard Review of Psychiatry*, Vol. 1, 5, pp. 253–62.

van Manen, M. (1995) On the Epistemology of Reflective Practice. *Teachers and Teaching: Theory and Practice*, Vol. 1, 1, pp. 33–50.

van Manen, M. (1999) Knowledge, Reflection and Complexity in Teacher Practice. In M. Lang, J. Olson, H. Hansen and W. Bünder (eds) *Changing Schools / Changing Practices: Perspectives on Educational Reform and Teacher Professionalism*. Louvain: Garant, pp. 65–76.

van Veen, K., Sleegers, P. and van de Ven, P.-H. (2004) Caught Between a Rock and a Hard Place: The Emotions of a Reform Enthusiastic Teacher. *Teaching and Teacher Education* (forthcoming).

Vandenberghe, R. (1999) Motivating Teachers: An Important Aspect of School Policy. Paper presented to the meeting of the School Management Project, Catholic University, Leuven, Belgium.

Vandenberghe, R. and Huberman, A. M. (eds) (1999) *Understanding and Preventing Teacher Burnout: A Sourcebook of International Research and Practice*. Cambridge: Cambridge University Press.

Veninga, R. and Spradley, J. (1981) *The Work–Stress Connection*. Boston: Little Brown.

Vonk, J. H. C. (1995) Teacher Education and Reform in Western Europe. In N. K. Shimahara and I. Z. Holowinsky (eds) *Teacher Education in Industrialised Nations: Issues in Changing Social Contexts*. New York: Garland Publishing Inc, pp. 255–312.

Wang, M. C., Haertel, G. D. and Walberg, H. J. (1997) Learning Influences. In H. J. Walberg and G. D. Haertel (eds) *Psychology and Educational Practice*. Berkeley, CA: McCulchan, pp. 199–211.

Wellington, B. and Austin, P. (1996) Orientations to Reflective Practice. *Educational Research*, 38, 3, pp. 307–16.

Wheatley, M. (1992) *Leadership and the New Science: Learning about Organizations From an Orderly Universe*. San Francisco: Berrett-Koehler.

White, J. (2000) *Do Howard Gardner's Multiple Intelligences Add Up?* Perspectives on Education Policy. London: Institute of Education.

White, J. J. and Roesch, M. (1993) *Listening to the Voices of Teachers: Examining Connections Between Student Performance, Quality of Teaching and Educational Policies in Seven Fairfax County (VA) Elementary and Middle Public Schools*. University of Maryland, Baltimore County, Fairfax (VA) County Public Schools, USA.

White, R. C. (2000) *The School of Tomorrow: Values and Vision*. Buckingham: Open University Press.

Wolfe, P. (2001) *Brain Matters: Translating Research into Classroom Practice*. Alexandra, VA: ASCD.

Woods, P. (1978) Negotiating the Demands of Schoolwork. *Curriculum Studies*, 10, 4, pp. 309–27.

Woods, P. (1979) *The Divided School*. London: Routledge & Kegan Paul.

Woods, P. (1999) Intensification and Stress in Teaching. In R. Vandenberghe and A. M. Huberman (eds), op. cit.

Woods, P. and Jeffrey, B. (1996) *Teachable Moments: The Art of Teaching in Primary Schools*. Buckingham: Open University Press.

Woods, P., Jeffrey, B. and Troman, G. (1997) *Restructuring Schools, Reconstructing Teachers*. Buckingham: Open University Press.

Woolfolk, A. E., Rosoff, B. and Hoy, W. K. (1990) Teachers' Sense of Efficacy and Their Beliefs About Managing Students. *Teaching and Teacher Education*, Vol. 6, pp. 137–48.

Yinger, R. (1979) Routines in Teacher Planning. *Theory into Practice*, 18, pp. 163–9.

Zehm, S. J. and Kottler, J. A. (1993) *On Being a Teacher: The Human Dimension*. California: Corwin Press, Inc.

Zeichner, K. M. (1993) Action Research: Personal Renewal and Social Reconstruction. *Educational Action Research*, 1, 2, pp. 199–200.

Zeichner, K. M. and Liston, D. P. (1996) *Reflective Teaching: An Introduction*. New Jersey: Laurence Erlbaum Associates.

Zembylas, M. (2003) Emotions and Teacher Identity: A Poststructural Perspective. *Teachers and Teaching: Theory and Practice*, Vol. 9, 3, August 2003, pp. 213–38.

Zohar, D. and Marshall I. (2000) *Spiritual Intelligence: The Ultimate Intelligence*. London: Bloomsbury Publishing.

Index